USING ENGLISH WORDS

# USING ENGLISH WORDS

*by*

DAVID CORSON
*The Ontario Institute for Studies in Education*

KLUWER ACADEMIC PUBLISHERS
DORDRECHT / BOSTON / LONDON

A C.I.P. Catalogue record for this book is available from the Library of Congress.

ISBN 0-7923-3710-7 (Hb)
ISBN 0-7923-3711-5 (Pb)

Published by Kluwer Academic Publishers,
P.O. Box 17, 3300 AA Dordrecht, The Netherlands.

Kluwer Academic Publishers incorporates
the publishing programmes of
D. Reidel, Martinus Nijhoff, Dr W. Junk and MTP Press.

Sold and distributed in the U.S.A. and Canada
by Kluwer Academic Publishers,
101 Philip Drive, Norwell, MA 02061, U.S.A.

In all other countries, sold and distributed
by Kluwer Academic Publishers Group,
P.O. Box 322, 3300 AH Dordrecht, The Netherlands.

*Printed on acid-free paper*

*To the Memory of*
WILLIAM SANDS CORSON

# Contents

# Introduction

*Using English Words* examines the impact that the life histories of people have on their vocabulary. Its starting point is the taken-for-granted fact that the vocabulary of English falls into two very different sections. Randolph Quirk mentions this striking incompatibility between the Anglo-Saxon and the Latinate elements in English: "the familiar homely-sounding and typically very short words" that we learn very early in life and use for most everyday purposes; and "the more learned, foreign-sounding and characteristically rather long words" (1974, p. 138). It is mainly the second type of word that native speakers start learning relatively late in their use of English, usually in the adolescent years of education, and keep on learning. It is mainly the one type of word, rather than the other, that ESL/EFL students have more difficulty with, depending on their language background.

This book shows how discursive relations, outside education, 'position' people through their vocabularies. Some are prepared for easy entry into lifetime prospects of relative privilege and educational success, while others are denied entry. In writing this book, I share an aim with other writers who observe the many discontinuities that exist between discursive practices in communities outside schools, and the discursive demands that schools make (e.g. Hamilton et al. [1993], Heath [1983], Luke [1994], Philips [1983], Romaine [1984], Scollon & Scollon [1981]). I argue that education fails to take account of the fact that many children's discursive relations, before and outside schools, are inconsistent with the kinds of lexico-semantic demands that schools and their high-status culture of literacy place upon them, often unnecessarily. Partly as a result of this, many English-as-a-first language and English-as-a-second language students, from some cultural, linguistic and social backgrounds, are almost guaranteed to fail in the middle levels of present-day education, before they have a chance to show that they can succeed.

1

## The Lexical Bar

This book is a fully revised, rewritten, updated, re-theorized, and so, very different version of an earlier book: *The Lexical Bar* (Corson, 1985). The period between the writing of that book and the writing of this one, has seen remarkable developments worldwide in our understanding of the intricate links between language, mind, the brain, education, society, and culture. The vastness of these developments prompted me at first to bypass the idea of a new book on this topic, once the earlier one had sold out completely. Another deterrent was the fact that the publishing house, that brought out the earlier book, no longer exists in its independent state. That publishing house was part of the holdings of a now deceased and very controversial publishing figure. With him, it disappeared as an independent entity, along with many of his other enterprises. I have no idea what impact the reputation of that publisher had on the earlier book's distribution, although one anonymous reviewer of the manuscript of *Using English Words* noted that *The Lexical Bar* "suffered from being overpriced and was probably undermarketed". In spite of all this, as I explain below, events influenced me into seeing this complete rewrite and update of the book as a very worthwhile undertaking.

In ways that I could not have foreseen (and in other ways that I should have foreseen), *The Lexical Bar* was a very controversial book. No doubt its examination of words seen from an interdisciplinary viewpoint, meant that it was conceived and published about ten years ahead of its time. But its timing was also inopportune for other reasons. Its development and release took place during the first two Thatcher governments in Britain. This was a time of great ideological and social change, much of it unhappy, and most of it harmful to education and to social policy generally in Britain. It was a time when the forces of educational conservatism were in the ascendancy, and they were running rampant.

*The Lexical Bar*'s message seemed to speak unambiguously in support of the egalitarian view that schools and school systems need to reform themselves in order to treat children from different sociocultural positions more justly. Educators need to moderate the discontinuities that exist between home and school as much as possible, and make schools more organic to their sociocultural communities. In spite of these messages, some commentators found they were able to read their own rather illiberal and élitist prejudices into the book. Indeed, some had their own prejudices strengthened by what could only have been a very superficial reading of it. By the time the book was released, I was already based again in Australia and then New Zealand, driven by the ravishing of higher education in Britain that accompanied the above changes, and which followed me to those countries. My physical distance from Britain made it much easier for people there to take wrong messages from the book, and to circulate those messages without contradiction.

The book's starting point was the simple division in English between the Graeco-Latin and the Anglo-Saxon vocabularies. Naturally such a topic attracted the curiosity of classicists, who were then understandably casting about for a means of survival, at a time when the historical moment of the classics seemed well passed. Some even saw the book as a kind of rallying point for 'the last charge of the classicists'. But, in fact, *The Lexical Bar* gave little or no encouragement to the cause of the classics. A footnote in this book, reproduced from *The Lexical Bar*, makes this point strongly (see footnote 1 of Chapter 5). Nevertheless many classicists still saw their interests represented in the book. Their enthusiasm for it spread quickly, and since classicists are sometimes rather conservative in their views about educational issues and in their associations, their reports quickly reached other more partisan commentators writing for the élite and conservative media. These commentators had various educational axes to grind. But among the second-hand or third-hand reports of the book that they received, the main idea that grabbed their attention was what some classicists wanted to believe they saw in it: that the book in some way supported a return to the widespread teaching of the classical languages. This wrong inference gave the media commentators one more argument for advocating back-to-basics and élitist educational policies and ideas.

At the same time, others misread the book's evidence quite innocently, and used their misreading in the service of more laudable educational aims. For example, one widely distributed book that argued for more foreign language education in schools, drew a very inaccurate conclusion. It said that David Corson "observed a qualitative difference (a 'lexical barrier') between pupils who had studied Latin and those who had not" (Hawkins, 1988 p. 79). Yet the salient and (may I say) most dramatic point in the research studies, a point that is really a central theme of this book too, was that *none* of the children had a background in Latin, even those who favoured a Latinate orientation in their oral and written English. Indeed the reasons for the differences are not due in any way to school experience of Latin (or Greek), a point sometimes lost on people who feel that there is no connection between wider social structures, different discursive practices, and the actual language that different groups of people use. In fact, most people tend to take language differences for granted in this way, and we might be forgiven for thinking that some of them should know better.

In many places, this book and the earlier one borrow from the work of Pierre Bourdieu. Like me and the many other 'discontinuity theorists' listed above, Bourdieu is very interested in the discontinuities in discourse that arise between the home, the community, and the school; and in how education unfairly rewards some forms of cultural capital that children bring to school, more than it does other forms. Now because Bourdieu's early ideas on language and cultural reproduction were widely misinterpreted, they do offer a good illustration of a major misunderstanding that also affected reception of *The Lexical Bar*. His idea of 'cultural capital' has been difficult for some to fit into their schemes of reference, especially when those schemes embrace class distinctions in a single society, but not cultural distinctions as well. An early criticism of the idea of 'cultural capital' was little more than a misinterpretation. This was probably an understandable misreading in the late 1970s and early 1980s, when the existence and influence of major cultural differences in monolingual societies was not widely appreciated. For instance, an important theorist like Michael Apple, in his early work, misread Bourdieu's use of cultural capital, seeing it as something only possessed by educationally dominant groups: "students without it are, by definition, deviant" he says (1982 p. 45). Similar misreadings appear elsewhere. Stanley Aronowitz wrote of schools as sites "where cultural capital may be wrested from those who hold it under lock and key" (1981 p. 4).

These and other writers seemed to miss Bourdieu's central point, which is really an anthropological one: *All* sociocultural groups possess esteemed cultural capital, including a linguistic capital of their own, but it is not always the same form of capital that is recognized and valued in education, and esteemed in other formal sites. By moving from one cultural 'field' or context to another, power relationships change, and different types of cultural capital become more or less valued. In *The Lexical Bar*, my concern was to show how schools value one kind of vocabulary as high status linguistic capital, although that vocabulary is unequally used by people from different sociocultural positions and is not at all regarded as high status cultural capital in many important human contexts. Like Bourdieu's, this interest of mine in vocabulary discontinuities was misunderstood, especially in England and especially by linguists. This was a curious misunderstanding, since the book explicitly concentrated on vocabulary differences that inevitably and every-where arise from the discontinuities between the home, the community, and the school.

Along with all this controversy and misunderstanding, the book was also being praised, especially again in England but elsewhere too. Sample comments from the reviews give a counterpoint to the criticisms. Meara wrote that if the work survived the savaging it would undoubtedly get, "it should lead to a revival of interest in how vocabularies grow, and how word knowledge affects educational attainment" (1986 p. 5). McCarthy noted that Corson asks "some important questions about the nature of the specialised vocabulary which many children first encounter at middle or secondary school" and his "historical outline of the development in England of an élitist vocabulary from the Renaissance onwards is well drawn and makes its point" (1988 pp. 143-4). Addressing a later discussion of the book, Marland remarked on the unusual emphasis on vocabulary knowledge that was in his view "very practical", saying that what Corson "aptly calls 'the lexical bar' must be crossed by all students" (1990 p. B11). Ridge believed the book presented "exciting challenges to researchers and policy makers" (1986 p. 33), while Robinson also called it "an exciting set of ideas" that was directly relevant to the fate of pupils whose school achievements are its central concerns (1986 p. 326).

This point about the book's direct relevance to educational practice and to real people, was echoed elsewhere too. In the United States, Roberts observed that "the research front on which he works is intriguing in that it forces us to look across the walls between the disciplines; and, of course, there are some real life consequences - the lives and futures of the children" (1986, p. 94). In Australia, Bradley saw the book as "a useful contribution" that "documents in an innovative way the lexical aspect of the class difference in language which is the output of the current education system" (1987 p. 144). Finally, in New Zealand, Nash cautioned that "there is much work to be done, but here is a book facing in the right direction" (1987 p. 162).

As well as the many reviews, there was also much informal feedback that I received when addressing teachers and academics, in seminars, conferences, and workshops. The most common first reaction from teachers was fascination with the factual detail about the English vocabulary: 'why didn't someone tell us all this about our own language before?'. More important was the widespread agreement, especially among teachers of adolescents, that the book was an accurate portrayal of one of the key problems in secondary classrooms, a problem closely linked to educational failure. Teachers from all backgrounds, not just English and language specialists, but also mathematics and science teachers, were in agreement. Again and again, science teachers remarked that they could often tell from children's written use of vocabulary, at the beginning of a class term, who was likely to master the Latinate signs that are the conceptual stuff of the science curriculum, and who was not. Regrettably the book was not as accessible to these teachers as many would have liked, since, in advancing a tentative theory, my main audience was other researchers. Indeed the book was not well written. I hope that this book is much more accessible, both in its writing and in its distribution.

The informal responses that I had from a great diversity of academics were often very revealing about the respondents' own disciplinary or research allegiances. For example, one modern language professor, who is now very senior in Australian universities, wondered why I needed to go beyond the conceptual and historical evidence, since that really told him all he needed to know. At the same time, an educational psychologist in New Zealand, well known for her work in literacy education, was unconvinced by the historical and sociolinguistic material, and needed to see the psycholinguistic data. Also gender theorists asked if there was a sex-based dimension to the research findings. A re-analysis of the data by sex, reported and discussed in Chapter 5 of this book, found no sex differences and this is consistent with other research on children's vocabulary use. Finally several historians of education praised the historical chapter and its conclusions, but admitted to reading little of the rest.

These reactions were not surprising to me, since I had prepared myself to receive the inevitable blows and disappointments of doing inter-disciplinary research. Indeed the kinds of problems that I met, especially when publishing the material, were summed up rather nicely in the opening lines of a review published in the United States:

> In a discouraged moment, a friend in American Studies once remarked that cross-disciplinary work is a fool's game. He said it is like trying to get your sled from Anchorage to Nome with a team that has on it a leopard, a wolverine, a wolf, a hyena, a grizzly, and a tiger. You know that the trip will be exciting, he said, but you also know that by the time you get to Nome every one of those animals will have bitten the driver. Corson's *Lexical Bar* looks into a question on which a score of research disciplines speak with utter assurance in completely different ways (Roberts, 1986 p. 93).

But there was a dark side to all this too, and this did surprise me a little. It also offers a lesson about some of the realities of academic life. For example, while still in its rough thesis form, the British sections of the study had been rejected by a professor for inclusion in a book series that he edited. Although I made no reference to him in the work, he was influential for a time, and I took his written remarks and went elsewhere. But later, when *The Lexical Bar* was published, I found that its only unconstructively critical review came from the same person. Moreover it was clear from the review that little of his critique addressed the greatly revised and augmented book itself, only his reading of the original thesis.

A point in several of the critiques was that I had slighted the discipline of linguistics in some way. Certainly my original thesis speculated at many points about why vocabulary had received such little recent attention in a number of disciplines, including linguistics. But *The Lexical Bar* itself was rather silent on these matters. Looking back now, I think I can better understand what these reviewers were worried about: They were seeing my indifference to disciplinary boundaries in general, as hostility to the boundaries that surrounded linguistics in particular. Fortunately disciplinary territoriality of this kind is fading fast, especially in areas like applied linguistics where the framework is now almost totally permeable, and almost anything goes. But it is also true that the recent British tradition in linguistics, up to the early 1980s, offered surprisingly little that was relevant to my work, even though I thoroughly ransacked that material in the University of London Senate House Library, hoping to find its relevance. Chapter 2 of *Using English Words*, confirms how recent the explosion of research on vocabulary has been, at least in applied linguistics.

### Using English Words

The motivation for producing this fully revised and updated book, came from three broadly different directions. None of these is more influential than the others, but taken together they made me feel that the project was definitely worth another look.

Firstly, in recent years *The Lexical Bar* began to receive a lot of attention in published research and scholarship. In particular, several studies that are mentioned in this book used that earlier book as their springboard. They also advanced its ideas in promising directions. At the same time, many citations of the book began to appear in the social science literature, especially in the years 1990-1994. This happened at about the time that the renewed interest in vocabulary studies, which developed in the mid-1980s, began to spread from applied linguistics and psycholinguistics, stimulating research in other areas.

Secondly, in the last decade, there has been a dramatic change in academic and policy attitudes to interdisciplinary studies. In both England and Canada, the major research funding bodies now lay special stress on interdisciplinary studies: by creating categories of funding for them, or by setting up centres of excellence in interdisciplinary studies, or by giving them priority alongside other narrower forms of inquiry. This trend is beginning to spread in the United States and in Australasia. No doubt it is more than an academic fashion, since it is underpinned by recent developments in the philosophy of social research. It probably heralds a major paradigm shift for doing any research in the social sciences and the humanities that is aimed at addressing real problems to do with improving the human condition. Human problems are almost inevitably interdisciplinary, so they are rather different from the more abstracted problems of single disciplines.

Finally, a clear catalyst for this book was the recent development of 'discursive psychology', a fertile field of inquiry that should receive a great deal of deserved attention and acclaim. Discursive psychology is itself an interdisciplinary field of immense promise. Its attraction for me, of course, was the absolute priority that it gives to the human ability to make use of words and other signs. In discursive psychology, words are basic to understanding the development of mind, the development of consciousness, the development of 'the self', and especially, by extension, the development of human emancipation from the influence of oppressive dogmas, ideologies and fanaticisms. Rom Harré's reaction to my work on the lexico-semantic positioning of people from different sociocultural backgrounds, prompted me to see these studies as a small part of the prime data of discursive psychology.

*The Structure of this Book*

Chapter 1 begins with a short summary of discursive psychology, showing how it gives priority to the place of words in dealing with the world and how it sees them as symbols for forming and refining thought. I then argue that formal education's definitions of success demand competence in the dominant vocabularies of a language. The chapter turns next to another very relevant interdisciplinary field: the sociology of language. This is also central to the study of word use, because over time different sociocultural groups shape the different vocabularies of a language. Sociology of language also highlights the divisive place that words have as tools of social and cultural stratification. Formal education is the key institution in society reinforcing this 'stratification through words'.

Chapter 2 is a synthesis from relevant topics and disciplines, of data and assumptions about the links between words, culture, education, and society. Its review of many disciplines builds a comprehensive picture of the place of words in research and theory. While it deals with English words in particular, it also assembles a more general research basis for understanding how lexico-semantic positioning, outside formal education, routinely creates major vocabulary discontinuities. These vocabulary discontinuities can exist between the home community and the school, or between the structure of the first language of ESL students and the English vocabulary of the school.

Chapter 3 describes the processes of invasion, conquest, renaissance and oppression that equipped the English vocabulary with its unique division into a more everyday Anglo-Saxon section and a more specialist, largely Graeco-Latin section (G-L). It draws a direct link between the flood of G-L words into English and the sociocultural positioning of present-day users of English as a first language. Formal education itself has had the influential role in creating a lexical bar.

Chapter 4 examines present-day factors operating in the English language and among its users, that combine to reinforce the bar and its effects. The first group of factors is linguistic. Their marks in the semantic, morphological, and phonological features of English are fairly clear. The second group of factors is both sociological and intrapersonal. These relate to the differences in engagement that different sociocultural groups have with different meaning systems and their signs. When combined, these factors lead to differences in linguistic capital that occur across social contexts. The chapter relates these factors to first language speakers of English, but it is also very relevant to vocabulary learning by ESL/EFL children and adults.

Chapter 5 presents a range of empirical studies undertaken between 1980 and 1989 confirming that groups of children from different sociocultural backgrounds differ systematically in their use of words that are drawn from the knowledge categories of the secondary school curriculum. These differences appear at the crucial moment in children's school careers. They offer evidence of discontinuities between the lexico-semantic positioning of people outside formal education, and the lexical demands that formal education places upon them.

Chapter 6 looks more closely at lexico-semantic differences between individual children at 12 and 15 years. It tries to show how individual children's different uses of words in discourse combine to create the patterns of word use that appear in the group data of Chapter 5. The chapter's evidence is of two main types: a number of complete interview transcripts that contrast with one another lexico-semantically, as larger units of discourse; and many smaller fragments of discourse, set against other fragments produced by other children in response to similar discursive contexts and tasks.

Chapter 7 has its basis in the very recent but well attested claim that the brain's neurobiological mechanisms can alter as a result of different social environments and discursive practices. It assembles state-of-the-art evidence suggesting that the mental lexicon adapts in this way too, as the brain changes in response to language experiences, especially the words and other signs that it encounters. Since sociocultural positioning affects language experiences, then discursive practices encountered over a lifetime will arrange different people's mental lexicons very differently, so that they come to process words very differently as well. Morphological complexity and semantic opaqueness are key factors in the processing difficulty of specialist G-L words. The chapter highlights the effects of different kinds of language experiences and the likely value that greater language awareness has for an individual word user.

Chapter 8 looks at the features that appear more often in specialist G-L words, as a group, than in other English words. It is especially concerned with the features that tend to make these words more difficult for some language users than for others. The chapter summarizes the impact of all these factors on word learning and use: in reading, writing, speaking, and listening. It ends by spelling out the two sides to the lexical bar.

Chapter 9 suggests areas for further research and recommendations for changing practices in education. These recommendations are relevant to both English-as-a-first language education and ESL/EFL education. They highlight important roles that formal education needs to assume more purposefully: valuing vocabulary differences among students; providing studies in language awareness; and giving more attention to oral language activities, to literacy extension, and to the study of other languages in general. The book ends by asking about the existence of lexical bars in other languages.

*Acknowledgments*
My thanks to the following for their help in various ways with the development of this book: Rom Harré, Oxford University; Bruce Maylath, University of Minnesota; Paul Nation, Victoria University of Wellington; Dominiek Sandra, University of Antwerp; Marcus Taft, University of New South Wales; Jim Cummins, Birgitt Harley, Sylvie Lemay, David Olson, and Keith Stanovich, Ontario Institute for Studies in Education. My thanks too to Kluwer's two anonymous reviewers for their very full and useful comments; and to Tim Corson for producing the final manuscript and the Index.

# 1

# The Place of Words in Discourse and in Education

By examining the place of words in the discourses of English, this book follows the 'discursive turn' in the social sciences. Linguists, sociologists, historians, and anthropologists have long discovered important differences in the discursive practices of culturally, socially, and historically remote peoples, differences that no doubt have deep implications for differences in social cognition and human interests. Language offers the best evidence for seeing differences in social cognition more clearly, and for appreciating the range of human interests that can occupy even a single social space. In particular, by studying the lexico-semantic range of people who are positioned differently by their sociocultural experiences and discursive practices, we can establish with a little more certainty the different ways that different peoples use different meaning systems to interpret their world.

Insight into these matters has great relevance for education and society, since formal education at every level brings its own special meaning systems to the task of interpreting the world. But because of their different discursive positioning and material conditions, many people see these academic meaning systems as rather remote and alien ways of interpreting their own worlds.

## Discursive Psychology and the Discursive Mind

The 'discursive turn' occurring across the social sciences and humanities, could not come soon enough for many commentators in the human sciences. It has been delayed mainly by institutional forces to do with the boundaries between academic disciplines and with the interests of those tied to earlier ways of perceiving the world. Its arrival is having an impact even on the most conservative of disciplines.

An important book *The Discursive Mind* signals the appearance and rapid rise of a genuinely new psychology: 'discursive psychology' (Harré & Gillett, 1994; Corson, 1995b). While the book's focus seems to be on psychology, this new field extends to all branches of the human sciences, involving anthropology, sociology, and linguistics in a synthesis of trends that are already appearing or established. "It is both remarkable and interesting that the old psychologies continue to exist alongside the new" say the authors, and they begin their description with a critical look at "the traditional experimentalist psychology that still exists, particularly in the United States" (1994 p. 2).

Although my treatment of the place of words in English discourse, goes well outside the present discursive psychology literature, the two have a common source. The source of discursive psychology is in the idea of the social world as a discursive construction. This idea has many antecedents: Vygotsky, Wittgenstein, Gramsci, Luria, Bourdieu and many others. The work of these theorists links into my theme at different points in this book. But in recent psychology itself, it is the work of Jerome Bruner (1973; 1990) that opened the way for thinking about human cognition in other than the methods and the metaphysics of the experimentalist tradition.

Discursive psychology has already gone beyond Bruner's path-breaking work by discarding the twin dogmas of cognitive science: that inner mental states and processes exist; and that they are much the same for all human beings. In so doing, discursive psychology becomes a truly interdisciplinary field by acknowledging the reality and importance of those differences that linguists, sociologists, historians, and anthropologists have long discovered in the social cognition, the human interests, and the discursive practices of people. As Wittgenstein argued, we understand the way people act and behave when we grasp the meanings that inform that behaviour.

*Rule-Following and Words as Signs*

Wittgenstein's simple idea of following a rule is at the root of the whole discursive revolution: Mental activity is not tied to some internal set of processes; it is a range of moves set against a background of human activity governed by informal conventions or rules, especially rules to do with the ways in which words and other symbols are used within the structures of a language. Since the meaning of a word is its 'use' in a language, people have to adopt normative attitudes to their own responses when they try to use a word to structure mental activity: They have to conform in some way to its rules of use. These norms or rules are set within some language game or other, where words have their meanings and in which the range of moves and rule-following takes place. These language games include the language people use to do complex things and the relevant tools and actions that form a backdrop to those discursive practices. In Chapter 2, I give some examples of words and the rules that give them communicative sense.

For Harré and Gillett, whatever existence the psychological world might have, it is not reducible or replaceable by explanations based on physiology, or any materialist discipline that does not get to grips with the structure of meanings in the lives of the cultural group to which a subject belongs. Getting inside those structures involves getting inside the forms of life, the norms, conventions, and rules, and seeing them as the subject does. Discourse provides the raw material for doing this, since its public face tells us much about its inner use. In fact discourse itself is both public and private: When public, it is behaviour; when private, it is thought. As Vygotsky noted of children acquiring language: "the system of signs restructures the whole process" of intellectual development; the skillful use of those signs against a background of publicly meaningful rules, is central to human thought (1962 p. 35).

The subject matter of the social sciences in general is changing radically to include discourses, significations, subjectivities, and positionings, since this is where mental events are really located. For some time, discourse analysts, ethnomethodologists, conversation analysts, and sociologists of language have been setting this new course for the social sciences. But now all these viewpoints are coalescing in a more coherent way. As Harré and Gillett conclude: "the study of the mind is a way of understanding the phenomena that arise when different sociocultural discourses are integrated within an identifiable human individual situated in relation to those discourses" (1994 p. 22). The mind of an individual becomes a nexus or meeting point of social relations and past and present discursive practices and subjectivities. So each human individual stands at a unique intersection of discourses and relationships: a 'position' embedded in historical, political, cultural, social and interpersonal contexts, that largely determines mind.

The place of words as signs is central in all this. They provide most of the important symbols for forming and refining thought, based on meanings that are a function of their use in discourse. So words are at the heart of the new discursive psychology. For Harré & Gillett, the role of words in forming and refining thought is increasingly confirmed across a range of disciplines. Thinkers are competent managers of systems of signs, and our most efficient signs are the words of a language: "To be able to think is to be a skilled user of these sign systems, that is, to be capable of managing them correctly" (1994 p. 49). This is not to say that words structure cognition, only that discourse itself is the medium in which cognitive activity takes shape. Harré & Gillett summarize it all this way:

> Thus the grasp of (the use of a word) [a concept] is an active discursive skill. It is selective in the face of a rich set of experiential possibilities. It is built on participation in discourse, and it is governed by rules or prescriptive norms that tell the thinker what counts as an item of this or that type (e.g. what counts as a DOG in the fireplace or in the kennel, a FROG in the pond or in the throat, or a HEAVY METAL BAND in the dance hall or around the ankle).

Thinkers' awareness of these rules shows in their recognition that there is a right and a wrong way to capture in thought the object or property that is thought about (p. 48).

## Words in Education

Success in education is highly dependent on people's ability to 'display' knowledge, usually through the spoken or written use of words. Young children's use of the signs of a language is often the first contact teachers have with them. In later stages of education, verbal contact through formal or informal assessments is sometimes the only link between students and the assessors who declare their educational fate. Indeed, as studies reported in later chapters of this book confirm, formal education is very largely a process of teaching the rules of use for words and then judging how well those rules have been acquired.

What formal education is looking for in people, is their ability to put meanings together in thought and to communicate them. Many other factors, of course, affect educational success, often unjustly. Matters of race, culture, gender, region of living, and class, often unfairly interfere with people's educational progress (Corson, 1993). But if these other things could be taken out of the equation, one thing would stand out as the most important factor in educational success or failure: The more diverse the meanings that people communicate, and the more appropriate those meanings are to the specialist meaning systems given high status in education, the more impressed and the more rewarding the institution of education will be.

The last sentence is not a prescriptive statement about formal education, only a normative one. That being so, and since formal education is as it is, this book looks at that most basic of points about formal education. In other words, this book assumes that educational failure or success depends to a very large extent on people having the words, wanting to use them, and being able to use them.

### Studying Lexico-Semantic Range

In spite of evidence to confirm the link between vocabulary and academic progress, the matter is more complex than just finding a simple correlational comparison of word diversity and school performance. Psychological studies commonly ask people to make selections from groups or pairs of words presented to them, often in response to a picture or some other stimulus. But these tests measure 'word recognition-potential', not meaning, since they ask for no meaning in use. What can we really decide from differences between people in their recognition of single words?

We can decide very little, because achievement for people in education depends on their verbal access to the rules of use, the life forms, and the discursive practices of entire knowledge categories, not to single words within those categories. This means that lexico-semantic research needs to look at people's readiness to enter and operate within the meaning systems of some knowledge categories or other. This is also the first aim of research in discursive psychology:

> 1.  One wants to find out what resources people have to accomplish their plans, projects and intentions. What repertoire of concepts do they have available as usable sign systems, and what are their capacities for the use of words and other signs? (Harré & Gillett, 1994 p. 98).

To be effective, lexico-semantic research needs to acknowledge key premises about word meaning that inform the language disciplines. Both linguistics and the philosophy of language offer similar premises in this area. Leech (1974) describes the premise upon which modern linguistic semantics is founded: "the meaning of a linguistic expression is precisely that knowledge which enables one to use it appropriately in linguistic communication, whether in everyday or specialist contexts" (p. 204). Platts (1979) corroborates Leech's judgment, but from the philosophy of language viewpoint: "the understanding of an expression is the ability to *use* it in saying things in an identifiable mode" (p. 232).

*Words as the Taken-for-Granted Markers of Educational Potential*

It is the content of language, the use and the diversity of vocabulary in particular, that teachers and academics look for when their students are communicating meaning (Graves, 1986; Isaacson, 1988; Nielsen & Piché, 1981). They do this believing, as did Vygotsky, that the skillful use of those signs against a background of publicly meaningful rules, is the most important evidence available about the quality of student thought. But they also do this while knowing that the special vocabulary they target is culturally bound and unevenly distributed among the population (Purves, 1988).

While many people in education are very sensitive to this problem, and to the contradictions it raises for educational policy and practice, others too readily take specialist words for granted in this way. They feel justified in judging people largely on the basis of this single criterion. Moreover they do so uncritically, perhaps because they themselves have come to see the world largely from within the discourses of the academic meaning systems that are also unequally available to different sociocultural groups. In fact, there is much evidence that vocabulary diversity is the most consistent marker of proficiency used throughout education. In written work, what teachers currently see as 'good' narrative writing is closely linked to vocabulary diversity (Grobe, 1988). Also in reading, it is content knowledge, especially knowledge of word meanings and the rules for their use, that is the key to mastering texts and gaining entry to the culture of literacy (Chall, 1987).

Sometimes alarms are raised about the improper emphasis placed on vocabulary skills in education. For instance, there are good reasons to target the verbal sections of the Scholastic Assessment Tests (SAT) that are used in the United States as gate-keeping measures for entrance to universities and colleges. Daniels (1983) describes these verbal tests as little more than a measure of 'lexical formality'. Informed by *The Lexical Bar*, Maylath (1994) adds that the SAT is mainly a test of fluency in the Graeco-Latin vocabulary of English. He says that in the United States this vocabulary has almost second language status for many people, so remote is it from their everyday language practices. He also observes that high school marks, based largely on tests of the Graeco-Latin (G-L) vocabulary, "combined with college entrance exams, like the SAT, do much to cull out those students who have avoided the G-L vocabulary, usually well before they might step into a college or university classroom" (p. 198).

In this book I pay a lot of attention to these issues of equity and fairness in judgments made about the use of words. The issues, of course, are directly relevant to the concerns of discursive psychology, since these issues link people's lexico-semantic range with their sociocultural positioning. But since broader cultural, social, and political questions are part of these issues too, I also discuss them from the viewpoint of another equally interdisciplinary field: the sociology of language.

### The Sociology of Language

Since the vocabulary of a language is moulded more by the demands and impulses of sociocultural groups than by any other factor or set of factors, a sociological approach to the study of vocabulary has much to recommend it. The sociology of language has a lot of common ground with anthropological linguistics, the social psychology of language, and the ethnography of speaking. It shares major interests too with social semiotics.

Trudgill (1983) describes the sociology of language as the subdivision of the study of 'language and society' that is both sociological and linguistic in intent. It is distinct from a second subdivision, 'sociolinguistics', that is purely 'linguistic'; and it is also distinct from a third subdivision that is 'social' rather than linguistic in intent. This last area includes ethnomethodology and conversational analysis.

A. D. Edwards (1976) describes the sociology of language as including matters not normally considered in linguistics, like language loyalty, language as source and symbol of group solidarity, and language as an instrument of stratification. The central domain of a sociology of language is its concern with the social, political, and educational aspects of the relationship between language and society. Differences in access to the meaning systems of a society rank high among its interests.

### Words, the Sociology of Language, and Education

A brief look at the work of four contemporary contributors to the sociology of language will set the scene for cross-disciplinary discussion in later chapters. These four are Dell Hymes, William Labov, Pierre Bourdieu, and Basil Bernstein. Hymes (1974) was influential in re-identifying the importance of vocabulary in the language disciplines and urging that more attention be given to the formal study of words:

If linguists were to cease treating vocabulary as functionally perfect by definition, returning to the study of lexical creation and change and the more general question of a theory of vocabularies, a great deal of good might result (p. 318).

*Hymes and Labov*

By introducing the idea of 'communicative competence' to language studies, Hymes (1972) encouraged a move beyond the ground rules of language to an enlarged perspective, including the habits and attitudes that accompany language in use.   He proposed that members of a speech community acquire a set of sociolinguistic rules for the appropriate use of language.  These enable language users to know when to speak and when to remain silent, which code to use, when, where and to whom.  Part of this proposal was the expectation that members of a speech community, coming from different sociocultural backgrounds, will acquire different communicative competencies or different degrees of the same competency.

His interest in context of situation is central to what he called the 'ethnography of speaking' (Hymes, 1968). Context of situation is also basic to his ideas on communicative competence itself. This phrase 'context of situation' has a long history in ethnographic research.  It suggests that speakers bring to any situation their own knowledge about when to speak, what about, at what level of formality, and with what degree of explicitness. For example, when people enter a speech situation where the communicative demands are largely defined for them, such as the extralinguistic context of a formal educational institution, their communicative competencies will vary according to the rules of appropriateness for such situations that each one has acquired in the school or in the wider language community.

These ideas from Hymes were influenced by his observations and work as an anthropological linguist, among aboriginal peoples in the United States. I return to the idea of 'extralinguistic context' and its impact on rules of use in Chapter 2 and elsewhere.

Labov's studies in descriptive linguistics, comparing Black American and Puerto Rican vernaculars of English, and other varieties (1966; 1972), offered the sociology of language many original insights. In particular, he found that people from different sociocultural backgrounds speak different kinds of English that in all important respects deviate systematically and regularly from each other. His findings helped overturn the common stereotype that these and many other varieties of language are incorrect forms of a language. Rather, they are varieties with their own norms and rules of use. Accordingly they deserve respect and valuation, although education itself, as a standard practice, disvalues varieties that are very different from the dominant norm (Corson, 1993).

Matters of syntax, accent, and pronunciation can offer markers of prestige in language to teachers who then make imprecise and unfair judgments about the educational potential of children.  Labov (1972b) successfully argued that there is no real basis for attributing poor performance to the grammatical and phonological characteristics of any non-standard variety of English.  He used this evidence in successful challenges against discriminatory language practices in schools and school systems (Labov, 1982). But the status of vocabulary in Labov's account is left open.

He explicitly allowed that certain key aspects of words and their meanings, including mastery of the very different morphosemantic features of Latinate words in English, may be critical attainments for educational success (1972b).  He also proposed that the internal representations of words in the brain are coded on semantic principles like a thesaurus and should be accessed accordingly. He pointed out that, in verbal production, the problem is to locate words that express a given meaning (1978). I return to this point about the role that meaning must play in processing words in the mental lexicon, in Chapter 7; and to other aspects of Labov's work in Chapter 2.

## Bourdieu and Bernstein

Bourdieu's compelling arguments about language and education touch directly on the use of vocabulary and on differences in meaning systems (1966; 1977; 1981; 1984). Like Hymes, Bourdieu's earlier experiences as an ethnographer (in francophone parts of North Africa) inform his work and his conclusions. He argues that all forms of power that impose meanings in such a way as to legitimate those meanings and conceal the relations that underlie the exercise of power itself, add their own specifically symbolic force to those relations of power. In this way, dominant ideas reinforce the power of the same forces exercising it. He sees the culture of education as a creation of the dominant culture.

His special term 'habitus' names a system of durable dispositions at the core of a person's behaviour. He argues that the habitus shared by members of dominant groups permeates every aspect of formal education. This limits the educational opportunities of people from non-dominant groups, because the school demands competence in the dominant language and culture which can only be acquired through family upbringing. While education might not openly stress this culture, it implicitly demands it through its definitions of success. So groups who are capable of transmitting through the family the habitus necessary for the reception of the school's messages, come to monopolize the system of schooling. Those with alternative dispositions or habitus, have little purchase on the culture of education, or on the social rewards that that culture makes available.

Different sociocultural groups have different relations to language. These differences emerge from different sets of dispositions and attitudes towards the material world and towards other people. As a result, different groups of people pass on different meaning systems to their offspring and often there are social advantages in those systems that are passed on with them. Bourdieu is much concerned with this handing on of esteemed social attributes, and the allocation of social and cultural power that it implies.

To help describe the relations between language and sociocultural influence, Bourdieu uses an apt economic analogy: He presents culture metaphorically as an 'economic system' and looks at the way a person's resources of culture are used in the social system. He introduces the phrase 'cultural capital' (1966) to describe those culturally esteemed advantages that people acquire as a part of their life experiences, their peer group contacts, and their family backgrounds: such things as 'good taste', 'style', certain kinds of knowledge, abilities, and presentation of self.

'Academic capital' is closely related to the cultural capital inherited from the family. This is the guaranteed product of the combined effects of cultural transmission by the family, and cultural transmission by the school. Most relevant here, Bourdieu sees 'linguistic capital' as the key part of the cultural heritage. But this linguistic capital is more than the competence to produce grammatically well-formed expressions and language forms. It also includes the ability to utilize appropriate norms for language use and to produce the right expressions at the right time for a particular 'linguistic market' or context of situation.

For Bourdieu, people who have appropriate linguistic capital in a given setting are favourably placed to exploit the system of differences that exists. They do this in two ways. On the one hand, profit or advantage in general accrues most from a use of those modes of expression that are the least equally distributed. For example, the use of rare or low frequency words can often give advantage in this way. On the other hand, the readiness of minority language or non-standard speakers to stigmatize their own language, means that they often condemn themselves to silence in public settings for fear of offending norms that they themselves sanction. Using Bourdieu's metaphor, there are many linguistic markets in which rare or high status forms result in profit for the user, and where non-standard or low-status language use is assigned a limited value (1977). As a result, children from non-privileged backgrounds are silent within those 'markets' or they withdraw from them.

Bourdieu argues that while the cultural or linguistic capital that is valued in education is not equally available to people from different backgrounds, education still operates as if everyone had equal access to it. By basing its assessments of success and failure on people's possession of this high status capital, education reproduces the sociocultural arrangements that create the situation in the first place. But the members of some sociocultural groups come to believe that their educational failure, rather than coming from their lowly esteemed social or cultural status, results from their natural inability: their lack of giftedness. They come to believe that social and cultural factors are somehow neutralized in the educational selection process and that the process itself is a fair one that is based on objective educational criteria.

Along with the obvious properties of language, like its syntax, sounds, and vocabulary, people acquire through their socialization certain attitudes towards words and their use. These give people criteria for judging which styles and forms of expression seem better than others. For Bourdieu, one of the surest distinctive signs of a speaker's social position is language use that is either reverential or casual, tense or detached, stilted or easy, heavy-handed or well-tempered, ostentatious or measured (1977). Labov also speaks of the "casual and intimate styles" that can be "stationed at one end of the continuum, and frozen, ritualistic styles at the other" (1972 p. 112). Central to all this is the significance allotted by formally educated social groups to academic culture, to the institutions set up to transmit it, and to the vocabulary needed to transmit it. In this book, I point to the educational significance of having a high-status vocabulary whose display can confer sociocultural prestige on those who know the appropriate place and the manner in which to use it.

Of the four theorists discussed here, Bernstein is perhaps the only one who would describe himself as a sociologist of language, and then only occasionally. His position within the sociology of language has similarities to Bourdieu's and he also offers a complex sociological and philosophical argument. Like Bourdieu too, his theories have been misinterpreted by some who take pieces out of the theories and critique them away from their original context: away from their original meaning system or language game.

Bernstein's project was to show how people from different class positions differ in the ways that they categorize and conceptually order the world. His theory seems fully consistent with the idea advanced in this book, that different cultural meaning systems are made available to different class fractions in societies through different discursive practices and material life forms. This happens routinely when people experience different meaning systems while moving across different cultures. But within a single culture, the key mechanism in this process of stratification is the division of labour. This is what separates people into various class categories: those who create the routines, those who supervise the routines, and those who carry them out. I return to the division of labour and its impact on sociocultural positioning and lexico-semantic range in Chapter 4.

It is only within this essentially sociological theory that Bernstein became concerned with language. His interest in meaning systems and the different orientations to the world that go with them, encouraged him to look for linguistic evidence of these differences. This led to a famous misunderstanding that he has been at pains to correct:

> What is at stake is not the issue of the intrinsic nature of different varieties of language but different modalities of privileged meanings, practices and social relations which act selectively upon shared linguistic resources . . . Educational failure (official pedagogic failure) is a complex function of the official transmission system of the school and the local acquisition process of the family/peer group/community (1990 p. 114).

The linguistic evidence that Bernstein and his associates gathered was used only illustratively to present his central idea of 'code'. He defines this complex notion as "a regulative principle, tacitly acquired, which selects and integrates relevant meanings, forms of realizations, and evoking contexts" (1990 p. 101). Since his concern was not with varieties of language, it is quite a distance from my interest in differences in access to academic meaning systems as revealed in people's active and passive lexico-semantic range. As he says, codes and varieties "belong to different theoretical discourses, to different theories, and address fundamentally different problematics" (p. 48).

Bernstein paid little explicit attention to lexico-semantic range in his studies. However, he does offer a useful definition of the key influence on lexico-semantic range: sociocultural 'positioning'. This definition fills out the concept that I have adopted from Harré & Gillett, who use it very widely in their work. It also helps place Bernstein's theory of codes into perspective:

> 'Positioning' is used here to refer to the establishing of a specific relation to other subjects and to the creating of specific relationships within subjects. In general, from this point of view, codes are culturally determined positioning devices. More specifically, class-regulated codes position subjects with respect to dominant and dominated forms of communication and to the relationships between them (1990 p. 13).

As argued in this book, the kind of complex meaning systems that Bernstein discusses are rather ephemeral for people who participate in them, if the same people do not have the support of the special vocabularies or other shared signs that are embedded within the systems. We need the signs if we really want to get inside the systems. This is because it is the rules of use for those special signs that make meaning systems coherent and durable. Not only do these rules of use give individual signs their sense within a language game, they also mark the relationships between words and other signs, against a background of material practices and life forms.

## Conclusion

Two interdisciplinary fields of study come together in this book: discursive psychology and the sociology of language. Discursive psychology gives real priority to the place of words in thought and in dealing with the world. Words provide most of the important symbols for forming and refining thought, while their meanings are a function of their use in public discourse. Thinkers are competent managers of systems of signs, and our most efficient signs are the words of a language. This is not to say that words structure thinking, only that discourse itself is the medium in which thinking takes shape.

The relevance of the sociology of language to all this, comes from the fact that over time different sociocultural groups shape the different vocabularies of a language. Sociocultural interests create, change, or eliminate the rules of use for words. Different sociocultural group discourses transmit those rules, including the rules of appropriateness for using language within specific contexts of situation. Unlike discursive psychology, the sociology of language also highlights the divisive place that words have: Often they are tools of sociocultural stratification and blatant injustice.

Strangely perhaps, considering its benign purpose, education is the key institution in society reinforcing this 'stratification through words'. This happens because education's definitions of success implicitly demand competence in the dominant vocabularies of a language, even though this verbal competence is ordinarily only acquired through the kinds of family upbringing not widely distributed in societies. Usually only members of privileged groups manage to acquire diverse competence in the dominant vocabularies of a language as a result of their family upbringing. Yet this aspect of linguistic capital is an esteemed social attribute, used in the allocation of social and cultural power and reward.

This book studies lexico-semantic access to knowledge categories or meaning systems. It does this by looking at the use of words in discursive contexts, by people from different sociocultural positions. In setting the course for the rest of this book, this chapter proposes that a cross-disciplinary study of vocabulary has important things to say about educational success and failure, whose importance goes well beyond the institution of education. The worth of this approach can be judged from the well-demonstrated centrality of words in interaction and assessment at every level in formal educational settings.

# 2

# A Multidisciplinary Review: Words, Culture, Education, and Society

This chapter is a synthesis, from relevant disciplines, of evidence and assumptions about the intricate links between words, culture, education, and society. In trying to give the interdisciplinary background to the study, I acknowledge that a discussion without disciplinary framework may be difficult, integrating as it does many rival discourses. But I agree with W.V.O. Quine (1966) that disciplines are mainly useful for deans and librarians, and that efforts to integrate rival frameworks are likely to increase the fruitfulness of the discussion. This is especially so in an area like the study of vocabulary, which inevitably overflows even the tightest of disciplinary boundaries. So my separation of this chapter into topics and 'disciplines' is in many places a rather arbitrary one. It is often used mainly to break up the text.

### Insights from the Philosophy of Language

The later Wittgenstein provides key insights. In his thinking about the links between language and knowledge, Wittgenstein underwent an intellectual transformation (1961 [1922]; 1953). He realized that his earlier view, that knowledge was a linguistic picture of reality, was untenable. So he put together quite a different philosophy: We are all participants in many different language games that are being played within fairly closed linguistic circles. When we have knowledge, we have it according to the linguistic rules that obtain in a given circle. In order to play the games, we need to learn the special rules of the circles in which we are operating, or in which we hope to operate. These rules are no more than conventions, laid down at some time by those who have the power to decide the rules in whatever circle they happen to be.

These rules are not as abstract as they might seem. Everyday words have quite basic and commonly agreed rules for their use, based on the tacit assumption of all language users that there are right and wrong ways to use all signs within language games. Harré & Gillett (1994) give some examples: They mention the rules behind the use of words like RED or SQUARE that prevent us from thinking of a red object as blue, or a square one as round. Similarly, the sentence 'sheep are carnivorous' is not false, but just senseless. This is because the rules governing the use of the sign SHEEP and the sign CARNIVOROUS are incompatible with placing the two words together in the sentence 'sheep are carnivorous'. The sentence is inexplicable because it is outside the language games and forms of life where people who follow these rules live their lives. Instead, the idea of 'carnivorous sheep' enters other realms where conventional rules of use are deliberately ignored, like science fiction, horror movies, or satire. In fact, the very thought of 'carnivorous sheep' could be very appropriate within the language game of a satirical show, like Monty Python, or in a child's cartoon where the prevailing rule is that the rules that apply in other language games can be ignored. So these ideas about words and their rules of use are not abstractions. Rather they are tied closely to the real world of life forms, material practices, and human interaction.

Elaborating on Wittgenstein's account, Rundle decides that 'meaning' and 'use' are not exact equivalents. But a consideration of 'use' opens our eyes to possibilities that we overlook if we concentrate only on 'meaning':

> Questions of meaning do appear to be, invariably, questions of use, but the converse does not hold: the use of a word, but not its meaning, can be fashionable, ill-advised, or unjustified; it can be encouraged or prohibited, accompanied by gestures, occasion disputes, and reveal something about the speaker. Not so its meaning (1990 p. 9).

When we think about a word's use, we must operate at the point where world and word meet, so as to keep in touch with its meaning. This returns a consideration of meaning to the real social contexts where words are used.

So there is need in the philosophy of language to escape from what Austin calls 'excessive abstraction', or the tendency to see language as an isolated phenomenon in abstraction from the wider context in which things are said. Language must be returned to the context of human behaviour and social interaction. We need to look at the speech act, rather than concentrate too much on any single item of discourse or simply upon words on their own (Austin, 1962a, 1962b; Searle, 1969). The prime importance of words, then, resides in the meanings they convey when used in a discursive or material context that displays their rules of use.

This is not to say that words in isolation are without meanings. Clearly word meanings are 'autonomous' items for which we can write dictionary entries. But even these dictionary entries have their meanings because words can be used in particular contexts. Yet in particular contexts, speakers could not mean something by the words they use if the words did not already have some established conventions for their use: prior meanings which individual speakers did not themselves make the words mean. Some common agreement on rules of use, in a variety of contexts, is a necessary preliminary to using words in sustained communication. Convention dictates the 'prior meaning' of words: meaning is determined by use.

When we become familiar with the conventions of use for words, we are able to understand the meanings of sentences. Platts cites Quine who acknowledges the priority that 'autonomous' words possess, but proceeds to put that priority pointedly in its place:

> "Sentences being limitless in number and words limited, we necessarily understand most sentences by construction from antecedently familiar words . . . Then we can say that knowing words is knowing how to work out the meanings of sentences containing them" (Platts, 1979, p. 24).

In the reverse activity of making up messages, our familiarity with the conventions of word use allows us to say original things. We show our knowledge of the meaning of a word by knowing how to use it within its appropriate language games.

For Wittgenstein, we learn the rules of any language game by watching it being played, and by playing it; not by being told how to play it. Still the sentence 'the meaning of a word is its use in a language', is not a definition of word meaning. Norms, rules, and values govern word use; they do not dictate it. Norms or rules do not lay down what must be done. Rather a norm or a rule is that which, once an action is done, can be said to display the meaning of that action. Putting a word to use is a way of making propaganda for a certain way of thinking. While the use must be public, it also represents the life forms in which our words are grounded and these are not necessarily public. Every explanation and every interpretation fits into a meaning system or language game.

So words have meaning depending on their 'fit' within the context and the meaning system of the utterance. This fit in turn depends upon conventions, rules and agreements arbitrarily reached at some stage. It is not important philosophically when this stage was reached. These enable the word user to communicate 'sense' to other people. By replying, the others acknowledge that they are party to the conventions, rules, and agreements that determine the fit of word meanings. Patterns of use determine meaning: the meaning of a word is its use in a language game.

## Insights from Linguistics and from Studies of Literacy

### Literacy and Sociocultural Position

The academic meaning systems, shaped by the special culture of academic literacy over several millennia, are the world's most influential language games. Getting access to those meaning systems is obviously tied to literacy in important ways. At the very least, access depends on participating orally in the culture of literacy and perhaps also on becoming literate.

The problems of those trying to master literacy are only superficially matters of linguistic behaviour. In becoming literate, adults and children pass through a sequence of cognitive, linguistic and social adjustments rather like those that occur in communicating across cultural boundaries. There are also epistemic and political dimensions to literacy that make it a complex practice that is embodied in individuals and groups in very different ways: "There is no such thing as reading *per se*, as skills or processes of reading independent of texts, discourses and ideologies" (Luke, 1994 p. 367). Indeed the evidence is now very strong that many speakers' discourse styles are not readily translatable into the expository written mode. As a result, children progress unequally towards academic literacy and towards success in the special literate culture that the school tries to create. The intricate factors underlying that inequality have recently come more to light through the work of Goody (1987), Gee (1988), Gumperz (1982), Hamilton et al. (1993), Heath (1983), Luke (1994), Philips (1983), Romaine (1984), Scribner & Cole (1981), Scollon & Scollon (1981), and Snow (1983) among many others.

From these and other studies spanning educational systems, disciplines, cognitive dimensions and sociocultural groups, an important link emerges between the mode and manner of literacy acquisition and sociocultural positioning: Literacy is learned in specific settings and the discursive practices for that learning vary across institutional and social networks in the critical purposes to which the literacy is put. In particular, the purposes, effects, and types of literacy for any single group may be very different from those established and recognized in schools. Accordingly the potential for achieving academic literacy and quick success in the literate culture of the school will vary, as sociocultural factors interact with cognitive factors in complex ways.

For example, Heath (1983) examines the ways of 'taking' from printed material that young children learn from their home settings. Often these ways of taking are inconsistent with the patterns of literate culture expected in schools. These patterns established in the home leave many children unconnected with the traditionally assigned rewards that come from literacy: things like job preparation, social mobility, intellectual creativity and information access. As a result, the motivation for reading and writing for many children is different. Literacy also has different meanings that correspond with variations in modes, functions, and uses.

In particular, the academic usefulness of immersion in the school's culture of literacy, holds little motivation for many children: The printed word, the knowledge categories, and the ways of taking meaning from the printed word, have little place in many children's worlds. In their place, they often have other culturally relevant skills including access to other meaning systems that are not required of them until later stages of schooling, if at all. But by the time these skills are required, many children have missed the foundation immersion in the school's culture of literacy that is needed to support the presentation of their special insights in school-acceptable ways.

Intricate sociocultural forces and discursive practices are at work positioning people close to or distant from dominant meaning systems. Depending on their sociocultural position, children may acquire a lexico-semantic range very different from that favoured by the special literate culture of the school. Although we know very little about the concrete effects of literacy on the lives of individuals (Kaestle, 1991), it is very likely that the acquisition of literacy in schools does little to change the active vocabularies of children who occupy sociocultural positions at a distance from the kinds of cultural capital given high status in the school.

I continue this discussion of literacy and vocabulary under 'Insights from Psychology' and return to it in the last chapter of the book. Second language research in applied linguistics has also become a rich source of insight into the study of words and society.

*Second Language Research*

English-as-a-second language (ESL) research now pays much closer attention to vocabulary acquisition (McCarthy, 1990; Nation, 1990; Nation & Carter, 1989; Carter & McCarthy, 1988; Meara, 1993). *The Lexical Bar* helped lend impetus to this revival (Meara, 1986). But this interest in lexical semantics among second language researchers is not new. Wilkins (1972) noted the broad importance lexical studies have in several areas: in understanding the process of translation; in seeing the way that words are organized; and in appreciating the range and subtlety of meaning that words possess.

Still the upsurge of interest in vocabulary in the 1980s and 1990s, among ESL and other second language researchers, has been remarkable. It has been prompted by studies like Saville-Troike's (1984) into academic success and failure in a second language. She confirmed that in learning another language, vocabulary knowledge is "the most important aspect of oral proficiency for academic achievement" (216). Confirmation comes from Garcia (1991) who finds that ESL students' dearth of adequate English vocabulary severely affects their reading comprehension and their academic progress. The reading performances of Latino students in the United States, for example, differs mainly in vocabulary range and conceptual development when compared with non-ESL students. These differences begin to grow rapidly at around 10 years of age (Applebee, Langer & Mullis, 1987). How does vocabulary knowledge discriminate between new and old learners of English?

Young ESL students and young native speakers of English acquire vocabulary at about the same rate, but because ESL students come later to learning the language, they take time to make up the gap that already exists (Goulden, Nation & Read, 1990). In Canada, Cummins (1981) shows that 'length of residence' has a substantial effect on the rate at which immigrant students approach grade norms in vocabulary, and that this length of residence effect is largely independent of the children's age on arrival. Older learners make almost the same progress as younger ones, and in fact acquire cognitive/academic second language skills more quickly. Cummins points out that since immigrant children arriving in English-dominant parts of Canada, take 5 to 7 years to bridge the vocabulary gap between themselves and Canadian-born children, then the two years of ESL education that they receive is quite inadequate. Because these children quickly master the surface features of English, they often seem more fluent than they really are. Cummins warns that this can also cause very misleading scores on verbal ability tests and serious mistakes in assessing educational potential.

These early findings from Cummins and others, underline the discriminatory effect that access to academic vocabulary can have. The first-language backgrounds of the students in Cummins' studies are not mentioned, although they were mainly European and Asian in origin. But the length of time that these ESL students needed to gain educationally relevant cognitive/academic skills in English, suggests that the lexical bar itself may be an important obstacle for many ESL students to negotiate. Obviously many older ESL children, and also adult learners about to enter complex knowledge areas, will come across this academic vocabulary barrier that intensifies the problems they already have starting on English itself.

Some ESL research draws an explicit link with the lexical bar studies. In Hong Kong, researchers studied 55 Cantonese-first-language ESL adolescents, sampled from schools across Hong Kong (Hsia, Chung & Wong, 1995). They looked at how these advanced students organize English words into lexico-semantic fields ready for learning. In particular the students have great difficulty in recognizing words that are Graeco-Latin (G-L) in origin. From their data, the researchers suggest that the specialist meanings of these words and the teaching approaches used to introduce them, place the words in rigid and isolated lexico-semantic categories within each student's mental lexicon, which makes them difficult to recall and use. This problem for Cantonese students contrasts with another problem to do with morphology differences in using G-L words, that is experienced by Dutch students.

Chapter 7 describes the psycholinguistic studies from the Netherlands more fully (Bergman, Hudson & Eling, 1988). It also describes the effects on word processing in the brain, of the basic morphological differences between specialist G-L words and other types of words in English. In brief, Dutch university students process morphologically complex Latinate-Dutch words much more slowly than morphologically complex Germanic-Dutch words of the same frequency in the language. But this is a very different kind of difficulty in using G-L words compared with the difficulty experienced by the Hong Kong students. In the Hong Kong case, it is the isolation of the G-L words in single specialist meaning systems that makes them difficult to use. In the Dutch case, the morphological complexity of the Latinate-Dutch words is intensified by the low frequency and moribund nature of their affixes and stems in Dutch. This is because the words are very different from other morphologically complex words in the students' Germanic language.

Hancin-Bhatt & Nagy (1994), Ard & Homburg (1983), and Sandra (1988; 1993) examine the value that a knowledge of morphology has as a natural aid in learning the vocabulary of a second language. From studies of Dutch students learning English vocabulary, Sandra reports that many older learners spontaneously rely on morphological knowledge to learn new words. Hancin-Bhatt & Nagy study the ability of Spanish-English bilingual students to locate Spanish cognate stems in suffixed English words. All of the target cognate words used in their study are Latinate. The researchers find that older students, in grades 6 and 8, and also students who keep on using their Spanish in school, are more able than younger students to 'translate' cognate words, even beyond any increase in their actual vocabulary knowledge. They also report development in the students' awareness of certain systematic relationships between suffixes in the two languages. In contrast, Ard & Homburg study adults, whose first languages are Spanish and Arabic. They look at the ability these adults have to recognize Latinate words in English that are also Spanish-English cognates. Not surprisingly, the Spanish-as-a-first-language speakers are significantly more proficient in recognizing the words. In all of these cases, the ESL speakers who have an advantage are getting linguistic 'motivation' from their morphological knowledge.

Just finding a 'motivation' for the presence of a G-L stem in a derived word helps its learning in direct ways. Later I discuss the use of 'motivation' in this special linguistic sense. I also return to Sandra's work in Chapter 7. Giving words increased linguistic motivation has much to do with the classroom context and the teaching methods used when formally introducing the vocabulary of a second language. Chapter 7 also concludes that language awareness of this kind, acquired at the time of putting G-L words into verbal memory, is very important for their later recognition and use.

In present-day education, the increased integration of ESL students into regular classrooms gives them wider opportunities to interact in natural language settings with native speakers. ESL students are now less often placed in withdrawal classes, where intrinsic (psychological) motivation can be low, and where wider social contacts and peer models of proficient usage are few. But there are reasons for this ESL reform that go well beyond the social and the motivational. Linguistic factors, related to extending students' lexico-semantic range, also support these changes.

For example, negotiated interaction between a native speaker and a second language learner, of the kind provided by teacher-to-pupil and often by pupil-to-pupil interaction, provides the vital moment for developing competence and spurring language acquisition (Swain, 1985). Research bears out the view that peer negotiation and any other accompanying speech adjustments, especially to do with 'talking about text', play a very importa t part in second language acquisition (Allwright & Bailey, 1991; Leung, 1993). These are the experiences that put the word learner in touch with the life forms and the rules of use that lie behind words. They also play the most important part in first language vocabulary development.

Yet research outside classrooms, on the close link between second language learning and social identity, suggests that these important linguistic arrangements are regularly missing from first or second language learning classrooms. Students always need genuine opportunities to use the newly acquired language material, but because their sociocultural positioning outside classrooms often denies them wide opportunities for natural interaction, many adult ESL students often make only slight gains in their English language proficiency, even after many years of formal instruction (Peirce, 1995).

What is needed in any vocabulary learning, is an opportunity to use the word for the first time in some motivated discursive context that sets the word against the rules of use that obtain in that context: to use it in the company of interlocutors who respond and thereby acknowledge, qualify, enrich, and reinforce that very first use of the word. I continue this discussion under 'Insights from Language in Education'.

## Differences Between Oral and Written Vocabularies

Studies on the linguistic differences between spoken and written texts give conflicting results. No single kind of variation between spoken and written texts adequately accounts for the differences (Biber, 1986). But most research finds that writing is more complex, explicit and integrated (Chafe & Danielewicz, 1985; Olson, 1977). Writing contains more novel content when length is controlled (Brown & Yule, 1983). It is also more highly organized (Akinnaso, 1982: Gumperz et al., 1984).

Vocabulary differences between speech and writing are widely noted. There is general agreement that certain vocabulary differences distinguish edited writing from spontaneous speech. This is because the extensive editing that careful writing allows, gives a high degree of lexical precision to most types of written text. Edited writing also allows more explicit levels of expression, as evidenced by more precise word choices, more high-content words per clause, and higher type/token ratios (ratios between the number of different words used and the total number of words). Greater word length is a characteristic that also distinguishes edited writing from spontaneous speech.

When taken together, all these features of writing allow a very exact presentation of information content in relatively few words. When longer words appear, they tend to have more specific meanings, allowing a unique expression of each thought within some specialist semantic field or meaning system. Shorter words always appear more often and tend to be more general in their meanings. The studies reported in Chapters 5 and 6 examine both speech and writing. They reveal very significant differences in G-L usage between the two modes. Chapters 4, 7 and 8 also treat word length more fully.

## Semantic Fields

Studying vocabulary is difficult because individual vocabularies vary so greatly, even between people of similar age, background, and experience. But in education what is really important is discursive access to entire knowledge categories. It is the induction of students into the language games of educationally relevant meaning systems that really matters for educational success in present-day schools. Semantic field theory gives a guide to studying the vocabularies of these knowledge categories.

The origins of field theory lie with Trier in the early 1930s. But Trier's interest was prompted by the German philosopher von Humboldt's much earlier search for the 'inner form of knowledge'. Although Trier's work has been heavily criticized (Vassilyev, 1974; Lehrer, 1974; Lyons, 1977; Ullmann, 1962; Leech, 1974; and Moravcsik, 1977), his theories are still an important stage in the development of structural semantics.

Work by Weisberger and by Hjelmslev gave semantic field theory two of its major divisions. These are paradigmatic fields and syntagmatic fields. Paradigmatic fields include words of the same form class that share semantic features (e.g. KITTEN and PUPPY). Syntagmatic fields include classes of word closely linked by usage, but never occurring in the same syntactic position (e.g. ANNOUNCE and MICROPHONE). In the category of paradigmatic fields, several further sub-divisions of field types appear, including 'lexico-semantic groups' and 'semantemes' (Vassilyev, 1974). Both these categories are important for this study, so I introduce them briefly here.

*Lexico-semantic groups* denote any class of words united in sense by at least one common idea. In Chapter 5, seven knowledge categories of the secondary school curriculum (mathematics, physical sciences etc.) provide the unifying ideas for the seven lexico-semantic groups explored. These are the semantic fields used in the study. Table 1 in Chapter 5 shows these seven fields, each one consisting of seven 'semantemes'.

A *semanteme* is a single word with two or more meanings. For example, in discussing Wittgenstein's philosophy of language, Rundle (1990) mentions the pattern of associations between one or more central meanings of the word PLATE, and its transferred or extended senses: The article of crockery is generalized to a COLLECTION PLATE, and then to a STEEL PLATE, and then on to its many more distant uses in photography, geology etc. In the studies reported in Chapter 5, I examine a number of semantemes to see if children from different ages and backgrounds differ in their access to these different meanings across different semantic fields. For example, three of the different meanings for the word OBSERVE extend its ordinary language sense, when the word is used in specialist semantic fields linked with the physical sciences, with religion, and with ethics.

These categories of 'lexico-semantic groups' and 'semantemes' seem relatively uncontroversial in semantic field theory, although as a whole it is an area affected by all sorts of confusions in definition and meaning. Perhaps this is understandable in an area where abstraction is at a premium.

Lyons (1977) distinguishes 'designation' from 'meaning' within field theory, and he focuses on the latter. This removes field theory from confusion with associationist investigations in psychology, by making the idea of 'field' distinct from the idea of 'semantic network' explored by psychologists. Since 'semantic field' is only a lexical category, it is identical with the term 'lexical field' as Lyons expresses it: Words and other units that are semantically related within a given language-system "can be said to belong to, or to be members of, the same (semantic) field; and a field whose members are lexemes is a lexical field" (1977, p. 268).

So for Lyons, words semantically related in any sense are said to belong to the same semantic field. Also field theory is not restricted to particular sections of the vocabulary.  Relevant to my theme, Lyons relates semantic field theory directly to differences in sociocultural meaning systems:

> If the natural and cultural habitat of a particular society does not present instances of certain flora and fauna, of certain climatic conditions, of certain social institutions or artefacts etc., these things simply do not exist for that society (260).

So semantic fields allow comparisons to be made about meaning systems that exist or do not exist across social groups or between cultures. They also help uncover change or decay in meaning systems, at different historical points. While Lyons looks across the space dimension, Ullmann looks across time:

> A semantic field does not merely reflect the ideas, values and outlook of contemporary society, but it crystallizes and perpetuates them: it hands down to the oncoming generation a ready-made analysis of experience through which the world will be viewed until the analysis becomes so palpably inadequate and out-of-date that the whole field has to be re-cast (1962, p. 250).

The close overlap in meaning here with 'language games' and 'meaning systems' should not be missed. A relevant difference between 'semantic fields' as used in linguistics, and 'language game' from philosophy, or 'meaning system' from anthropology, is that semantic field is only a linguistic category. It takes little account of the non-linguistic life forms and  rules of use, set against a background of material conditions, that tend to unify cognate signs within the other types of system.

A person's lexico-semantic development within semantic fields depends directly upon life encounters with those systems. Like any essentially 'psycholinguistic' system, these are rather arbitrary organizations of words that groups of individuals tacitly agree to share, and whose status as enduring systems of meaning depends on conventions of use in the language games of the culture.

Nevertheless a conceptual analysis of the term 'semantic field', integrating views from semanticists such as Vassilyev (1974), Lehrer (1974), Lyons (1977), Ullmann (1962), Leech (1974), and Moravcsik (1977), reveals common ground that all these users of the expression 'semantic field' intend by it. This basic meaning is the useful and simple contention that it is possible to make generalizations about semantically related words and notionally to group them according to those generalizations.

While semantic field theory is an area of controversy in linguistics, it would be out of place to say more about the controversy and of the competing claims of theorists.  But 'semantic field' is a very useful organizing idea. Its point is nothing more than an analysis of word meanings that is compatible with speakers' intuitions about word usage. Because our intuitions about word usage are uncertain, we often need an 'authority' whose judgment is accepted as authoritative depending on whether or not the conventions of word usage are represented accurately in that authority. Ullmann (1962) cites conceptual dictionaries as authoritative collections of semantic fields and their components. In Chapters 5 and 8, I use a conceptual dictionary as an aid to inquiry.

*Morphology and Word Motivation*

In descriptive linguistics, morphology is the study of inflection, word shape and formation: the study of the properties of morphemes and their combination. Early work tried to develop an inventory of morphemes and an all-encompassing definition of the morpheme (Nida, 1948). After a period of decline (Anderson, 1982), the study of morphology revived through the work of Aronoff (1976), Halle (1973) and Jackendoff (1975). This revival matched the growth of interest in vocabulary more generally (Selkirk, 1982; Bauer, 1983).

The revival also occurred at the same time as interest grew in the mental lexicon among psycholinguists. But linguists and psycholinguists studying morphology and the brain have very different interests: The latter inherit a legacy from tachistoscopic studies of the link between perception and the mental lexicon. But the former are interested in fully developed linguistic representations of words in the mind (Sandra, 1994) and especially in words as part of language as a system.

Relevant to the representation of words in the mental lexicon, two main linguistic models have dominated debate: The 'impoverished-entry theory' assumes that only the stem of words is fully entered in the lexicon; and the 'full entry theory' assumes that all words, including complex and derived forms, have full entries (Jackendoff, 1975). Psycholinguistic research into the arrangement of the mental lexicon took over these two models and assimilated them. I describe relevant aspects of this burgeoning research in Chapters 7 and 8 and draw conclusions from it. Again, psycholinguistic research is more concerned with the actual representation of words in the brain than with their abstract characteristics.

These abstract aspects of words include their compositionality, their transparency, and their productivity (Bergman, Hudson & Eling, 1988). Bauer says that semantic 'compositionality' suggests that the meaning of the whole is predictable from the sum of its parts (1983). This relates closely to the idea of semantic or structural 'transparency' in which the meaning of a word is enhanced by the way its component morphemes combine in form or sense (e.g. the morphemes in LIGHTSHADE). 'Productivity' refers to the frequency of use of the same morphemes in the words of a language (e.g. the -PROACH in APPROACH and REPROACH). A morpheme is productive if it appears often in familiar words and also in new words in a language. All of these aspects of morphology relate to the idea of word 'motivation': the degree to which words 'speak' their meanings to people meeting them for the first time.

Words have three common types of 'motivation' that can make their meanings more transparent, even to people who are unfamiliar with them (Ullmann, 1951, 1962). Firstly, in 'phonetic motivation', the pattern of sound in the word suggests a noise associated in some way with the word's meaning (e.g. THUMP, HUMP, DUMP, CLUMP). Then, in 'semantic motivation', a clue to a word's meaning comes from some similarity discernible between the word and some other object referred to (i.e. through metaphor or metonymy). Finally, in morphological motivation, the parts of a word have  meanings of their own and the meaning of the word depends in some way upon a summation of the meanings of its parts (i.e. HEADSTAND, LOINCLOTH, SUBWAY).

Morphological motivation will sometimes give only an imprecise and even misleading guide to a word's meaning. In some compound words like LADYBIRD, BUTTERFLY and BLACKMAIL, there are many possible semantic relationships between the parts of the words. So the semantic value of this kind of motivation can depend on extralinguistic cues that are strong enough to supplement or even correct cues offered by the morphological motivation. This need for contextual support argues for the representation of the whole word in the mental lexicon, not just its component parts (Sandra, 1994). I return to this discussion about morphological motivation in Chapters 4, 7 and 8. Again the role of wider context, both larger linguistic units of meaning and extralinguistic context, is central to this discussion.

*Vocabulary and Discourse*

Interest in the relationship between vocabulary and larger units of meaning, has grown apace with the growth of interest in discourse analysis (Corson, 1995a).  In important ways, the text-binding quality of vocabulary relations provides insights into the rules of use of meaning systems that go well beyond the lexical and the linguistic. Recognition of this fact has caused linguists to look beyond language for insights into many of the more important questions about language that go outside language itself. Sometimes they call this the study of 'social semiotics' (Halliday, 1978) or more recently 'critical linguistics' (Fairclough, 1992).

A relevant example here is Benson & Greaves' (1981) work. They look at how lexical fields of discourse link up with social actions that occur within an institution. To understand a text, its readers or hearers have to discover its institutional field by looking for lexical signs that are located close to one another within the text. The fit between these collocated words helps create a lexical field of discourse. That fit is established over time within a social institution, like any other convention of use. As Wittgenstein suggests, playing the language game of the institution, or being allowed to play it, gives access to the conventional rules of word use. This improves people's place within the game and makes them more a part of its particular meaning system.

The growing links between these extra-linguistic interests of linguists and questions of access to knowledge, power, and social justice, take linguistics away from a preoccupation with language as a system. The research methods used in Chapters 5 and 6 try to stress the intricate links between word meaning and wider units of discourse and social formations. But I introduce these issues in depth at this point by discussing other disciplines that theorize matters of ideology, belief system, cultural meaning system, power, and language.

### Insights from the Sociology of Language and Education

There is a major shift in attitude to the language activities that schools take for granted as part of their mandate. This extends even to literacy, the very thing that schools were organized to pass on:

> literacy has been used, in age after age, to solidify the social hierarchy, empower élites, and ensure that people lower in the hierarchy accept the values, norms, and beliefs of the élites, even when it is not in their self-interest (Gee, 1988 p. 205).

By showing how access to the academic culture of literacy has helped stratify society, Chapter 3 lends historical support to this claim, although the point has not often been made by historians themselves who always count among the literate. But prominent theorists in anthropology, like Leach and Goody, were often critical of the central place that literacy gets in formal education (Musgrove, 1982). These critiques had a direct impact on the 'new' sociology of education that developed in England in the 1970s (Young, 1971) and which began to question the taken-for-granted aspects of formal education. Two theorists in particular were very influential in shaping this work. Both look at language from a sociological point of view: Bourdieu (1971; 1977; 1981) and Bernstein (1973; 1977; 1990). This section links their work with other related work.

### *Words as Linguistic Capital*

Clearly the special culture of literacy, given high status in schools, is well removed from the cultural capital valued by many people who occupy sociocultural positions remote from academic cultures. Compared with the culture of poorer working class people, the ruling group's cultural capital in a society is an 'academic' one:

> Those whose 'culture' . . . is academic culture conveyed by the school have a system of categories of perception, language, thought and appreciation that sets them apart from those whose only training has been through their work and their social contacts with people of their own kind (Bourdieu, 1971, p. 200).

In an earlier section, I discussed different ways of 'taking' literacy, and I mentioned groups of people who are set apart in these way from important basic aspects of academic culture. Many children may have only an intermittent experience of discursive practices, before and outside schooling, that promote acquisition and use of the specialist vocabularies that the literate culture of the school requires them to use.

Already in Chapter 1, I outlined Bourdieu's compelling arguments about language and education: Different sociocultural groups have different relations to language that are embedded in different sets of dispositions and attitudes towards the material world, ideas, and other people. As a result they value language in different ways. They have different kinds of linguistic capital which often contrast greatly with the high status forms of linguistic capital favoured in schools. But this academic linguistic capital is more than the competence to produce grammatically well-formed expressions and vocabulary. It also includes the ability to use appropriate norms for language use, and to produce the right expressions at the right time for a particular 'linguistic market'. So this linguistic capital that is valued in schools, is not equally available to children from different backgrounds, yet schools still operate as if all children had equal access to it.

The display of a high status vocabulary confers sociocultural prestige on those who know the appropriate place and the way in which to use it. Its possession favours some, while non-possession discriminates against the many. A theme of this book is that coincidences of social and linguistic history have combined to create a lexical situation in English that is unique among languages: Most of the specialist and high status vocabulary of English is G-L in origin, and most of its more everyday vocabulary is Anglo-Saxon in origin.

Relative to other languages, English has a fairly clear boundary drawn between its everyday and its high status vocabularies. As Chapter 3 argues, this creates a barrier between one form of linguistic capital and another. If children of certain sociocultural groups, in their final years of schooling, have unequal active access to a use of the high status words that provide linguistic capital in the 'field' of education, and if teachers assess their students' grasp of the culture through their public use of this vocabulary, then high status word usage stands as a key mediating factor between sociocultural background and educational success or failure.

These points about the lexical bar offer strong support to Bourdieu's ideas. In his book *Distinction* (1984), he studies artefacts of 'taste' taken from across the spectrum of social and cultural practices. These configurations of taste relate to specific social fractions and probably have many counterparts in configurations of vocabulary usage. I say more about the over-formality and pseudo-prestige of the G-L vocabulary in Chapters 4 and 6. But if present-day educational selection processes are based upon a long-term display of access to the high status vocabulary of the language, then this lexical bar in English stands as a key mediating factor between the different attainment rates in education achieved by children who are socialized into the different meaning systems of different groups.

A powerful implication of all this coincides with a basic tenet of the 'new' sociology of education. This is the view that rather than changing the children in some way, to suit the school, we need to think more about changing the forms of education and the institutions that unfairly disvalue what many children bring to school with them. There are close parallels here too with some of Bernstein's ideas. In his theorizing, he observes that "what is at issue is the social distribution of privilege and privileging meanings" and then later goes on to say:

> Success or failure is a function of the school's dominant curriculum, which acts selectively upon those who can acquire it. The dominant code modality of the school regulates its communicative relations, demands, evaluations, and positioning of the family and of its students" (1990 p. 118).

## Extralinguistic Context

I introduced Bernstein's theory of codes in Chapter 1 and explained why that theory of his has only an indirect bearing on the lexical bar studies. A decided shift in Bernstein's stance in the development of his theory of codes, came with his growing recognition of context as a prime unit of analysis. But this contextual unit of analysis "is not an abstracted utterance or a single context but relationships between contexts. Code is a regulator of the relationships *between* contexts and, through that relationship, a regulator of relationships *within* contexts". So what counts as a context for him depends upon these relationships between contexts, which "create markers whereby specific contexts are distinguished by their specialized meanings and realizations" (1990 p. 101). So Bernstein's emphasis here seems to be on what happens to differently positioned people's discourse practices, in the widest sense, when contexts or fields are changed or overlapped. When I am looking at vocabulary use within some specific meaning system, I use the phrase 'extralinguistic context' in a somewhat similar way. But like Bernstein's definition, mine is also difficult to approach because it is determined as much by psychological constraints as by sociological or linguistic ones.

The meaning of context in this sense is a form of extralinguistic control on the encoder. It is largely an involuntary constraint, so this idea is somewhat different from the idea of 'register'. Register is some variation in person, place, or topic that affects the language variant selected, but in a more voluntary way. In register there is emphasis on a changing choice of language that is made as a result of a change in extralinguistic context, rather than on involuntary control by it. In relation to controlling vocabulary, if a changed extralinguistic context affects word selection, the speaker in that new context consistently relegates certain words that could be available for active use, to a passive vocabulary. I discuss active and passive vocabulary in a later section. But a simple example of extralinguistic context at work is its effect on a person who swears a lot, and does so habitually. When a changed context of some kind, such as entry into a religious gathering or into some other formal occasion, constrains that person into choosing words more carefully and not swearing, this is extralinguistic context at work.

Many factors combine in extralinguistic context: the setting of the communication; the status and degree of intimacy of participants in the communication process; the level of interest and the familiarity of the subject matter to be communicated; and the language function being served. This last factor is an important one, since clearly language varies depending on the use to which it is put. For example, the vocabulary selections prompted in using the functions of 'describing' and 'explaining' are different, even for similar subject matter. The studies presented in Chapters 5 and 6 look at language used to serve these two different functions.

There is no doubt that making even the slightest changes in extralinguistic contexts will affect sociocultural groups differently in their language use (Corson, 1993). It is important for education to know how changing the context of schooling affects different children's vocabulary use, allowing some groups more ready active access than others to vocabularies that they hold in verbal memory. Schools could then think about deliberately changing the extralinguistic contexts that they create, thereby removing unwanted controls and allowing a more free-flowing use of language by all children in a setting that pays high regard to differences in group discourse norms.

*Social Influences on Vocabulary Acquisition and Use*

There are good reasons to think that the peer group is a most important influence in the acquisition of language (Trudgill, 1975). Many children do take their peers rather than their parents as models sooner or later, certainly before six years and perhaps much sooner (Samuels, 1972; Hudson, 1980). Probably children's oral vocabulary is mainly restricted to those words reinforced by the peer group, while words despised or avoided by the peer group will have much less appeal. But for some groups, this 'lexicon of avoidance' may well include the fundamental vocabulary of the school.

The impact of peer group pressures on a sociocultural group's vocabulary is obvious, especially where groups live in separate areas, as is common in English-speaking countries. Vocabulary changes intensify and accelerate in this peer group form of language contact (Samuels, 1972), as the roles for language use are defined by the innovative uses to which words are put within the unique meaning systems created by the sociocultural group. Role conflict can affect group members who venture outside the group into the meaning systems of other groups, and who return to the group after experiencing other ways of looking at the world.

This idea of 'role conflict' has great power in explaining the influence of peer groups on language. Failure to conform to the peer group's closed role system in lexical selection (by choosing to use the 'group-despised' vocabulary of the school, for example) can lead to a control which is much less subtle than that exercised in the family, and more immediate. The discourses of peer groups are clearly important in motivating the use of a differentiated vocabulary, but there are wider forces and discourses again that influence peer groups and the discourses they develop.

These wider forces relate to cultural and class divisions in society. Most people, for most of the time, try to conform to the language practices of those around them. For much of the time too, they do it subconsciously. Even when language practices serve the interests of powerful influences that are oppressive to them, most people seek the comfort that comes from conforming to sociocultural divisions by not challenging or even explicitly recognizing hegemonic relations. This is one of the influential ideas that Gramsci (1948) developed to help interpret social and political behaviour. But when people do recognize injustices in their sociocultural position and begin to resist the effects of cultural and class divisions on their language, they may begin to use vocabularies very different from those they normally use. The very act of resisting takes them into a different context and into meaning systems that were previously not their own. This can result in an active use of words very unlike those that may be legitimated by the peer group.

To resist the oppressive effects that some forms of schooling can have on their lives, people may have to use a language of resistance that borrows powerful vocabularies from more dominant discourses. Outside assessors may see these discourses as beyond the level of fluency expected from that group. Balester (1991) discusses what he calls 'hyperfluent discourse': Even when students in schools use words appropriately that are unusual for them, they may be engaged in an act of resistance, identifying with the language of the oppressors in order to turn it against them.

Yet children and adults are only able to do this if their life experiences have positioned them in contexts to acquire the rules for wielding those discourses. More than this, as part of the rules of use, they need to acquire the motivation to do so. C. Wright Mills stresses the role of 'vocabularies of motive' that have ascertainable functions in situated actions, and influence their users and those around them: "a motive tends to be one which is to the actor and to the other members of a situation an unquestioned answer to questions concerning social or lingual conduct" (1940: 907). Words, through their rules of use, have a power to motivate behaviour, which people only begin to appreciate when they try to play in the language games that establish the rules of use for those words.

There is a remarkable example of this in Willis's book *Learning to Labour* (1977). A 15 year old working class boy, Joey, uses a stream of G-L words very appropriately to help justify his peer group's lifestyle of resistance: DISCRETE, AUTHORITY, ESTABLISHMENT, RESENT, SUBMISSIVE, EMOTIONS, FRUSTRATIONS, DISPLEASURES, EXHILARATING, DEFYING etc. By using these words, like RESENT, DEFY, EXHILARATE, and FRUSTRATE, this boy gives voice to feelings that may be only vaguely sensed by him and his peergroup without the words themselves. His speech uses these vocabularies of motive to influence himself and those around him in ways that could be emancipatory and empowering for him and his mates. This is only a rare instance in which a young person's emancipated eloquence and broad vocabulary combine to meet the needs of an adolescent resister.

In fact, this form of resistance, couched in a rather aggressive and uncompromising challenge to authority, can have a disempowering effect, by reinforcing the conditions of subordination that help stratify schools and societies in unjust ways. While the more privileged students in schools also resist, they tend to do so in ways that allow them and their teachers to 'ignore' the results of the resistance, and even to incorporate it into their definitions of school success. Gramsci (1948) might call this boy, who comes from a far-from-privileged background, a budding 'organic intellectual' of the kind that relatively powerless groups produce, since the boy rises from an oppressed sociocultural group to speak up in its behalf. But Willis is careful to describe Joey as 'not typical' of his peergroup.

For most of the time, children from marginalized minority groups, or from poorer working class backgrounds in general, tend to conform, remain silent, opt out, or drop out of discursive settings of this kind. The evidence clearly shows that they tend to have less experience inside the kind of abstract and decontextualized discursive practices that schools set great store by and try to develop (Heath, 1983; Snow, 1983; Ogbu, 1981; 1985). As Bourdieu observes, they have different dispositions about what counts as important linguistic capital for them and about the appropriate occasions for using it. But what are the sociological variables that most affect word selection, use, and, as a result, lexico-semantic positioning? Does children's vocabulary use vary by sex, and across sociocultural groups?

*Sex Differences*

A summary of early studies comparing the vocabulary of boys and girls in middle and later childhood, finds few differences between the sexes in vocabulary diversity, and none that are significant (Corson, 1985). Later vocabulary studies by Anglin (1993) look at children from grades 1, 3 and 5. While there are slight differences among the youngest children, he reports no significant sex effects among the older children. In general, Anglin confirms that the lack of significant sex differences in his research is consistent with earlier studies. It is certainly consistent with evidence more generally to suggest that there are few overt language differences between boys and girls, although significant differences do exist in discourse norms between boys and girls, probably modelled through socialization on the differences between men and women (Corson, 1993). While some gender theorists may find this summary of the vocabulary evidence surprising, as it was to me, to date there is no evidence to suggest that boys and girls raised in one another's company differ much in their lexico-semantic orientation. But it is certainly likely that because of their broad differences in discourse norms, girls and boys would acquire different rules of use in different contexts for certain words, as they grow older.

*Quantitative and Qualitative Variations by Class and Cultural Background*

A summary of early research suggests that a much more differentiated vocabulary is available to some groups of children than to others (Corson, 1985). Later studies on differentiation in vocabulary by social class and minority culture background, lend strong support to this conclusion (White, Graves & Slater, 1990). Anglin (1993) also reports significant variations in favour of upper socioeconomic status children in the diversity of their recognition vocabulary (see Chapter 4).

Many studies report variations in form class usage by social class background, especially in the use of uncommon adjectives (Bernstein, 1977; Hawkins, 1977; Lawton, 1968; Robinson, 1978) and in the use of adverbs of manner and location (Turner, in Brandis and Henderson, 1970). Significant differences in mean word length also appear (Bernstein, 1977). Clearly there is something going on here, but the many researchers are unsure what it is.

Little evidence is available about 'qualitative' differences in word usage, either by sociocultural group or by gender. The same summary of early research concludes that suitable instruments for measuring qualitative word use in texts are not widely available (Corson, 1985). Although many researchers can see clear differences, they say that finding a means of comparison between qualitatively different words has not been easy.

Oevermann makes an early effort to overcome this difficult problem of measuring qualitative verbal differentiation (in Dittmar, 1976). He tries to differentiate word use according to semantic and not grammatical categories. From his study of the relative use of verbs of intention and emotion, Oevermann reports significant differences in vocabulary use. In doing so, he tacitly adopts a measure designed to investigate two specific semantic fields.

These points about the qualitative representation of meaning systems in words, take discussion a little away from the lived social world and its material events. Later in this chapter, I look again at these questions when discussing cultural meaning systems in anthropology. At this point, I return to the role of words in the mind.

## Insights from Psychology and Cognitive Studies of Literacy

Vygotsky (1962) and Luria (1956) share the view that we use socially invented signs as instruments of thought, mainly in the form of the words of a language whose rules of use we acquire in discursive practice. In any of the ways in which people experience words, against the backdrop of some meaning system or other, they pick up clues about these rules of use so that once an action is done, the rule becomes the thing that displays the meaning of that action within its own meaning system. But when represented in the brain itself, meanings are groupings and orderings of stimulus patterns and connections between them:

> Just such a view is suggested by Luria's characterization of a word as a "complex multidimensional matrix of different cues and connections" ([Luria, 1973] p. 306). Neural network theory enables us to hazard a guess as to how meanings, construed in this way, could shape or influence the microprocessing structure of the brain by setting up nodes or configurations of sensitivities to patterns of information and then forming connections between those functional nodes (Harré & Gillett, 1994 p. 72).

I return to all these matters (cues, connections, activations, and nodes) when discussing the internal ordering of the mental lexicon later in this section and more extensively in Chapter 7.

Specific to rules of use, the learning of words provides the focus for making sense of the rules. But this process of word acquisition is a dynamic one, not a single act of mastery. It proceeds against a backdrop of rules known only imprecisely at first. Word meanings remain unstable until the network of rules becomes more interlocked. However the more words that people learn, and the more thoroughly they learn their rules of use, the more seamless becomes the fabric of rules that comprise a meaning system. As children become more adept at 'taking' the words of a language, they learn that their own utterances also have meaning in a certain way, as exemplars of certain rules, and against the backdrop of certain meaning systems and contexts.

*Quantitative Studies of Vocabulary*

The study of vocabulary growth is one of the oldest lines of research in language development. Estimates of adolescent vocabulary size, drawn from many of these early studies by Nagy & Herman (1987), suggest that the average high school senior's vocabulary is around 40,000 words, and that a child at only the 25th percentile in vocabulary size would perhaps possess only 5,000 fewer words. This is not a great difference in size, yet the value of those extra 5000 words may confer great social rewards.

Unfortunately these and the many other early studies of vocabulary conducted in psychology prior to 1970 (Palermo & Molfese, 1972), miss many aspects of semantic development. There are several reasons for this: first, the presence of a word in a child's recognition vocabulary by itself, does not say much about the child's grasp of that word. Second, simple vocabulary counts ignore important relations between word meanings, since a person's knowledge of vocabulary goes well beyond a list of words. Third, earlier vocabulary studies do not provide information on the vital process by which word meanings are combined into sentence meanings (Dale, 1976). How to develop adequate instruments for measuring the semantic aspects of vocabulary, and its role in discourse, has been a challenging problem.

Many studies of vocabulary confine themselves to various manifestations of simple 'word count' procedures. Here, in designing measures, little concession is made to distinctions like 'levels of lexical difficulty', 'the influence of extralinguistic context', and 'passive or active vocabulary'. Many psychological tests of vocabulary are framed largely as simple checklists for measuring recognition vocabulary (Zimmerman et al., 1977) or as standardized reading vocabulary tests that require only a moderate amount of information about a word's meaning in order to answer correctly (Curtis, 1987). Often the tests concentrate on more 'picturable' word meanings, which means a heavy bias towards nouns. One study of the form classes of words that appear in many different vocabulary-based tests, found none of the tests was representative: Nouns dominated the word lists, even though nouns as a group are less 'difficult' than other parts of speech (Roberts, 1970).

In particular, standardized attainment tests often give only a crude basis for numerical count and show nothing about relations among ideas. They can also create problems of cultural bias and other biases. But studies do suggest that the checklist-with-foils method, in which words and non-words are randomly mixed in a list, has some value for assessing differences between individuals in vocabulary knowledge (Meara & Buxton, 1987; White, Slater & Graves, 1989; Allen, Cipielewski & Stanovich, 1992). This is no doubt true, but there seems to be something important missing from a study of the words that people are thought to 'have', if the rules for using the words are not considered.

*Qualitative Studies of Vocabulary*

More qualitative measures of vocabulary are attempted by some. The use of a 'common versus uncommon' dichotomy is one solution offered. While there are "no formal criteria for deciding what is common or uncommon" (Hawkins, 1977, p. 14), some researchers appeal to word frequency in the language as an important characteristic of commonness (White, Graves & Slater, 1990; Graves et al., 1987) using various word frequency catalogues (Thorndike and Lorge, 1944; Carroll *et al.*, 1971; Kucera and Francis, 1967; Dictionnaire des Fréquences, 1971). Whyte (1983) looks at the interpretative language of adults who are normal readers and adults who are poor readers. In his study, normal readers use more abstract/psychological referents, while poor readers use more concrete sensory referents. So Whyte is looking more towards the content domain, or the meaning system that usually embeds the words. This is an interesting departure. As Drum & Konopak note: "the influence of content domain on vocabulary learning has not been examined closely" (1987, 78).

Informed by *The Lexical Bar,* Olson & Astington (1990) examine adolescents' familiarity with two types of verbs: 'mental state' verbs and 'speech act' verbs. They invite children to choose appropriate verbs from a list that includes distractors, to fill spaces in a written passage. Although in their study, vocabulary proficiency clearly increases with age, the 12 year old children only perform at around chance level on this task, as do the 12 year olds in the lexical bar studies (see Chapter 5). Elsewhere Allen, Cipielewski & Stanovich (1992) also use a measure of mental state words, which is based in turn on the Olson & Astington measure. They supplement it with a revised version of the Peabody Picture Vocabulary Test (Dunn & Dunn, 1981) and several other normed tests of vocabulary achievement. Their study confirms that a strong correlational link exists between children's exposure to print material and their recognition vocabulary. Other researchers prefer a combination of interviews and multiple choice tests (White, Graves & Slater, 1990), and perhaps in this way they overcome some of the problems other researchers have distinguishing the different meanings that polysemantic words often have across meaning systems.

*Passive and Active Vocabulary*

It is clear that early in their development, children's comprehension vocabularies are larger than their production vocabularies (Benedict, 1979). It is also clear that older children's comprehension of morphologically complex words exceeds their ability to produce them (Clark & Berman, 1987). Yet outside the lexical bar studies, I know of no attempt to distinguish between words passively held and words used actively.

Many researchers confirm that recognition vocabulary knowledge expands greatly in the middle school years, as Anglin argues (1993). But he also acknowledges that the kinds of tests used to measure recognition vocabulary fail to show that words have been learned previous to the test. They also fail to show that the words are 'psychologically basic' in the sense of having been stored in long-term memory as unitary wholes. He estimates that children's recognition vocabularies are 10,000, 20,000 and 40,000 words at grades 1, 3, and 5 respectively. However he warns that these vocabularies include words that are 'known' in the sense that their meanings have been learned previously and can be used in an active way; and others too that are only potentially knowable, in the sense that their meanings could be worked out at the time of testing, through morphological cues.

Getting people to display their active vocabulary is rather easy. But as I have suggested, a single word response to a picture or query is not really enough to assess someone's grasp of that word's rules of use. The word really has to be used in some linguistic context: in some discursive practice. Much the same can be said for eliciting passive vocabulary, but that task is complicated by the additional need to elicit words that may be only partly known on the one hand, or held passively for reasons of extralinguistic context on the other. What I mean here are the constraints of the various closed role systems discussed above, in the sociology section. For example, the common reluctance that people have to swear and curse in public, makes many taboo words inactive, yet almost everyone has those words passively and can recognize them when heard. As Harré & Gillett note: "human rule-followers not only follow rules, but conceive of themselves as under discursive constraints" (1994 p. 76).

In general, a study of vocabulary that tries to meet the 'use' theory of vocabulary meaning, should meet these two requirements. First, the study needs to verify that respondents have some minimal familiarity with the rules of use for the words studied within the relevant meaning systems. Second, as well as eliciting active vocabulary, it needs to elicit that kind of word that is stored in verbal memory but not readily available for active use. This vocabulary may be passive for one or both of the following reasons.

On the one hand, passive words may be low frequency words in the person's mental lexicon. These are words that can be activated in principle, if the stimulation and the length of activation is great enough. But for most of the time, they stay unactivated, except for rare use as recognition vocabulary when making sense of an incoming message that can be slowed down to allow time for greater activation. On the other hand, these passive words may be part of a 'lexicon of avoidance', like swear words, that are available for use if the constraints of extralinguistic context are removed. The words affected by these two factors are what I mean by a person's passive vocabulary. Is there more to say about this distinction between 'active vocabulary' and 'passive vocabulary'?

An active vocabulary covers all those words people need to use and have no reservations about using to communicate with others on an everyday basis. The range of people's active vocabulary is a unique reflection of their sociocultural position and the range of discursive practices engaged in. In other words, it depends on the range of relations people contract as a part of everyday existence, over a lifetime. Except for people who frequently make contact with the specialist meaning systems of professions or of other special knowledge categories, most people's active words are high frequency words in the language and need little stimulus to activate them in the mental lexicon. They are ready for use in incoming and outgoing messages, with no noticeable effort.

A passive vocabulary also includes the words stored in verbal memory that people partially 'understand', but not well enough for active use. These are words that people meet less often and they may be low frequency words in the language as a whole. In other words, activating them takes longer and it demands greater stimulus than most textual contexts provide. Words stop being passive if people are regularly contracting relations that activate them, since this lowers the amount of stimulus needed to put them to use. A facility in using the words develops. Again constraints of another kind in the extralinguistic context may also restrict the active use of some words. This can happen even when words are available for active use in principle, such as cultural taboo words that most people know but rarely use outside certain settings.

Following the immense vocabulary growth of the middle years, when children's verbal memories rapidly expand, they enter adolescence with a very high proportion of their words still lodged in their passive vocabularies. What do we know about the growth of word meaning in adolescence?

*Mature Concept Formation in the Adolescent Years*

Formation of concepts (or 'word meanings') depends on "the development of many intellectual functions: deliberate attention, logical memory, abstraction, the ability to compare and to differentiate" (Vygotsky, 1962, p. 83). Chomsky notes that "the rate of vocabulary acquisition is so high at certain stages of life, and the precision and delicacy of the concepts acquired so remarkable, that it seems necessary to conclude that in some manner the conceptual system with which lexical items are connected is already substantially in place" (1980, p. 139). All these things seem to come together developmentally during the adolescent years. They may take longer for some children than for others, because of differences in language experience. But if adequate verbal stimulation is present in the adolescent environment, all normal children become capable of mature concept formation somewhere after their twelfth and before their seventeenth year.

A fruitful source of insights about adolescent concept formation is the series of studies in Britain by Peel and his associates (1971, 1972, 1975, 1978). His conclusion confirms the results of earlier research that mature concept formation from contextual material alone, is only achieved at the earliest by the age of 15 years. A corollary of this research is that when higher level concepts are first introduced to younger children, they need to be supplemented by more than the contextual prose in which they first appear. An example may help: Although most 6 year olds really do appreciate the role in gathering information, of complex behavioural ideas like perceiving, communicating, and inferring, the concepts named by related words, like PERCEIVE, INTERPRET and INFER, are rarely present in children's active vocabularies before middle adolescence (Wimmer, Hogrefe & Sodian, 1988).

This difficulty in learning words only from their textual context, is clear from a study by Nagy, Herman & Anderson (1985). Using multiple choice questions and interviews about word knowledge, they estimate the percentage chance of learning a word from textual context alone, after only one encounter with it, at between 10% and 15%. So while a great many words may go into children's passive vocabularies while they read, only a few new ones that are met over and over again will actually be learned in the sense that they become available for ready use. Something more is needed to promote wider and greater conceptual development. Clearly the textual context for word learning needs supplementing through motivated activities using dialogue around that textual material: by talking about text.

*The Academic Culture of Literacy: Talking about Text*

Olson & Astington believe that participation in the discursive practices of a literate culture promotes an active use of the metalinguistic distinctions named by abstract words:

> Although it is likely that the knowledge of such terms is more characteristic of the speech of educated middle class families, we see this knowledge as a direct reflection of the literate habits of families rather than as a general characteristic of a social class (1990 p. 717).

Putting 'the world on paper' is an apt metaphor for the process by which representations of the world, recorded in literate texts, have created entire meaning systems within and across the academic culture of literacy. Olson speaks of the innovators of this culture of literacy: "What they invented, it turned out, was not a royal road to the ultimate truth of things but a new mode of discourse" (1994 p. 197). This new mode of discourse reshaped the structure of knowledge and the ways of thinking about representing and using knowledge. As Luke notes, the bias of literacy is "towards the 'autonomous text', abstract, decontextualized and aligned with a scientific will to truth" (1994, p. 375).

These new literate interpretations of the world became the specialist meaning systems of education. Olson traces the history of some of these systems: There is the 'mathematization of motion' wherein properties of motion were reconstructed in terms of the structures of formalized written languages. There is the 'taxonomization of the natural world' when drawings were coordinated with the texts of scientific description. There is the 'reifying of imaginary worlds' when distinctive literary forms began to use literal meanings that normally report truth, to report things known to be false. And there is the 'representation of the mind and mental states' which gave us culturally idiosyncratic ways for thinking about the mind. This last development yielded results that are still with us: It produced the twin beliefs of experimental psychology, mentioned in Chapter 1, that allow people to think of the mind as independent of the world and not as a positioned product of the discourses in which they have engaged.

What does all this have to do with specialist vocabulary learning? Olson's main point again is that it is mainly participation in the discursive practices of a literate culture that promotes conceptual development and the learning of words appropriate to this culture of literacy. For him there is no better way into it. There is confirmation of this view in the wideranging work of Bruner. He wonders about the strange priority given in recent decades to a search for the underlying genetic program for language acquisition and development:

> How puzzling that there should be . . . so *little* [emphasis] on the ways in which the culture, the parents and more "expert" speakers (including other, older children) help the genetic program to find expression in *actual language use*. The educational level of parents deeply affects how well, richly and abstractly their children will talk (and listen). It is not just the *grammar of sentences* that is at issue, but discourse, dialogue, the capacity to interpret spoken and written language (Bruner, 1983 p. 173).

These views go beyond recommendations about how to promote vocabulary development that other researchers in the psychology of education offer. Some of these researchers give high priority to wide reading (Hayes, 1988; Nagy, Anderson & Herman, 1987). Some also find strong connections between exposure to print and the development of certain, if not all, verbal skills (Stanovich & Cunningham, 1992; Stanovich, 1993: and see Chapter 9). Some recommend direct vocabulary instruction (Beck, Perfetti & McKeown, 1982; Beck, McKeown & Omanson, 1987) or instruction in morphological structure (Anglin, 1993; Henry, 1993). Some favour a combination of word instruction, wider reading, and the explicit teaching of word strategies (White, Graves & Slater, 1990).

Granting the merits of these contrasting views, along with Olson I rank oral participation in an English-speaking culture of literacy, and its mediated benefits, more highly as a factor in English vocabulary growth. Even without acquiring literacy (Goody, 1987; Scribner & Cole, 1981), oral participation in a culture of literacy seems at least as important for vocabulary acquisition as some of the work that schools concentrate on, in the formal teaching of reading or in direct vocabulary instruction. In fact, a rather worrying finding from a study of children's out-of-school experiences, tends to confirm me in the view that just participating in the discursive practices of a literate culture is more important for vocabulary growth than most school-related things.

Looking at thousands of students in New York, Hayes & Grether (1983) compared all the students' vocabulary development during the vacation period with their vocabulary development during the school term. Remarkably the vocabulary gap between high-achieving and low-achieving students increases more during the holiday period. The researchers conclude from this that most of the difference in word knowledge performance comes from events outside school, not from school itself.

This is also strong evidence to support the view that differences in the discursive practices of children positioned differently by their sociocultural relations, are the key to understanding differences in their lexico-semantic range. Chapters 3 and 4 discuss how differences in discursive positioning have come about for speakers of English. Chapters 7 and 8 discuss how the two sets of differences, the discursive and the sociocultural, show up in different arrangements of the mental lexicon, linked especially with the storage and retrieval of morphologically complex words.

## Morphological Processing

Evidence confirms that after children's earliest years, vocabulary growth is related to the ability to handle greater morphemic complexity. This development is also associated with greater language knowledge (Clark & Berman, 1987; Clark, Hecht & Mulford, 1986; Hancin-Bhatt & Nagy, 1994). Different word types and differences in knowledge of morphology affect the growth of vocabulary. In general, derived words seem to be acquired later than inflected and compound words, and polymorphemic words later still.

Anglin (1993) finds that the recognition and comprehension of derived words shows a ninefold increase between grades 1 and 5; and that recognition and comprehension of words consisting of three or more morphemes increase eightfold between these grade levels. But directly relevant to my theme, relatively few of the early words in Anglin's sample of test words are G-L in origin. These words that are so characteristic of academic meaning systems, are not recognised or understood very much by pre-adolescents. In their verbal recognition, hardly any children at these grade levels reach the G-L words in Anglin's test sample. Why should these more morphologically complex words present difficulties to young children in their verbal recall and comprehension?

There are strong indications that the human brain uses an interactive-activation system to process words (see Chapter 7). The mental lexicon analyzes words as whole units, or as letters, syllables, or blends of sounds and morphemes. At the same time, other evidence strongly suggests that the brain's neurobiological mechanisms can alter as a result of different social environments and discursive practices (Harré & Gillett, 1994). It follows that since the mental lexicon is one of the entities in the brain, it also adapts in this way. The lexicon responds to language experiences and then changes the ways that it organizes and processes morphemic units of words, consisting of their stems and affixes, and especially any transparent meanings that those morphemes carry for the language user. This alteration gives the mental lexicon more nodes of activation for processing individual words. The more forms of stimulation available for any word entry, the more readily it will be activated and the more readily it will become available for use on incoming or outgoing messages. Since most G-L words, at least, have great meaning potential in their morphemic structure, a person's storage of this potential in verbal memory can facilitate the acquisition and use of these words within specialist meaning systems.

## Insights from Anthropology: Cultural Meaning Systems

Throughout this section and the rest of the book, I use the word 'culture' to suggest an organization of shared meanings (LeVine, 1984) forming systems that are learned and communicated by means of natural language and other symbol systems (D'Andrade, 1984).

### Words and Cultural Meaning Systems

The conceptual world of a culture includes meaning systems that are often transparent to those who participate in them. Once they are acquired, they become ways of seeing, but often the meaning systems themselves are not apprehended. They become taken-for-granted and unquestioned. Most of these systems are expressed or supported in the language of the culture.

Early efforts in cultural anthropology to understand cultural meaning systems, tried to describe the semantic structure of lexical domains or semantic fields across each system (Quinn & Holland, 1987). These studies assumed that by piecing together the labels for bits of the system, this would give a map or model for the meaning system as a whole. Formal semantic analysis of these lexical systems did yield insights, especially in domains like 'kinship' and 'ethnobotany' in which the tasks of labelling and classification are important lexical functions (LeVine, 1984). But more generally, the studies yielded only limited insights into the organization of cultural knowledge, since they ignored the multiple meanings of words, which are the things that make metaphor possible, and especially the non-linguistic rules of use that link signs together within a system and which change from context to context.

The things that words themselves label are rarely the most important aspects of cultural meaning or cultural psychology. As a result, the things that members of a culture take from their meaning systems, and the things that they use on an everyday basis to categorize, reason, remember, solve, decide and learn, go way beyond what is represented in the isolated meanings of fields of words divorced from their rules of use and their location in relevant material life forms.

Cultural psychology assumes that there is not just one psychology, but many cultural psychologies, overlapping each other, but far from identical. Each is concerned with its own cultural meaning systems (Kakar, 1982; Much,

1992). Directly relevant to my theme, cultural psychology is not confined just to distant cultures: Any interplay between people, social structure, and cultural meaning systems, is ripe territory for study (Stigler, Shweder & Herdt, 1990; Tannen, 1990). Since my concern is with the lexico-semantic structures and processes of people, who come from different sociocultural positions but live within the same cultural space, then my theme seems as compatible with cultural psychology as it is with discursive psychology. Perhaps as the disciplines grow closer to one another, these two tags will be recognised as different names for the same area of inquiry. Nor is the traditional work of anthropologists distant in any sense from my theme.

Meaning systems are a cultural product. Along with language itself, they provide the best evidence of a culture's distinctness. As shared symbol systems, meaning systems exist long before we do. Although they have bewildering surface differences and change greatly over time, cultural meaning systems are shared, collective, and enduring. While they operate on a plane that is independent and outside of the individual (LeVine, 1984), different sets of meaning systems are taught to us as individuals through the many discursive practices that our life experiences give us. In this discussion, discursive practices are not limited to 'language' or 'speech acts'. Discursive practices extend to routine and special actions and customs that carry individual and sociocultural meanings. Thumbing your nose is a discursive act. So is washing a relative's feet in some cultures; or serving yourself last at mealtimes (Much, 1992). All such practices are filled with meaning.

Because most of these actions can also be described in the words of a language, albeit with less drama and eloquence, the way people use language, and the language they use provides a means for identifying and interpreting their meaning systems. People's discourse continually reveals information about their sociocultural meaning systems, exuding far more information value than it seems to on the surface. Many examples of this appear in research: Mühlhausler & Harré (1991) look for insights into social relations in the alternative use of pronouns of power and solidarity, as speakers switch from the familiar to the formal use of the second person pronoun. Ervin-Tripp (1972) examines terms of address as indices of attitude and bias. Labov & Fanshel (1977) combine insights of these kinds with assumptions about knowledge shared by participants in an interaction, looking for some aspect of the cultural meaning system that they have in common.

## Academic Meaning Systems

Western categories of thought, like medicine, religion and psychology are rooted in the history of Western institutions. They have become much more differentiated than in many other cultures (LeVine, 1984). This complex differentiation also extends into other areas of Western thought: areas that form knowledge categories comprising the high status specialist meaning systems that developed along with the academic culture of literacy. Like all meaning systems, these specialist domains have at least four types of cultural force (D'Andrade, 1984): They represent the world by activating complex mental processes; they create cultural entities; they direct people to do certain things, to follow rules more like obligations and pressures than like prescriptions; and they evoke certain feelings.

Although from the inside, cultural meaning systems often appear to be the only fully logical and rational way of representing the world, they are the product of institutional forces and experiences not shared by all cultures. So they are hardly logical and rational in every setting, since they represent sectional interests. Similarly academic meaning systems and the knowledge categories of education, are conventional creations, open to change, challenge, renewal, reform, or decay. Moving freely within those meaning systems is much easier for those reared within and around the institutional forces and experiences that produced them. These people already have the appropriate habitus, while the meaning systems themselves are already an important part of their acquired cultural capital. In short, those admitted by sociocultural positioning to these language games have more ready access to all the rules of use needed to play in the games proficiently across many different contexts.

*Words as Signs in Meaning Systems*

Meanings are marked by conventional but rather arbitrary symbols. The words of a language are the conventional symbols most often used in the process of following rules within shared meaning systems. Thinkers in any culture are competent managers of systems of signs, and our most efficient signs are the words of a language. "To be able to think is to be a skilled user of these sign systems, that is, to be capable of managing them correctly" (Harré & Gillett, 1994 p. 49). Moreover, these symbols that collocate in meaning systems are more than just representational in character. They also have the directive, creative, evocative, as well as the representational functions that D'Andrade mentions. Their interlocking rules and relations are broad indeed. Meaning systems go well beyond the sum of the meanings of all the words on their own that they contain, since they penetrate life forms, material conditions, and human relations.

A study of the meaning systems that embed gender typologies offers an example here. Holland & Skinner (1987) argue that the words that make up the lexical domain of gender labels used by students, relate only obliquely to the meaning system that supports the students' knowledge of gender relations. The words themselves label people who infringe cultural norms about gender relations. But understanding those words means understanding the relations, not just the words as labels. The meaning of a sign cannot be fully grasped independent of the background of assumptions, ideologies, values, beliefs and cultural experiences that comprise the meaning system. The meaning of a sign is its use against this backdrop. Its rules of use change in subtle and blatant ways from context to context of word use. The word user who really knows a word, knows its possible rules of use across all possible contexts. This is a relatively rare achievement, but it is one that competent managers of sign systems must come close to.

The intricate link between human meanings (the main determinants of human action) and human sign systems (especially the words of a language), means that we study human differences very largely by studying different meaning systems. It is different languages and discursive practices that transmit different meaning systems, notably, in this context, the academic meaning systems of education.

## Insights from Language in Education

From their extraordinary study of different literacy practices among the Vai in Africa, Scribner & Cole (1981) conclude that the important and general cognitive effects that come from schooling derive not from learning to read and write as techniques, but through participation in educational discourse. For education, this conclusion directs attention to the vital role of talk as the practical discourse of schooling.

### Talking about Texts

In an earlier section, I mentioned Heath's work on the different meanings for literacy that correspond with variations in its modes, functions, and uses. Olson & Astington (1990) draw a helpful link between Scribner & Cole's above conclusion and a suggestion from Heath: that it is not just talk about things in general that matters, but 'talk about text'. This is a kind of discourse where knowledge gained from texts can be talked about repeatedly, using an acquired metalanguage set against a meaning system that is used to interpret and extend understanding (Heath, 1986). Putting it another way, this is the way we get inside the language games of meaning systems.

Kuhn (1962) observed that becoming literate in a scientific meaning system is to learn to share its paradigm. As a test of membership, a scientific community uses a person's broad acquaintance with a set of shared texts, interpretations and beliefs. Arguing from this, Olson reckons that "to be literate it is not enough to know the words; one must learn how to participate in the discourse of some textual community" (1994, p. 273). So again, we have to know the rules of use to use the words. Learning the rules of use comes from talking about texts that embed the signs to be learned, especially words that are unfamiliar in form and meaning.

### Education and the Two Types of Word in English

There is an incompatibility between the two major strands of the English lexicon: the native Anglo-Saxon vocabulary and the Renaissance and post-Renaissance vocabulary of Graeco-Latin (G-L) origin. According to Skeat (1917) there are 178 Anglo-Saxon roots in English, and 280 others, almost all G-L. In Skeat's day, traditional and accepted educational practice held that giving students a knowledge of word roots helped them to understand unfamiliar words. But are there other ways of getting this knowledge?

The roots of Anglo-Saxon words become very familiar to young children through their early, informal contacts with English. These are like the Italian dialect words that Meneghello calls 'ancient wounds' that carve out a place in verbal memory (see the next section). By perceiving common features in the sounds, shapes, meanings and uses of all the Anglo-Saxon words that are repeated continually across many contexts and everyday meaning systems, children acquire a tacit understanding of their roots in the most natural way possible. In fact, sometimes it is not quite so tacit, since many perceptive young children can point out these roots and draw complex relations between them. But the ability to do this seems to be developmental, affected by the wide language experiences which every speaker of English gets with Anglo-Saxon words. On the other hand, the specialist G-L vocabulary that is learned later is incompatible in sound, shape, meaning and use with these Anglo-Saxon roots. In general, only formal contact with etymology will give a broad knowledge of the G-L roots of English.

Quirk describes these two types of words in English as "the familiar homely-sounding and typically very short words" and "the more learned, foreign-sounding and characteristically rather long words" (1974, p. 138). This sums up the differences and marks out the problem. He says that it is chiefly the second type of word that we start learning relatively late in our use of English, usually during the adolescent years of secondary education, and keep on learning. If the words are part of the academic language game being played, then acquire them we must if we want to do more than watch that game. But it is an accidental fact of English that the many academic language games are all played using the rules of G-L words. At the same time, if we played the games in other ways, it would not be in English. So if users of English do not come from backgrounds where discourses using both types of word are the norm, or if they have not been exposed to formal contact with the G-L root metaphors, then it is likely that they will have a less motivated use of those vocabularies than someone with either or both of these socialization experiences.

Classroom curriculum change and evaluation research gives a guide to the benefits that a wide and continuous exposure to the etymology of English can bring to the language competencies of children. The members of a wide range of social groups benefit, in their practical language skills, from an acquaintance with etymology and word relationships, if this contact is a regular part of classroom experiences. Long after Skeat's day, this still seems a useful adjunct to education at upper primary levels and throughout the middle and senior years of secondary education (Corson, 1972; Henderson, 1985; 1990; Miller, 1991; Henry, 1993; Mason, Mason & Quayle, 1992). The results of these various studies bear out Labov's conclusion: "Precision in spelling, practice in handling abstract symbols, the ability to state explicitly the meaning of words, and a richer knowledge of the Latinate vocabulary may all be useful acquisitions" (Labov, 1972b, p. 192).

What I am talking about here, is talking with children explicitly about English word relationships and their etymologies, and doing so, if possible, at the very moment when they put the words into their verbal memories. But others go way beyond this simple emphasis on teaching etymology and word relationships; they draw a link between these various points and a return to the formal teaching of the classical languages.

*Teaching the Classical Languages*

In the 1970s and 1980s, Latin was introduced to senior elementary classes in many United States cities. The stated aim of these changes was not to teach Latin as a language, but to promote English language and literacy development among inner-city children (see Carlisle & Liberman, 1989). Evaluation of the programs shows changes in students receiving this introductory contact with Latin, when compared with control groups: improvements in their knowledge of vocabulary, grammar, reading skills, comprehension, cultural awareness, spelling, maths computation, problem solving, science, and social studies. The programs appear to develop the basic skills of children from a range of sociocultural groups and at all ability levels (Masciantonio, 1977; Mavrogenes, 1987). Clearly something interesting was going on in these programs, but what was it?

Olson's and Heath's conclusions, mentioned earlier in this section, help to make sense of the above results. What these Latin programs were doing, was what all good first, second, or foreign language programs always do: first they gave the students some relevant knowledge in the form of written texts, or texts spoken by a teacher; then they asked the students, in a range of ways, to talk about that textual information repeatedly, using an acquired metalanguage to interpret and extend understanding. So these programs certainly had the necessary quality 'input' (Krashen, 1989) from the teachers, and from the written texts too: Everyone was striving to show Latin's relevance to English, since this was the aim of the programs. But more important than this input, was the discussion and dialogue that took place in these classes about the meanings of Latin words and their links with the rules of use for words in English. This meant that quality 'output' came from the students, as they made the subject matter of these classroom interactions part of their own lexico-semantic experience and competence.

This kind of quality output is often missing from regular classrooms, as it is often missing from modern language classrooms (Swain, 1985). It is also often missing from special classes provided for ESL children and adults. I noted already that because ESL students often miss natural opportunities outside classrooms to turn their quality input into quality output (Peirce, 1995), graduates from these language classes sometimes leave them with their language proficiency little improved.

What I am saying here, is that it was not the Latin itself that mattered so much in the American programs, at least not for vocabulary learning. It was the purposeful talk about word meanings, word shapes, sounds, and the links between Latin and English words, that produced these improvements. While the students clearly developed their vocabulary knowledge through participation in these interactions, they were also enjoying the discussion format (Henry, 1993) and the interesting topics dealing with fascinating aspects of their own language. These experiences, at the very moment of learning many new words, gave them rich contact with many of the hidden roots of their own language and, in the process, with the rules of use for words across different academic meaning systems and different contexts. But this conclusion of mine is no more than an elaboration of a key insight for vocabulary learning that also comes from research on second language acquisition: "the more words are analyzed or enriched by imagistic and other associations, the more likely it is that they will be retained" (Carter & McCarthy, 1988 p. 12).

I am not in favour of the re-introduction or the general extension of Latin within the compulsory curriculum of English-speaking schools. This is partly because my memories of lessons in Latin and Greek are rather like those of Edward Gibbon: They involved much sweat, many tears, and even some blood. So I would not want to foist that form of schooling on any modern young person. More to the point, I suspect that very few modern young people would tolerate it, since Latin has had its day. It has lost its educational motivation, except perhaps as an important part of the education of English or ESL teachers, and of course teachers of the Romance languages.

The good input that these Latin programs in the United States were providing, can more easily be provided in other ways: in language awareness courses, exploring the Latin basis of families of specialist words in English (Henry, 1993; Corson, 1990; Mason, Mason & Quayle, 1992: also see Chapter 9) or the Greek basis (Spooner, 1988). What really matters for vocabulary development, and for all the other areas of improvement that the American studies noted, is motivated student participation in educational discourse using the lexico-semantic content as its beginning, not its end.

### Insights from Languages other than English

Many languages borrow major sections of their vocabularies from other languages, while others preserve the integrity of their vocabulary against disruptions by foreign invasion words. The dominant languages of their former colonial masters fill up the contemporary vocabularies of many of the world's newer nations, especially in high status and powerful meaning systems introduced by the colonizers. Similar things have happened in European countries too. Many times, through the actions of a dominant central power or some process of unification of disparate regions, a dominant variety has extended its influence and its vocabularies into other languages or other varieties of the same language.

*Italian*

Italy's creation of a national language based on the Florentine dialect, as part of its 'risorgimento' in the nineteenth century, offers a clear example of a dominant vocabulary spreading into distant regional varieties and carrying with it various high status meaning systems borrowed from the culture of learning and literacy.

For Italian 'dialetti' there is a super-imposed 'language of reasoning' that Meneghello characterizes as "le ferite superficiali, in italiano, in francese, in latino" [flesh wounds, in Italian, in French, in Latin]. But underneath are "le ferite antiche che rimarginandosi hanno fatto queste croste delle parole in dialetto" [ancient wounds that in the course of healing have left these deep scars that are words from the dialect]. For Italian speakers of remote regional varieties, the dialect is their contact with the cultural reality and meaning systems of their roots, but its vocabulary needs supplementing if they are to enter academic meaning systems distant from the local culture. According to Meneghello, this calls for word-meanings, which only the French, 'Italian' and Latin words supply, to augment the 'ancient wounds' (1963, pp. 47-48).

*Czech and Russian*

The Slavonic languages, notably Czech and Russian, have deliberately augmented their vocabularies by going to Greek and Latin sources. In both languages the G-L elements perform vital functions: They are said to allow greater precision and sometimes greater generalization than their nearest native synonyms. They have great word-forming potential, which is a characteristic of G-L words when they appear in other languages, since they consist of word formative elements (bases and affixes) each of which regularly conveys its own meaning. Finally these elements give greater flexibility in compound structuring for the host languages, because of the compounding facility of their polysyllabic word forms (Rolfe, 1978). But even in Czech and Russian, the incidence of G-L words approaches nowhere near half the total vocabulary and they are certainly not the majority as they are in English.

*German*

Germanic languages, other than English, resist widespread disruption by invasion words. German itself is relatively reluctant to borrow G-L words, preferring to derive words through its own compounding processes. German regularly builds its more complex words on others whose meanings are more elemental and denotatory: MUND (mouth) is embedded in MÜNDLICH (oral); STADT (town) is embedded in STÄDTLICH (urban); SPRACHE (language) is embedded in SPRACHLICH (linguistic). Speakers of German have a ready access to the meaning of many German abstract words by way of the more elemental morphemes embedded in them.

In contrast, influential users of English, through much of its history, have looked to earlier and much admired cultures, especially the Roman and the Greek, as sources for most of the abstract terminology of English. Consider the English words for the German words cited above. I give the elemental word first, then the more complex and less concrete word: MOUTH-ORAL, TOWN-URBAN, LANGUAGE-LINGUISTIC. In each case, the more abstract word is drawn from a Latinate root, embedding a Latinate morpheme and ignoring the metaphor offered by its 'native' counterpart.

Most of the abstract terminology of English lacks the motivation that comes from the more elemental metaphors embedded in the abstract words of other languages. Vygotsky likens the agglutination found in the speech of the very young child to the compounding process used in languages like German to express complex ideas but with transparent effect:

> When several words are merged into one word, the new word not only expresses a rather complex idea, but designates all the separate elements contained in that idea. Because the stress is always on the main root or idea, such languages are easy to understand (1962 p. 246).

Preferring to return to their own resources for word creation, German speakers established no stress patterns for the acceptance of foreign words in large numbers, allowing native word formation to remain the norm (Samuels, 1972). So G-L words in German have only random value, as individual words. They appear at around 3% to 6% of total vocabulary, based on a small analysis of technical texts drawn from the realms of psychology, philosophy, literature and social science (Corson, 1981). Taken as a group, German G-L words seem to have no obvious connection with general levels of textual complexity.

Modern Icelandic, a Germanic language as close to Anglo-Saxon as any, has a very conservative morphological system that would be disrupted if the number of new words that do not conform to the inherited pattern were to rise above a certain level. So there is no obvious G-L lexical bar in Icelandic either, although there may be in other languages. While Chapter 9 looks at other kinds of lexical bars that may exist in other languages, some of them Germanic, it is clear that real 'disruptions' have happened in English, imposed upon the language by invasion and conquest, leaving it open to a flood of loan words for centuries.

## Conclusion

Knowing the meaning of a word is knowing how to use it within an appropriate language game or meaning system. We get access to the academic language games given high status in culture and society, by participating, at least orally, in the culture of literacy. Many people are well placed to do this. From their earliest years, they receive a natural immersion in the culture of literacy, since sociocultural forces and discursive practices position them in a favourable relationship to that culture. Others, depending on their position, may acquire a lexico-semantic range very different from that favoured in the special literate culture of the school and in its academic meaning systems.

Word meanings remain unstable for language users, if the network of rules behind the words, and the life forms in which they are embedded, are not learned along with the words. As children become more adept at 'taking' the words of a language, they learn that their own utterances also have meaning in a certain way, as exemplars of certain rules, and against the backdrop of certain meaning systems across contexts. In any of the ways in which people experience words, against the backdrop of some meaning system or other, they pick up clues about these rules of use, so that once an action is done, the rule becomes the thing that displays the meaning of that action within its own meaning system.

Meaning systems, language games, knowledge categories, and semantic fields are all closely related, if ab tract, ideas. Each one in its own way suggests linked complexes of conventional signs and their meanings. As a result, they are sometimes used almost synonymously by different people working in different disciplines. For this book's purposes, they do convey slightly different but largely overlapping ideas. So my use of them will not be arbitrary. In some places, I find that one or other of these expressions suits the context of the discussion a little better than the others: Its rules of use in that context display my meaning better.

Two features of G-L words in English emerge from the cross-disciplinary discussion in this chapter. First, they tend to appear far more often within academic meaning systems created by the academic culture of literacy than they do in everyday discourse. Second, as a group they are very different morphologically from the rest of the vocabulary of English. Because coincidences of social and linguistic history have combined to create a lexical situation in English in which most of the specialist and high status vocabulary is G-L in origin, and most of its more everyday vocabulary is Anglo-Saxon in origin, this creates a barrier between one form of linguistic capital and the other.

Those whose lexico-semantic positioning gives them greater access to the one form of linguistic capital, rather than the other, may be at a disadvantage in educational settings that give a higher status to that other form of linguistic capital. It is clear that differences in the discursive practices of children, positioned differently by their sociocultural relations, are the key to understanding differences in their lexico-semantic range.

This review of disciplines and topics helps establish the links between words, culture, education, and society. Chapter 3 now describes the processes of invasion, conquest and renaissance that changed the English vocabulary. It draws a direct link between the flood of G-L words into English and the sociocultural positioning of present-day users of English as a mother tongue.

# 3

# The Historical Development of the Lexical Bar

This chapter examines the introduction of G-L words into English. It identifies the sociohistorical events that have positioned some social groups at a distance in their discursive practices from specialist and learned words. The events distancing G-L words in this way get special treatment, since they stand out in an historical analysis. They are mostly to do with the development in Britain of a rather exclusive culture of literacy and its associated meaning systems: a culture that spread later to newly founded or colonized English-speaking countries. This culture of literacy became institutionalized in formal education where high value was placed on the daily use of Latin for all spoken purposes and on the rigorous study of Greek. It then became the basis for an enlarged English vocabulary drawn from those languages. This process excluded the many, who received no education, from the new vocabularies of the few who did. The many continued to use a very Germanic vocabulary which became less and less central to the formal expression of the meaning systems of the literate culture.

**Before the Renaissance Period**

Anglo-Saxon was itself an invasion language. It mingled with and almost extinguished the Celtic which preceded it in Britain. Only a few Latin words from the Romans became a part of Celtic, as a result of the centuries of Romanization of Britain, and then became part of Anglo-Saxon. Tribal Celtic and the language of the 'English' invaders were kept functionally apart, although previously Celtic and the Latin of Rome had greatly intermingled.

The language of the Anglo-Saxon invaders itself brought the first great corpus of Latinate words to Britain. These had been adopted by the Germanic tribes from those aspects of Roman civilization that impressed them most: Roman roads, warfare, buildings, and food. They are such ancient words in Anglo-Saxon as to be almost genuine. They come down to us as mainly monosyllabic, everyday words like PILE, STREET, WALL, TILE, CHALK, MILL, PIT, POUND, MILE, CHEAP, MONGER, MINT, KETTLE, DISH, PEPPER, PEAS, CHEESE, BUTTER, PLUM, APPLE and WINE (Barber, 1965).

Like other Germanic peoples, the Anglo-Saxons found Latin a difficult language to learn. In this they were unlike other peoples in Western Europe who spoke dialects based on Latin. As a result, very early in the history of English, a tradition arose of writing and using comprehensive textbooks for teaching Latin, and thereby gaining access to the desirable knowledge resources of the Latin-based academic culture of Western Europe. So it was in the British Isles, for the first time in history, that Latin grammars were used to teach Latin-as-a-second language. Furthermore, to make this Latin teaching easier, Anglo-Saxon scholars and teachers also began to use the Latin alphabet for writing their Old English (Orme, 1989). Slight though these changes were, they opened the way for the vocabulary of Latin to begin to have its relentless impact on the vocabulary of English.

*The Anglo-Norman Period*

Latinate words began to have a heavier impact on the language of Britain after the Norman invasion in the eleventh century. This was partly because the Normans brought with them a mainly Latinate dialect of French, and partly because both conqueror and conquered found a common vehicle for communication in Latin, a language still recognized because of church usage. While the Normans were used to literature and documents in Latin, rather than in their own language (Orme, 1989), even the common people in Britain saw Latin as 'a living language', although as little more than that. As late as 1188, Giraldus Cambrensis recorded that in preaching crusade for the liberation of the Holy Land, he was always most successful when he delivered his sermon in Latin. In Grove's words: "the people were moved to tears, and took the cross in crowds, in spite of the fact . . . that they did not understand a word of what he had said" (1949, p. 10).

Though submerged, the popular tongue lived its own life in an oral tradition through the twelfth century, not much influenced by Norman French. Nevertheless, it was the Norman invasion, if not the French of the Normans, that was both root and catalyst in what was to follow. The Normans themselves, as an invading teutonic people in the first place in France, adopted the language of the conquered there, but not the language of the conquered in Britain, even though it was so near to their original tongue.

Norman French was retained as the language of the Norman ruling classes, while the growing strength of monasticism throughout the Anglo-

Norman period ensured the dominance of French or Latin in all official contexts. But King John's loss of Normandy in 1204 loosened the hold that French had, even among the influential classes. By the end of that century, manuals of instruction in French-as-a-foreign language were beginning to appear (Alexander, 1990) and in 1337 the outbreak of the Hundred Years War between England and France, brought the era of strong French language influence to a gradual close. Yet, although the earliest surviving petition in English dates from 1344 (Alexander, 1990), French was still used in the courts alongside Latin until 1400, long after its meaning was lost on the common people. This was also long after English had supplanted French as the medium of instruction in schools in 1349.

But the results for English were already grave. When the Act of 1362 permitted the use of English in courts of law, because most people no longer understood French, the law could not be adequately expressed in English, and pleadings had to continue in French. In fact, the decree was not finally enforced until 1731 (sic), creating a lucrative profession for lawyers serving as French/English interpreters in the courts (Maylath, 1994). French also remained the language of most books owned by the nobility, until at least the 1470s (Orme, 1989). Nevertheless, Henry IV ascended the throne in 1399 as the first sovereign since 1066 who spoke English as his mother tongue.

The G-L content of Norman French left little impression on the Old English vocabulary. Borrowings included more everyday words than the later borrowings from Central French: "presumably because they were in many cases introduced by the Norman rank and file who came over at the Conquest" (Barber, 1965, p. 164). These loans added a vocabulary we can hardly do without in everyday discourse: PEOPLE, GARDEN, MARKET, HOUR, CATCH, CATTLE, WARDEN and WAGES. But during this Middle English period, Central French exerted a critical influence, displacing Old English words entirely where they were synonymous.

Central French was closer to the source of Latin, both geographically and politically. It provided words to fill gaps in existing semantic fields: religious words like REQUIEM and GLORIA; legal words like CLIENT, EXECUTOR, CONVICTION and MEMORANDUM; medical and scientific words like RECIPE, DISSOLVE, DISTILLATION, CONCRETE, COMET and EQUATOR; and many 'mental act' words like ADOPTION, CONFLICT, DISSENT, IMAGINARY, IMPLICATION. Contemporary developments in commerce and its associated activities, promoted a huge increase in 'speech act' verbs. Traugott (1987) finds that Latinate verbs needed for clarifying claims, for asserting rights, for reporting, assuring and promising, flooded into the language between 1100 and 1400. Now for the first time, Latinate words began to fill the role that they assumed more fully later on: providing the English lexicon with much of its learned and difficult terminology, founding and populating the semantic fields of a spreading literate culture in the process.

The more subtle influence in this invasion was that these early French loan words were so well assimilated into English that later G-L loan words found English a more hospitable host. English became less ready to use its own resources for word innovation.  At the same time, a gradual process began of stripping English of many of its native inflections, since the loan words could not be inflected in the native manner (Samuels, 1972). This eroding process made the language even more amenable to further foreign influence. Rapid vocabulary change now became possible and this dynamism in the language arrived at the same moment as broad cultural changes that rapidly promoted the obsolescence of literary works.  Lawson & Silver note the wide range of vernacular works available in the fourteenth and fifteenth centuries: romances and chronicles, religious and secular lyrics, popular songs and ballads, Chaucer and his fifteenth-century imitators (1973, p. 84).  But with the massive vocabulary changes occurring and about to occur, these works in English quickly became archaic; demand for them fell away; and the vernacular's influence declined.

### Education from 1300 to 1500

Prior to the Renaissance, lasting changes in education were already taking place.  Later patterns of discriminatory school system organization and curricular design had their roots in the century immediately before the Greek and Ciceronian Renaissance reached Britain, at the end of the fifteenth century. It is already possible to see in this period three types of education appearing that were stratified by social position, creating levels that would not be formalized until the nineteenth century.

For aristocratic children in late medieval England, literacy and Latin were inseparable:

> when they learned to read, they learned the alphabet in Latin; when they first practised recognizing and pronouncing words, the texts were also in Latin, so that every literate child was a minimal reader and speaker of that language. Literacy, and the elementary knowledge of Latin it involved, were probably universal among the later medieval aristocracy of both sexes (Orme, 1989 p. 170).

The evidence suggests that the nobility did all these things at a very early age, with literacy training in Latin often beginning well before 5 years, and more formal tutoring for both girls and boys at around 5 years. Children were often writing letters and reading liturgical texts in Latin soon afterwards. Most formal reading and writing was in Latin, although the preferred languages for recreational reading and writing were French and English.

Writing his account in the sixteenth century, Sir Thomas Elyot was able to look back on these educational customs of the nobility, that had already been developing for more than two centuries. Based on his observations, he compiled recommendations for the tutoring of noble children of his own day in the home.  In *The Boke Named the Governour*, he set out the language environment that was appropriate for those of high birth who must acquire their Latin early:

> And if a childe do begyn therin at seven yeres of age, he may continually lerne greke autours thre yeres, and in the meane tyme use the latin tonge as a familiar langage: whiche in a noble mannes sonne may well come to passe havynge none other persons to serve him or kepyng hym company, but suche as can speake latine elegantly (1531 p. 53).

Elyot's aim here was to turn out aristocratic children who were naturally bilingual in Latin and English, by having them immersed in Latin from an early age, and then using their Latin to learn Greek. But this type of immersion education was hardly possible for children who came from families of more modest means. These needed to get their Latin in the form of a taught second language, provided in an institution designed for the purpose. In these new schools of the fourteenth century, created for the middle levels of society, students would enter at about age 7. They would first be taught the Latin alphabet and the proper pronunciation of Latin, which was clearly a very useful and very desirable second language:

> It would have been a rare child who heard Latin spoken in the home. The child's language would have been French or English, depending on the social or cultural background of the family . . . Latin was taught by means of French until, in the second half of the [fourteenth] century, it was gradually replaced by English . . . Latin was the language of church and state, the language in which one wrote and in which there was something to be read (Courtenay, 1987 p. 16).

In this way, the new schools converted the longstanding but informal customs of the nobility into formal practices that were institutionalized for those who were not of noble birth. Founded in the service of the realm, the new schools tried to produce an educated élite whose training and accomplishments were modelled on those of the nobility. But to do this, the schools started students later on their Latin, at 7 years. Beyond this primary level, at ages 8 or 9, students entered the secondary level of schooling which was concerned wholly with Latin grammar. Lasting for up to 10 more years, this course was almost fully linguistic and literary. The course itself was taught in Latin and since the complete mastery of Latin grammar was their purpose, the schools became known as grammar schools.

The hundred or so grammar schools, which nominally owed their origin to Edward VI as new foundations in the mid-sixteenth century, were older institutions reaching well back into the mid-fifteenth century. But the aims for their all-male scholars were the same in both eras. The boys began by learning to speak Latin, taught to them at first through the oral medium of English. After these preliminaries, all lessons were conducted on the direct method using Latin. For much of the time, the student was "engaged on original composition in Latin, either letter writing . . . or theme-writing" and from an early age "he would also have turned his hand to the composition of original Latin verse". Ogilvie notes that "a similar course in Greek was also prescribed" but in this period, at least "knowledge of that language was more envied than attained" (1964, pp. 5-6).

Trevelyan illustrates the discriminatory effects of the early grammar school system for the children of families without means. He begins by showing that the "fine system of secondary education" acquired at this time, with schools endowed to teach 'the poor' free of fee, was discriminatory in the extreme. The poor who benefited were the 'relatively poor': the 'lower middle class', small gentry, yeomen and burghers, whose offspring took a part in the government of the land as a result of their education. For the rest, there was nothing, or the next-to-nothing provided by petty schools in villages. Nor was there any access to that distinctive, central facet of the endowed schools' curriculum, its Latin-based culture of literacy:

> Boys in the grammar schools wrote Latin verse and prose compositions, and stood up in class to translate the Latin authors into English. But out of school hours no language must be talked except Latin! For some centuries to come this amazing rule was sanctioned by the usual brutalities of flogging . . . How fully, one wonders, did this harsh prohibition actually take effect? Was Latin less 'a dead language' and more a real medium of speech to the grammar school boy of the fifteenth century than to the public school boy of the nineteenth? There are many reason to suppose that it was (Trevelyan, 1978, pp. 70-71).

The G-L element in the language of boys educated in this way, was as active a part of their vocabulary as the English element. Perhaps in some boys' vocabulary the two strains, the native and the G-L, merged and became indistinguishable.

At the same time, the petty schools' curriculum, in those villages where they existed, covered spelling and reading in the vernacular, taught to fee-payers and paupers' children, by teachers who were often paupers and menials themselves. Poor boys left at 7 or 8 years, after learning to read "any whit well" (Lawson & Silver, 1973, p. 115) and returned to take part in language practices more appropriate to their sociocultural position.

While for this mass of the people, the foundation Saxon was enough, for many others Latin became the vehicle of literate thought and for educated discourse of all kinds, largely displacing English. Discussing the education available in the first half of the fifteenth century, Watson suggests how the classical curriculum encouraged a wide decline in the status of English among the educated classes:

> The use of Latin for reading and writing exercises, probably accounts for the rarity of instances of English epistles . . . No English Composition was taught and as a matter of fact no well-instructed man or woman was particularly concerned to show that he could use his mother tongue (1908, p. 139).

## The Renaissance Period

Yet traces of native English vitality did begin to reappear by the late fifteenth century. More chroniclers turned to English as a source of new words, while noting its inadequacy for expressing literate ideas without word innovation (Grove, 1949). They finally rejected French, and English began to flourish. Although the great mass of published material sold in England at this time, was still being published on the continent and in Latin (Febvre & Martin, 1976), English literacy levels may have been greater in the sixteenth century than in the early nineteenth. Lawson & Silver cite Sir Thomas More in 1533 (unreliably) estimating that over 50 percent of the population could read English, while a 1543 Act of Parliament restricted access to the English Great Bible to certain classes "to safeguard orthodoxy from promiscuous Bible study" (1973, p. 85). Other draconian legal restrictions, aimed at curbing the production of 'seditious pamphlets', severely limited the number of presses in England, confining them to London, Oxford and Cambridge until well into the seventeenth century. These and other constraints meant that booksellers did not begin to find a market for works in English until the second half of the sixteenth century (Febvre & Martin, 1976). But no sooner did this interest in the vernacular re-appear, than the rise of English was again impeded by the Renaissance, which spread to England, from Italy via France, reviving classical ideas to add to the classical languages.

*The Rebirth of Classical Ideas*

Greek and Latin were fostered more enthusiastically than ever, and the native tongue was treated disparagingly by the 'literati' who declared it unfit for the expression of intellectual and emotional complexities. Gusdorf describes the background to this process:

> The immense upheaval of the Renaissance, indeed, finds in the birth of modern philology not only its symbol, but perhaps its essence. The learned henceforth are no longer theologians and debaters, but the men of letters, erudite men who set out to revive dead languages. First of all, Latin: now, there is a living Latin, Church Latin, mother tongue of the liturgy and of scholasticism. The humanists assert that this idiom is a decadent form of Latin. Beyond low medieval Latin, they recommend the return to Ciceronian purity. The study of Latin henceforth is complemented by the study of Greek, neglected by the Western Church . . .
> . . . The new understanding of ancient language enlarges the horizons of thought: the creation of philology is here a sort of equivalent to the great discoveries which, in the same period, by modifying the structures of the world, prepare that new self-consciousness characteristic of modern man (1965, pp. 23-24).

These new segmentations of metaphysical space hardened into meaning systems of great power and durability. The complexities that they contained needed new words to express them. This new vocabulary came from Latin and Greek, while English was deprived of its native, lexical dynamism, replaced by a bar which even today keeps many native speakers at a distance from discourse within those new "horizons of thought" that mainly had their origins in the world of Classical Greece.

In the early sixteenth century, William Lily, headmaster of St Paul's School, became one of the first to instruct his students in Greek. Lily was also the author of an influential textbook for Latin grammar, published in 1515. This was joined by Edward Grant's textbook for Greek in 1575 and William Camden's Greek text in 1597. These allowed Greek studies to become permanently established in the grammar schools (Alexander, 1990). But as early as the last decade of Henry VIII's reign, Greek was already firmly established in the universities. So at around this time, an intellectual climate emerged where Greek borrowings could come into their own. Word innovators began to go direct to Greek, rather than by way of Latin.

The rediscovery, via Arab sources, of the lost writings of the classical Greek philosopher-scientists, provided an irresistible inducement. For a minority of people, who were already inducted into the literate and scholastic culture, social and political conditions during the Renaissance matched that all-too-brief moment in Greek history. These conditions combined to produce an era of word innovation, comparable with its paradigm:

> A highly abstract vocabulary would only become important when man had gained some freedom from the daily subsistence grind — as the pre-Socratic Greeks had done. It would then be possible for some members of the community to stand back a little and try to understand the world (Brown, 1959, p. 283).

The apparent simplicity of the Greek words, for those familiar with their source, made them attractive to the innovators of the Renaissance. In fact this simplicity had been the hinge of Hellenic intellectual progress, since for the Greeks the vocabulary of learned discourse was the vocabulary of ordinary language reapplied. The words were available for use by all the Greeks, yielding direct popular access to learned discourse with no hint of a 'lexical bar' like that for many users of English.

Brown verifies the simplicity that Greek words often possess, when used abstractly in English by someone familiar with their source. He recalls Havelock describing the evolution of the concept of 'cosmos', through its Greek origins as a 'woman's headdress' or a 'horse's harness', with the general sense of a 'cluster'. Later it was used both for 'decoratively ornamental' and for the 'ranks of an army', pursuing its ascent towards abstraction, as Ionian thinkers put it to work with the sense of 'physical order', until finally it achieves a notion of 'the order' (Brown, 1959, p. 273). This progress from the concrete to the abstract is a characteristic of the semantic development of many Greek words. But it can be lost on those unfamiliar with Greek etymologies, or without a wide vocabulary sufficient to see the patterns independently, yet required to wrestle with Greek words lodged in their own language. For the Greeks, these words impinged on their cultural roots as much as the homely words of regional varieties. This partly explains the Greeks' ability to wrestle with them and to erect shared communication upon them. As important here, is Steiner's point:

> Granted the fact that fundamental intellectual insights and psychological attitudes are of a limited order, the Greeks had found for both means of plastic and verbal expression which were supreme and which had exhausted the likely possibilities. What came after was [mere] variation . . . (1975, p. 463).

By 1600, the trickle of loan words became a flood. As English gradually began to replace Latin as the language of learning, "the influx of Latinate words into English reached its highest level" (Samuels, 1972, p. 94). Stevenson (1983) sets the figure at more than 10,000 new words introduced from Latin between 1500 and 1650. Catalogues of these appear in many sources, and mention here of the semantic fields they 'created' and expanded in English is enough. The scientific realms of biology, botany, chemistry, physics, and medicine are favoured; while mathematical, legal, and abstract vocabularies, useful for 'talking about texts', are added from the Latin. Olson & Astington (1990) find that many borrowings around this time are 'speech act' and 'mental state' verbs that are central to the discourses of modern psychology and philosophy of mind: speech act verbs that substitute for the verb TO SAY but add a greater subtlety of connotation, such as ASSERT, CONCEDE, CONTRADICT, CRITICIZE, EXPLAIN, SUGGEST; and mental state verbs that substitute for the verb TO THINK, such as ASSUME, INFER, and PREDICT.

Also from the Greek came technical terms for use in literary criticism, rhetoric, and the natural sciences. They entered English easily, for reasons already mentioned. While in other languages, 'Greek and Roman antiquity' remained more or less a separate domain, in Britain the language "constituted a reservoir into which Greek and Roman material . . . could easily drift and be readily absorbed" (Grove: 1949, p. 76). But the words absorbed were of a type most used at the time in written language, not in the language of speech. Their circulation, at least initially, was restricted to those who met them in their literary context: educated readers who found little difficulty in assimilating words which the language needed and which served "a precise and useful purpose" (Ogilvie, 1964, p. 19). Other users of English were held at a distance by the vocabulary of a language that was their own, but seemed not to be.

Sir Thomas Browne in 1646 noted the prevalence of the invasion words and his own realization that his language barred him from the people:

> Although I confess, the quality of the Subject will sometimes carry us into expressions beyond mere English apprehensions, and indeed if elegancie still proceedeth and English Pens maintain that stream we have of late observed to flow from many, we shall within few years be fain to learn Latine to understand English, and a work will prove of equal facility in either . . .
> . . . Nor have we addressed our Pen or Stile unto the people (whom books do not redress and are incapable of reduction), but unto the knowing and reading party of Learning (1646, 'To the Reader').

Now the lexical bar began to assert itself, as the vocabularies of the learned and their literate culture drifted further from the vocabularies of the common people.

The vocabulary of non-readers was held at the greatest distance. Perhaps literacy levels declined in the early seventeenth century because of the lexical dynamism affecting the standard variety. The scanty evidence for literacy levels contrasts markedly with that of the previous century. Wills of the period reveal yeomen as often literate, but labourers as generally illiterate. In the New Model Army of 1645, the majority of infantry privates who were poor men by birth, could not write their names (Lawson & Silver, 1973). No doubt the reasons for this decline included the strangeness of the 'new' language of books. Even those with some small measure of literacy began to find that literary words were more than hard; they were foreign. This was complicated even more by the forms of education and of religious worship current in the seventeenth century.

### The Influence of Religion

Religious practices tended to nourish the Anglo-Saxon roots of English. Since the 1540s, the Latin litany had been superseded by Cranmer's *Book of Common Prayer*, which marked a clear advance in the progress of the vernacular. But the great event for English was the 1611 *Authorized Version of The Bible* which was translated from the Greek and Hebrew originals. Of course, there had been several earlier English translations of the bible, including a version widely disseminated from Caxton's presses, and there had also been bibles in English translated from the Latin Vulgate during the reigns of Henry VIII and Elizabeth I. But because of its much wider availability at this time, and because it had King James's imprimatur, the authorized version was set to become one of the most formative forces in English life and language.

As *the* book of the poor, the Bible is simple and Anglo-Saxon. Unburdened in its Hebrew and Greek version with a philosophical and scientific vocabulary, the Bible is adequately expressed in the vocabulary of Anglo-Saxon. Its meanings are concrete and picturesque, as is Anglo-Saxon, while its sentence structure is simple. Febvre & Martin (1976) note that the vocabulary used in the Bible and in the *Book of Common Prayer* was all the more readily understood because both works used no more than 6,500 different words in total. This vocabulary range contrasts remarkably, in size and in kind, with the written vocabularies of the clerics who made it their business to add commentaries to the bible. Olson & Astington (1990) draw a sharp contrast when they examine the vocabulary of the book of Job, and compare it with its own chapter glosses that were inserted into the *English Bible*: They find the speech act and mental state verbs in the text of Job itself to be rigorously Anglo-Saxon, but the verbs in the glosses are heavily Latinate. These glosses were written, of course, by commentators trained within the literate culture of scholarship.

Probably had the King James Bible been the work of a more modern age, its non-Germanic vocabulary would be larger. But in its era of greatest linguistic influence, the Bible stood as the main literary source for the vocabulary of the common people, joined only by the *Book of Common Prayer*, Bunyan's *Pilgrim's Progress* (1678-9), and sundry pamphlets and tracts. The common feature of all these was the simplicity and very English nature of their vocabularies. So the lexical distancing was reinforced as a result, fostered in the very institution of society that sought to elevate the lot of the ordinary person.

## The Influence of Education

In education the trend was not always one way. Richard Mulcaster, headmaster of St Paul's, asked that a person's mind should be built up and trained in its own congenial medium of expression: the mother tongue. He conveyed this sentiment in a treatise published in 1582:

> I love Rome, but London better, I favor Italie, but England more, I honor the Latin, but I worship the English (p. 254).

Mulcaster's entreaty "to read that first which we speak first" was not a wholly isolated one. John Brinsley published his *Ludus Literarius* ['The Grammar School'] in 1612. This influential book was an extensive manual for teachers in grammar schools. It set out the curriculum and teaching methods for giving boys all that they required from grammar schools: a firm grounding in the classical languages. But if that grounding also had some incidental impact on their English, then that was a useful bonus:

> The daily use, and practise of Grammaticall translation in English, of all the Schoole [Latin] Authours, which the yonger sort doe learne; causing them each day out of those to construe and repeate, whatsoever they learne. This I also have proved by happy experience, to be a rare helpe to make young Schollars to grow very much, both in English and Latine (1612 p. 23).

Beyond any benefits that might come from this 'dual system of translation' out of English to Latin and back again, Brinsley expressly left the job of seeing that boys were well grounded in oral and written English, to their parents. In fact, he laid the blame on parents if the boys' English suffered because of the school's concentration on Latin:

> concerning the complaint of the Parents, for their children going backward in English, when they first learne latine; the chief fault in truth is in the Parents themselves . . . For if such murmuring Parents, would but cause their children, every day after dinner or supper, or both, to reade a Chapter of the Bible . . . then I say, this complaint would soon be at an end: for they should either see then, their children to increase in this, or else they should discerne the fault to be in their childrens dulnesse, and not in our neglect (p. 24).

The impact of all this on the English vocabulary of grammar school students can be readily inferred, I think. It seems likely that in looking for a word in English to translate a Latin word, students would look no further than some similar word in English that displayed the same Latin roots, especially since their schoolmasters were constantly urging them to use the Latin or the Greek as exemplary models for English (Orme, 1989). Much the same could be said for the reverse process of translating from English into Latin or Greek. As a result, the English of grammar school graduates became

more and more Latinate. At the same time, any original English words that
were near synonyms for the new words, were overlooked. In many instances,
these Anglo-Saxon words either dropped out of the language or their rules of
use shifted more and more into the everyday contexts of ordinary language.
Not surprisingly, with repeated emphasis, writers regretted that the power of
forming new words from native roots, by creation or derivation, was being
lost or suspended. Supported by the educational doctrines of the day, words
from Greek and Latin became ready tools for word creation or derivation in
all academic contexts.

   Down to 1660 there is no evidence that the curriculum of grammar
schools gave English even the standing of a separate subject. Henry Peacham
in *The Compleat Gentleman* lamented:

> I have knowne even excellent Schollers so defective . . . that when they have been
> beating their braines twentie or foure and twentie yeeres about Greeke Etymologies . . .
> could neither write true English nor true Orthographie . . . (1622, p. 53).

On the other hand, the prominence of Latin in schools was unchallenged.
The methodologies trialled in the fifteenth century, had now been codified
and had taken on the status of educational dogma:

> The chief teaching methods for the speaking of Latin, in the 16th and 17th centuries,
> were founded on principles such as those laid down by Sir Thomas Elyot and Montaigne,
> viz the provision of an atmosphere of Latin-speaking (Watson, 1908, p. 312).

With the aim of relieving the universities of the actual teaching of Latin,
school students now received a comprehensive preparation in the language.
It consisted of colloquies, catechisms, making of verses, other 'pueriles
confabulatiunculae' and, culminated in the sixth form in the making and
delivery of original orations (Watson, 1908; Adamson, 1922). By 1542,
uniform elementary and advanced grammars had been prescribed for use by
every school (Orme, 1989), so that as early as 1549, universities were able to
remove Latin grammar from their curriculum, since mastery of it had by
then become a basic prerequisite for admission (Alexander, 1990). For the
scholarly, Latin was now truly the 'mother tongue' of learning.

   Bolstered by these policy changes, schools pursued a Latin curriculum
with a zeal sanctioned by their own statutes. Watson (1908) cites the extant
rules of eighteen separate schools, framed between 1524 and 1644, which
insisted on the use of Latin for all spoken purposes. Still, from a comment by
Brinsley, we can judge how difficult it often was to translate this Latin-only
policy into practice:

> if we could bring them to speake Latine continually, from that time that they beginne to
> parse in Latine: but this I have had too much experience of, that without great severity
> they will not be brought unto: but they will speake English, and one will winke at
> another, if they be out of the Masters hearing (1612 p. 219).

No doubt like Brinsley, most teachers of the period experienced this enduring problem of turning educational policy into classroom practice. Nevertheless it does seem likely that many well educated people of the time actually became fully functioning bilinguals in English and in Latin, just as their noble predecessors had tried to be. Indeed both the anecdotal and the monumental evidence suggests something of the sort. For example, Watson quotes D'Arcy Power, biographer of Dr William Harvey (1578-1657):

> He "was so good a Latin scholar and . . . had acquired such a perfect colloquial knowledge of the language that it is clear he thought with equal facility in latin or English, so that it is immaterial into which language he puts his ideas" (1908, p. 312).

Again, the closeness of the Latin and the English at this time, is clear from a striking inscription dating from 1633, during the reign of Charles I. This gilded carving runs around the exterior walls of the former Leominster town hall in Herefordshire. Erected by the 'King's Carpenter', the building is still in use for civic offices. Its inscription shows the ease with which the Latin and the English could be meshed in formal language. It suggests a widespread level of bilingualism among the influential members of Leominster's society, or, at the very least, it offers official confirmation that bilingualism was thought a desirable attainment for the privileged to have:

> VIVE DEO GRATVS. TOTI MVNDO TVMVLATVS CRIMINE MVNDATVS SEMPER TRANSIRE PARATVS. WHERE IVSTICE RVLE THERE VERTVE FLOW. VIVE VT POST VIVAS. SAT CITO SI SAT BENE. LIKE COLLVMNES DW VPPROP THE FRABRIK OF A BILDING SO NOBLE GENTRI DW SVPPORT THE HONOR OF A KINGDOM. IN MEMORIA AETERNA ERIT IVSTVS.

While making propaganda for the ruling élite of the day, the inscription's English sentences include nine Middle English words borrowed from Latin, in a total of only 25 English words. I wonder how many literate members of the lower orders of the day could make good sense of its English, let alone its Latin?

## Literary Effects

For writers of the period, the reading public in English was small, while authors who used Latin addressed themselves to the readers of the entire Western world. Febvre & Martin summarize the situation:

> Shakespeare and the Tudor drama were more or less unknown on the continent at this time, while Camden, Hobbes, Barclay and even John Owen the epigrammatist, enjoyed a popularity equal to that of any other European writer because they wrote in Latin (1976 pp. 330-331).

The attraction of Latin lay also in its precision and clarity. In contrast to modern languages that were constantly developing, Latin's vocabulary was fixed and easily determined by reference to authoritative texts that were widely available. But when English was used in written texts, its learned vocabulary now looked more like the vocabulary of Latin than ever.

In spite of attacks by linguistic patriots, like Philip Sidney and George Gascoigne, over the prevalence of 'inkhorn terms' in the English writings of scholars, notable attempts at mother tongue literature became more common. But the inkhorn terms had now become endemic. They were part of educated, literary English. Even those who criticized the use of intruder words, could not avoid using them when mounting an argument, as the following example reveals:

> ". . . to *recover* its primitive *flexibility* and *plastic power*, to *discard* the *adventitious aids* and *ornaments* borrowed from Greece and Rome, to *supply* the *place* of *foreign* by *domestic compounds*, to clothe again our thoughts and our feelings *exclusively* in a garb of living, *organic, native* growth" (Grove, 1949, pp. 97-98).

As late as the nineteenth century, a range of Anglo-Saxon substitutes was suggested: SKY-SILL for HORIZON; GLEECRAFT for MUSIC; FIREGHOST for ELECTRICITY; FOURWINKLE for QUADRANGLE; ONHENGE for APPENDIX etc. While picturesque, their silliness seems obvious today, in the light of modern knowledge about the complex sociocultural and sociopolitical processes that bring about lexical change. Hope's conclusion seems a sound one here:

> Purists' efforts to find a suitable native word often end by demonstrating how appropriate the foreign word is and so confirm its intrinsic semantic value and its right to be accepted (1971, p. 712).

### Into the Early Modern Period

I have argued that the lexical bar was first erected in the fifteenth to seventeenth centuries. The following centuries were the period of its reinforcement; and the Church and education continued as the tools of that reinforcement.

On the one hand, where the common people received an education, they got it in a few charity schools. I discuss the curriculum of one of these a little later. But even these schools were rare. When at their peak of influence, at the end of the eighteenth century, their spread was so restricted that Beilby, Bishop of Chester, complained:

> In many towns, and by far the greatest number of villages, there are no Charity schools at all. In London, and the other great cities of the kingdom, where they are in general established, they can take in only a very small part of the children of the poor. The rest are left of course to themselves, without education, without instruction in the great duties of morality and religion . . . (1786, pp. 6-7).

Sentiment similar to this created enthusiasm for Sunday Schools. These began in 1780 and spread rapidly. They emphasized basic literacy, and they did so with some success. Yet even these were 'selective' schools, since children had to pay a shilling for each Sunday attendance, their parents had to be of good character, agreeing to attend church services, and a reference was needed before each child was accepted.  The literacy development and lexical reinforcement centred on bible reading, while the rest of the curriculum aimed to foster "habits of piety and devotion", "the practice of catechizing", "grounding them well in sound evangelical principles", and above all "keep them firm to the church" (Beilby, 1786, pp. 12-17).

Meanwhile, gentlemen in their grammar schools relentlessly applied themselves to the classics, although the practice was at last becoming the butt of mild but influential ridicule.  Daniel Defoe complained that "students come away masters of Science, critics of Greek and Hebrew, perfect in language, and perfectly ignorant of their mother tongue".  Trevelyan draws attention to the possible consequences of this educational apartheid, which appeared to separate not just the high and the lowly, but, on a different plane, the sexes as well:

> It was even declared by some that "a girl which is educated at home with her mother is wiser at twelve than a boy at sixteen who knows only Latin" (1978, p. 272).

Certainly in the previous century, as Lawson & Silver confirm, well-born women generally were educated to a higher level of literacy than was usual again until the late Victorian era. For poorer children of both sexes, about a dozen new schools had been founded between 1603 and 1640. But as late as 1791, there was still significant difference in the curriculum provided by this type of school for the two sexes: boys received reading and arithmetic, with some history and writing; and girls received reading, sewing, spinning and knitting (Alexander, 1990)

There were already long-standing demands for reform in the education of the upper classes, some of the demands coming from citizens of influence who were witnesses to the obvious face of the bar. John Locke in *Some Thoughts Concerning Education* pressed for greater attention to English teaching, lamenting its universal neglect:

> If any one among us have a Facility or Purity more than ordinary in his Mother Tongue it is owing to Chance, or his Genius, or anything, rather than to his Education or any Care of his Teacher; to mind what English his Pupil speaks or writes, is below the Dignity of one bred up amongst Greek and Latin, though he have but little of them himself. These are the learned Languages fit only for learned men to meddle with and teach. English is the language of illiterate Vulgar . . . (1690, pp. 291-292)

Yet classics remained the common core curriculum of the grammar schools, its beginning and its end.  And it is important to see the agitation for school reform pursued by Locke and others in its true light.  Their aim was not to liberate education from the tyranny of Greek and Latin.  Education was to be reformed, but not by abolishing the classics.

Rather, curriculum objectives were redirected away from reading classics solely as works of literature, which merely taught a boy to express himself. Now they were to be studied "as sources of information, either on practical subjects like farming (Hesiod, Virgil), warfare (Livy, Frontinus, Aelian), mathematics (Euclid), architecture (Vitruvius), education (Plutarch), or on matters of moral and political behaviour" (Ogilvie, 1964, pp. 37-38). The effect was to open up these and other meaning systems to a further flow of specialist G-L words. But they remained semantic fields and meaning systems representative of knowledge areas of a curriculum and a vocabulary shared only by the nobility, the gentry, and the new middle classes. For the rest, where they were literate, the Bible, Bunyan, Blake, Wordsworth and a few other works formed the corpus of accessible, serious reading material.

Lawson & Silver give fairly accurate percentages of popular literacy, drawing on the records of seventeen rural parishes in the East Riding. These average 51 percent for both sexes in the 1750s, and 57 percent in the 1790s. They also list varieties of popular, poorer quality literature available during the period. In addition to the ballads, broadsheets and pamphlets common since Tudor times, the eighteenth century saw a great proliferation of spellers, writing sheets, fairy stories, moral tales, fables, and histories. Although they describe these as "hack-written", some part of the reading public were creating a demand for this material. But it was not the labouring classes: "even if the labourer could read, incessant physical labour left him with no leisure for reading such books as he possessed or could borrow" (Lawson & Silver, 1973, pp. 193-194).

For common readers without Latin or Greek, more serious reading became remote or irritating because the language of the page was not the language of the vernacular. Their vocabularies, though dynamic in their own ways, were relegated to peripheral areas not much recognised in the dominant culture of literacy. Their isolation from the innovations of the standard variety intensified their development in directions away from that variety.

## The Nineteenth Century
In the late eighteenth and nineteenth centuries, the situation remained, aggravated certainly by the Industrial Revolution. This upheaval closed off those narrow, traditional avenues which a largely agrarian economy allowed as a link between the poor and the wealthier. It herded the poorer people into urban conglomerations, where the undoubted lexical dynamism of their vernaculars continued to drive their vocabularies away from the discursive practices of the literate culture, and towards contacts with other vocabularies that were as intrinsically Anglo-Saxon as their own. Perhaps the Anglo-Saxon element intensified as a result of urban concentration in the new cities of Yorkshire. In the 1960s, Jackson & Marsden looked at a working class regional variety from a city "bred out of the Industrial Revolution" whose population quadrupled from 1800 to 1840. They record the following observation from a respondent:

"He was a year younger than me but he could understand the Chaucer I was doing. He spoke with a broad Yorkshire accent and he could understand it because the Chaucer was nearer to the way they spoke there" (1966, p. 47).

In the grammar schools, Latin lost its influence as a spoken language only at the time of the Industrial Revolution. Adamson records its passing:

Latin ceased to be spoken at Westminster in Vincent's time, 1788-1802; at that date it had so degenerated at the English universities that it was no longer worth speaking (1922, p. 227).

While not spoken, Latin's central place endured. Grammar school boys at this time were encouraged to regard Latin as the language of the mind, through "the practice which prevailed widely till the beginning of the nineteenth century of learning Greek through the medium of grammars and textbooks written in Latin. At both Eton and Winchester, it was customary to construe Greek into Latin" (Ogilvie, 1964, p. 83). This practice persevered in the United States too: Harvard College did not replace Latin and Greek with English composition until 1810 (Maylath, 1994). Indeed most of the founders of the American republic, including Jefferson, Hamilton and the Adams family, were 'conditioned' to seek models of excellence in patriotism, moral virtue, statesmanship, literary taste, and personal behaviour by looking to the classics for a sense of shared discourse. Arguing from this observation, Richard (1994) even recommends that the renewal and restoration of that republican tradition, in today's American life, might well come about through the teaching of the classics!

After nearly 400 years, Mulcaster's demand that English be given a prominent place in the education of English people, was still unmet, except in the schools provided for the children of the working classes, few though such' schools were. One model charity school for both sexes is an example here. St Anne's Parochial School in Soho opened for boys in 1699 and for girls in 1703. From the outset and for almost two centuries, the boys' curriculum was mainly reading, writing, and the 'grounds of arithmetic', with religious teaching on church lines. Textbooks were unavailable, and reading classes centred on holy writ, again remote from the flood of G-L sources which were influencing the language of the grammar and public school boys. The girls' curriculum was more than remote from the dominant vocabulary and its culture of literacy; it had few roots in language at all. While some reading was taught, writing was not, and industrial training and 'sampler' work formed the bulk of the girls' education. School priorities were peculiarly ordered: From the outset, more was spent annually by the trustees on the children's fancy and impractical school uniforms, than on their education (Cardwell, 1899). Oral language activities, so necessary for talking about text and assimilating a culture of literacy, were not in evidence. Instead, for most of every school day, oral language was outlawed, in the usual way.

National schools began by 1829, operating alongside charity schools. They developed quickly in the nineteenth century, educating upwards of

350,000 children in Sunday or daily attendance (Silver and Silver, 1974). Under their rigid monitorial system, 500 children could be efficiently controlled by one teacher, helped by child monitors. Again the twin features appeared of excessive concentration on religious instruction with minimal attention given to language and literacy. The National Society insisted that only religious tracts, sold by the Society for Promoting Christian Knowledge, were to be used in national schools. Moral and religious training formed at least the major part of the curriculum until the 1860s. Mary Sturt (1967) reflects on the inadequate, off-handed, and damaging language instruction available, with its elaborate methods for destroying meaning that were held to be a virtue. Again motivated participation in the kinds of discursive practices that position children closer to the school's culture of literacy, was unavailable.

Even well into the modern period, the little that the charity and national schools provided for some children of the poorer classes, was much more than most received. In 1816 a Select Committee of the House of Commons, established to inquire into the 'education of the lower orders', produced evidence which Adamson (1922) construes to show that not one in sixteen children in England and not one in twenty in Wales were receiving any education. As late as 1851, an analysis of the census of that year suggests that 40 percent of boys and 48 percent of girls were not receiving education, implying that these were poorer working class children (Hurt, 1979).

The age range of 6 to 10 years provided the peak period for the education of those working class children who did receive schooling. Above the age of 10, education became more and more a middle class prerogative. An 1861 Report on schools for the lower classes asserted that by the time the boy had reached his eleventh year, he should have acquired "all that it is necessary for him to possess in the shape of intellectual attainment". The text is quoted more fully by Lawton. His quote concludes, in part:

> " . . . and underlying all and not without its influence . . . he has acquaintance enough with the Holy Scriptures to follow the allusions and arguments of a *plain Saxon sermon* . . . " (1973, p. 80) (my emphasis).

The stress here is not to be missed. Contrast this curriculum fiat with the following, published only three years later as part of the Clarendon Report on endowed schools or public schools (the schools of the middle and upper classes):

> "If a youth, after four or five years spent at school, quits it at 19 unable to construe an easy piece of Latin or Greek without the help of a dictionary . . . his intellectual education must certainly by accounted a failure . . . " (Lawton, 1973, pp. 80-81).

The Grammar Schools Act of 1840 had overturned Lord Eldon's famous 1805 judgment that the school was only "for teaching grammatically the learned languages". It allowed schools to dispense with the teaching of Latin and Greek and encouraged the introduction of other subjects. Yet as late as 1864, the Clarendon Commission, denouncing the exclusiveness of classics in the grammar school curriculum, still agreed "that it should continue to hold the principal place" (Gordon and Lawton, 1978, pp. 6-13). Lawton (1973) comments that the Clarendon Commissioners accepted Latin and Greek as central to the curriculum because of their regard for these subjects as the best method of teaching pupils how to use their own language. In a century-long legitimation of this policy, Oxford and Cambridge still required undergraduate entry qualifications in Latin or Greek until the 1960s.

### A Modern Lexical Bar for English-Speaking Countries

So more formally than ever, in the late nineteenth century, British education, including its derivatives in the Empire's colonies and in much of the United States, institutionalized two educational cultures. By doing so, it guaranteed the maintenance of an already long established and deeply embedded lexical bar, which itself is reinforced by other institutions. Hurt returns to Horace Mann's contemporary account which seeks to explain class attitudes to formal education in that period. In general, a father as head of household, in whatever his station in life might have been,

> "takes himself and his own social *status* as the standard up to which he purposes to educate his offspring . . . ". Amongst the working classes this attitude was reinforced by the way in which they had "for some generations past been tutored not to look *beyond their station*". Hence the education of "the sons of all engaged in manual industry", that is, the unskilled was seen as completed "as soon as they possess the manual strength and skill required for such pursuits" (Hurt, 1979, p. 30).

Again the age of 12 years is implied here: that age when an ordinary child begins to display incipient puberty, physical strength, analytical reasoning, and the development of an abstract vocabulary.

The Taunton Report of 1864-8 institutionalized this lexical separation. It recommended three classes of school, to match the 'social ranking' of the pupils. Some working class boys were admitted to the lowest of these three grades, and their curriculum was spelt out as "reading, writing and arithmetic" or "a clerk's education" (Lawton, 1973). In framing the form of this "lowest type of school", the Taunton commissioners extensively consulted the wishes of working class parents themselves, who generally favoured nothing more than that the three Rs were taught as quickly as possible (Hurt, 1979). So in Gramscian fashion, cultural and lexical divisions were reinforced from both sides of the social barrier.

For the second grade schools, which were the schools of the middle class proper, a curriculum with both Latin and English was mandatory, in this way cementing the bond and reinforcing the bar. For the first grade schools, a classical education with no formal English, then followed by university, was the rule. These were to remain the schools of upper middle class children.

To a remarkable extent, what follows was more of the same. The impression gained from Hurt's summary is that syllabuses for the poorer working classes, where they existed, comprised the three Rs and very little else until the end of the century. It was not until 1918 that full-time education to the age of 14 years became the general rule in England and Wales, and the massive loopholes allowed by part-time work laws for manual workers were closed off, thus preventing half the children from leaving shortly after their twelfth birthday.

After World War I, discrimination no longer turned on access to elementary education. Access to minimum quality school environments, broad curricula, and senior level education now became the discriminatory factor. As late as 1929, Bernbaum was able to claim that:

> ... the conditions of schooling remained in many ways unchanged for the great majority of children ... poor facilities, sickness and irregularity of attendance in working class districts, difficulty of entry into the higher strata of education from the elementary school had hardly been tackled (1967, p. 50).

With only 10.7% of boys from the routine manual workers category obtaining secondary education in 1940, compared with 54.2% of boys from other categories, Bernbaum concludes that the children of unskilled manual workers were at an enormous disadvantage in securing secondary education. In many school systems, the habits of the past continued to direct the curriculum of the poor. But the need for change was gradually being recognised, as Hammond & Hammond describe:

> In the thirties, and still more in the forties, an attempt was made to relax the strict reference of all knowledge in the Lancasterian Schools to the Scriptures, and though no language was taught, ample explanations were given of the roots of words. This was probably not unconnected with the fact noticed by Kay-Shuttleworth: "Those who have had close intercourse with the labouring classes well know with what difficulty they comprehend words not of a Saxon origin, and how frequently addresses to them are unintelligible from the continual use of terms of a Latin or Greek derivation" (1947, p.146).

Certainly, then, teachers in schools in the 1940s were very aware of the inter-class differences in vocabulary use that had crept into English language communities. They were also aware of their subtle discriminatory effects.

On the one hand, like Kay-Shuttleworth himself, teachers noted that children from poorer working class backgrounds were almost systematically excluded from many activities requiring a motivated engagement with G-L vocabularies. On the other hand, teachers of children in upper middle class schools felt the need to warn their pupils that too great a use of the G-L vocabulary could be seen as pretentious and inconsistent with good style. Rom Harré recalls his own secondary education in a Public School in the early 1940s: "we were told that by implication good little members of the u-class would use the following rules for good writing: 1. prefer the Anglo-Saxon to the Latin; 2. prefer the simple to the complex; 3. prefer the concrete to the abstract". Harré and his classmates were told that these rules came from Winston Churchill (personal communication).

Clearly Churchill provided an influential and worthwhile model of plain speech, but it was a style also resonant with rhetorical eloquence, power, and conviction. So when they were recommending rules attributed to Churchill, Harré's teachers were hardly encouraging their students to speak more like working class people. Their aim was to inspire a plain but powerful style of communication that was deliberately understated by using G-L words sparingly, and so probably with more effect. But this form of voluntary lexical control, and the discretionary discursive power it licenses, was denied entirely to the labouring classes of the day, who would have had relatively little contact with the G-L, either in their own communities or in their schooling.

Writing in the 1960s, Eaglesham sees the associated problems, in Britain at least, as "manifestations of a deep underlying cleavage" that remains with us. He asks, "is 'comprehensive' schooling any more than an attempt to stretch the paper of a name over the reality of a huge social and educational gulf?" (1967, p. 108).

## Conclusion

Perhaps much sooner than in England, different arrangements in other English-speaking countries have modified the lexical bar somewhat. We might reasonably assume that the more egalitarian educational systems in some countries would allow users of English a more equal access to the rules of use for its words, and greater participation in the discursive practices necessary for engagement with the school's culture of literacy. But the evidence is against this view.

Fusserl (1983) in his study of 'class' in the United States, notes that the American middle classes even today prefer the cultural capital of G-L words for the prestige it confers, whenever they can get it. Even everyday American English prefers AUTOMOBILE and ELEVATOR to CAR and LIFT. This is because outside the school, the bar is already erected and maintained in the United States and almost everywhere else that English has penetrated. To a remarkable degree, it still distinguishes the high status from the low status discursive practices of English. This complex sociocultural phenomenon has resisted even the most egalitarian of educational policies. Comparative studies reported in Chapter 5 from England, the most class-divided English-speaking country, and from Australia, the most socially mobile, support this claim.

The introduction of comprehensive schooling, with its patchy history in England and Wales, Canada, Australia, New Zealand, and the United States, may have lowered the bar somewhat. But it has not seriously challenged it in a formal way. This is because the 'problem' is not recognized or formulated as a policy problem that education should address. The belief that large sections of the children of the poor and of other sociocultural minorities will routinely drop out, or fail in the literate culture of schools, is accepted almost everywhere as an educational given.

Britain enjoyed post-war egalitarian trends in education: Mixed ability grouping of children for the early years of secondary education became common; and more general forms of comprehensive education became available. But these reforms came to an abrupt end when élitist educational policies were introduced in the 1980s and the 1990s. These policies returned many schools to their former role as centres of sociocultural positioning and stratification: shaping the discursive practices of children to match prejudiced expectations about their life destinations.

As a widespread practice in North America, schools stream children for most of their secondary education into basic, general, and advanced tracks. This practice herds the children of the poor and the socioculturally different into basic and general tracks in hugely disproportionate numbers. It directly excludes the many from access to the high status meaning systems intended as the chief output of schooling, at the very time that children are almost ready to enter them.

Although there are many language-related reasons for this continuing discrimination (Corson, 1993), the problem is partly disguised by the present-day reinforcement of the lexical bar outside education. This operates to a lesser or greater extent in all countries where English is a major language of communication. This is the subject of the next chapter.

# 4

# Factors Reinforcing the Bar
# in the Present Day

If the lexical bar were no more than an historical detail, resident in the language over centuries but maintained by forces no longer operating, its contemporary effect would be a trivial one. Its implications for education and society would be slight and its marks on the English language would be rapidly disappearing. Linguistic evolution would have homogenized even the most distant vocabularies of English. Yet this has not been the case for some sociocultural group vocabularies, as studies reported in later chapters show. There are clear contemporary factors, operating in the language and among its users, that combine to maintain and reinforce the bar and its effects.

These factors are of two broad types, inseparable in effect but readily distinguishable in analysis. The first group of factors is linguistic. Their marks in the semantic, morphological, and phonological features of English are fairly clear, once exposed to inspection. The second group of factors is both sociological and intrapersonal. They relate to differences in engagement by different sociocultural groups with different cultural meaning systems and their signs, producing differences in habitus and in cultural capital.

A small clue to the distinction that I make here for the sake of analysis, lies in research studies from Hong Kong and the Netherlands discussed in Chapter 2. Both Cantonese-speaking second language users of English and also speakers of Dutch experience difficulties with G-L words. But there are different sources for these difficulties: Researchers argue that the Cantonese students keep G-L words within restricted specialist meaning systems in their mental lexicons and so they do not 'identify with' them very much. They do not put the words to use in ordinary language because they have not experienced them used in this way. There is a compartmentalization of meaning, which means the students recognize and use them less readily in general.

But the Dutch students have difficulty recognizing G-L words because they are different in form from Germanic words in Dutch, in much the same way as G-L words in English are different in form from the largely Germanic vocabularies of most speakers of English. This is because the similarity of words to the general form of a person's vocabulary is important for recognizing and remembering the words themselves. If they are too dissimilar, they become unmotivated words.

This chapter relates these factors to first language speakers of English, but, as the two examples above imply, the discussion is also very relevant to vocabulary learning by ESL children and adults. The chapter also covers the effects that the socio-economic and sociocultural orderings of English-speaking societies can have on vocabulary learning and use. Later I look at these social, cultural, and intrapersonal factors that especially impinge on differences in meaning systems and cultural capital. This first section deals with the more accessible linguistic factors reinforcing the bar. Chapters 7 and 8 also extend this discussion.

## Morphological and Phonological Factors

Steinberg and Jakobovits (1971) see two parts to knowing a word, the semantic and the phonetic. These operate alongside one another and it is difficult to separate their influence on word acquisition, retention, and use. Chapter 2 argued that the physical form of a word itself is also very important in helping to learn and use it. At all these linguistic levels, the lexical bar is reinforced in the English of English-speaking societies, and in the English of many associated cultures where it is a major second language. Most words of G-L origin are simply different in their physical form and sound from the rest of the vocabulary. Many speakers do not identify with them, since their sound and appearance are alien, and this contributes to their semantic strangeness. In this section, I deal first with word appearance, or morphology, and then with word sound.

### Identifying with the Morphology of Words

The relatively few abstract words of Anglo-Saxon origin left in English, like THOUGHT, UNDERSTANDING, LEARNING, KNOWLEDGE, are not systematically absent from people's vocabularies in spite of their abstractness. They are too morphologically motivated for people to find them strange. Indeed difficulties with G-L words, for many people, seem to be due largely to an interaction of form and meaning. Sometimes young students in literacy work, for example, are daunted even in their most basic attempts at making sense of words, by the very strangeness of the words themselves. Sometimes there are remarks like 'that's too hard for me' or 'I don't know what these long words mean', comments offered as rationalizations for what are perceived solely as difficulties in meaning. This problem carries over to adult students too. For several years, I supervised the adult literacy program of an Australian state. I was impressed by how often adult beginning readers associated word difficulty in their reading with word shape and length, even when the word was something everyday in meaning like MARMALADE. The morphology of some words seems to get in the way.

Tyler & Nagy (1989) see three types of knowledge of derivational morphology. First there is 'relational knowledge'. This is the ability to see relations in the shapes of two words that have a common stem, like CELEBRATE and CELEBRATORY. Then there is 'syntactic knowledge'. This is knowing that suffixes usually mark words as parts of speech, like the -ION in TRANSITION and IMMIGRATION. Finally there is 'distributional knowledge'. This is the ability to recognize that the use of affixes is usually restricted in the words that they can attach to. For example, the suffix -FUL can attach to verbs like HOPE but not to adjectives like QUIET. In tests based on these three categories, Tyler & Nagy report that children in grades 4, 6 & 8 are adept at using the first category, relational knowledge, but that syntactic and distributional knowledge increases with grade level. These two types of knowledge are developmental.

This kind of developmentally acquired knowledge about word morphology seems to be associated with socioeconomic factors. Anglin (1993) reports that grades 1, 3 and 5 children who differ in their socioeconomic background, reveal significant differences in knowledge of word morphology and these differences favour the more affluent. The differences cover the comprehension of inflected words, derived words, and words with three or more morphemes. Perhaps a partial explanation of these differences is that some groups of children just feel ill at ease with words of these types, which makes their comprehension that much more difficult. I come back to this point about socioeconomic background and word identification later in the chapter, since it relates directly to the barrier that this book addresses.

Potter (1966) and Quirk (1974) point out the striking incompatibility between the native and the Latinate elements in English. The G-L are very different morphemically and they are also very different in length. Samuels (1972) notes that with the loss of the final neutral vowel, English became the most monosyllabic language in Western Europe. But at the same time, the words that flooded into English around the time when that final neutral vowel disappeared, created a new kind of polymorphemic vocabulary for the language. The typical prefix-stem-suffix form of G-L words entering English was more than double the average length of earlier words still in the language. Does word length still separate the G-L from the Anglo-Saxon?

Word length certainly offers at least a superficial explanation for the reinforcement of the bar in the present day. Two sets of comparative studies of syllable length help support this claim. Firstly, from his studies of middle class and working class 15 year olds, Bernstein (1977) found mean total word lengths of 1.30 syllables for the middle class groups and 1.23 for the working class groups. But it is not these very slight differences between groups that concern me here. Rather, contrast Bernstein's findings with the mean syllable lengths of the G-L words used by 15 year olds in the London and Yorkshire studies reported in Chapter 5: a mean (G-L only) word length of 2.70 for the working class groups and 3.20 for the middle class groups. Middle class 12 year olds also returned a mean (G-L only) word length of 3.10 syllables. Clearly G-L words remain much longer than the rest of the vocabulary, and there is also a social dimension to their use. Unlike the speakers of many other languages, if random speakers of English are asked to name the most prominent feature of 'hard words', they usually say their length. This factor of word length alone suggests that many people find it difficult to identify with most G-L words.

## Identifying with the Sounds of Words

It is another peculiarity of English vocabulary that most of its specialist words do not sound English in origin. In this way they do not easily knit together with many people's active vocabularies, since they are not the more "ancient wounds" (Meneghello's "le ferite antiche") that leave marks in the verbal memories of people from their earliest contacts with language. Where met at all, they are usually experienced late and learned even later in life. Their frequent semantic strangeness, which comes from their regular use within specialist meaning systems, is reinforced by a phonaesthetic strangeness, and this strangeness takes several forms.

The typical vowel-consonant and consonant-consonant blends of G-L words, are very unlike the Anglo-Saxon. Children can find this an obstacle when adding them to their vocabularies, if they are not exposed to the blends often enough through contact with other higher frequency G-L words used in natural language. This idea of word frequency in the language is a very important factor in learning and using words. Not surprisingly, research confirms that speech errors occur more often with low-frequency words than with high-frequency ones (Stemberger & MacWhinney, 1986) and that the frequency of a word's occurrence determines its ease of production (Sandra, 1994). Although word frequency in research is usually assessed according to the word's frequency in computations of written English, it is the case that specialist G-L words appear even less frequently in spoken English and hardly at all in the everyday discourses of many sociocultural groups.

Even when the sounds of G-L words are similar to English sounds that are heard repeatedly throughout early childhood, they still cause difficulties when transferred to print symbols that children need to sound out when first learning to read the words. For example, low-frequency G-L words using the Greek digraphs PH, TH, CH and PS often seem anomalous if first met in print, even though the first three of these sounds are very high-frequency sounds in Anglo-Saxon words as well. Almost as alien are the many words that begin with Latin prefixes that are very different from the native, such as CIRCUM-,

CONTRA-, HOMO-, ULTRA-, SEMI-, SUB-, RETRO- and many more. Much the same can be said for Latin suffixes too, and for Greek affixes of both kinds

Is it surprising that children who are unused to these sounds and syllables, find difficulty in saying them when called upon to do so in formal educational settings? One long-term study, influential in British education (Davie, Butler and Goldstein, 1972), reports the administration of clinical speech tests to large groups of children from different backgrounds. Children were asked to repeat short sentences designed to cover most of the letter sounds and most of the combinations of sounds in 'normal spoken English'. Results reveal a marked social class trend: The average number of pronunciation errors declined markedly as tests were varied from poorer working class to upper middle class language groups. Nor do these differences disappear as a result of more years experience in the language. Jackson & Marsden (1966) report working class adults with larger vocabularies than they could easily pronounce. When attempts at pronunciation were made, the syllable lengths would be unusual in words like PREPARATORY or COMPROMISE.

While it is language experience that is the main factor at work here, it is not experience in the absolute sense. Extensive language experience is widely available to almost everyone in societies. But it is language experience that includes motivated use of the sounds of G-L words, that is not as widely distributed. The frequency of these sounds in the discursive events that children and adults take a part in, will affect their readiness to reproduce the sounds. It will also affect their ease of identification with the words.

Consider pre-school children whose language in the home and in the street, as speakers and listeners, is untrammeled by polysyllabic, prefix-base-suffix words. If they have had no experience playing those nonsense games with the sounds of long words that typify one formative stage of language development, around three to four years, these children will find this vocabulary strange when first met in school, or in a book, or in a newspaper. They may reject all three in consequence, to some extent. This rejection is easier for language users when words like 'high-brow' or 'posh talk' are part of the conventional rhetoric that allows the rationalization of the rejection. It is also easier when music hall entertainers, television comedians, and rap-artists take strange sounding words out of context and make fun of their use.

Bridging the phonetic and the semantic are phonosemantic factors that reinforce the bar. For example, often the initial cluster of consonants in words gives a hint about meanings of a rather special kind. Palmer (1976) cites the SL- initial cluster of consonants that connotes two ideas in English. One of these is 'slipperiness' appearing in SLIDE, SLIP, SLITHER, SLUSH, SLUICE, SLUDGE. The other is a 'general pejorative sense' as in SLATTERN, SLANG, SLY, SLOPPY, SLOVENLY, SLOUCH. Likewise, SK- can suggest either 'surfaces' or 'superficiality' as in SKATE, SKIMP, SKID, SKIM, SKIN etc. The ends of words can also show this phonosemantic factor at work. Words in -UMP suggest 'a roundish mass' as in PLUMP, CHUMP, HUMP, RUMP, STUMP.

For first language speakers of English, these and similar features offer additional semantic clues. They also increase the degree to which people identify with these words as a part of English. At the same time, first language speakers can readily derive cues of another kind from the phonosemantic features of many G-L words. But in the G-L, those features are very different in form and in connotation. If the words are not present in a person's mental lexicon in numbers sufficient for patterns of phonosemantic cues to be enlisted to help word activation (see Chapter 7), these very basic but supplementary phonosemantic cues are of no use.

When listeners do not recognize these sound cues in newly experienced G-L words, the words remain opaque and listeners identify with them less readily. Consider a low-frequency G-L word like CIRCUMSPECT for instance. It will lack this kind of motivation in a person's mental lexicon if the prefix CIRCUM- or the stem -SPECT are not already stored, either as high-frequency morphemes or as morphemes in other higher frequency words. These morphemes also appear in higher frequency G-L words like SUSPECT and CIRCUMSTANCE. But if these higher frequency words are only rarely encountered, any motivation in learning and using the new word may be lost. Moreover, a listener without this motivation and identification, who hears the word CIRCUMSPECT, may regard its use as bombastic, comic, or over-formal, whether its meaning is understood from the context or not.

### The Formality and Pseudo-Prestige of G-L Words

When thinking about the formality or informality of words, linguistic and functional factors merge. I think we can see the reason for this in Chapter 2's discussion 'Insights from the Philosophy of Language'. In that section, I present the prevailing view of philosophers that the meaning of a word is its use in a language. For example, Rundle's point about 'meaning' and 'use' relates directly to this question of formality: He says that the idea of a word's 'meaning' is best thought of as its 'use', partly because in looking at a word's use we find out something about the speaker or writer who uses it. This means we learn something about that word user's attitudes to the context in which he or she is placed, and about the power relationships that obtain. None of these things can really be disentangled from the meaning of the word as used on that single occasion.

Many Latinate words lend themselves phonetically to bombastic speech and to turgid prose. The sonority of strings of these words, coursing along like Latin hexameters, can turn off listeners or readers, especially where the subject matter and meaning are already difficult. To many people the statement 'they use big words', means 'they don't want us to understand' or 'we don't really want to understand them'. Technical G-L words, scattered across the texts of specialist subject areas, often seem "unnecessarily mysterious". They give the impression that the writer or speaker is covering "conceptual and empirical nakedness" (Edwards & Westgate, 1994 p. 18) with "verbal substitutions masquerading as knowledge" (Andreski, 1974 p. 58).

Certainly Latinate words are linked to formal and 'prestigeful language' (Giles & Powesland, 1975). But in English, formal style is more subtle than in languages where formality and informality are clearly marked by high status and low status varieties (Ferguson, 1959). This subtlety that English has, leads to difficulties of description, use, and acquisition, especially related to vocabulary (Levin & Novak, 1991). It is clear that readers of Latinate words see them as much more formal than Anglo-Saxon ones (Levin, Long & Shaffer, 1981). But this marked difference in formality is not due just to the relative low-frequency of most Latinate words. Levin & Novak (1991) report that interviewed respondents describe utterances that are high in Latinate words as being addressed to formal listeners, regardless of the frequencies of the Latinate words used. But the respondents even see very low-frequency Anglo-Saxon words as less formal than higher frequency Latinate words. Does this difference in formality and prestige between the two types of words have educational implications?

Basing his work on the lexical bar studies, Maylath (1994) examined the effect of the two types of vocabulary in English on university instructors' assessments of pieces of students' writing. The written texts were in three versions: one highly G-L; one highly Anglo-Saxon; and one a blend of the two types of vocabularies. Maylath compared the 90 instructors' assessments by their ages, years of teaching, sex, and places of schooling. All of the instructors who favoured the Anglo-Saxon texts were veteran teachers of writing, averaging more than 20 years experience. All of the instructors who favoured the G-L texts were novices at teaching writing, averaging just nine months' experience. A few more teachers preferred the mixed texts than either of the extremes, but male and female instructors reveal no differences in their preferences for any type of text. Later interviews conducted by Maylath, suggest that 'instructor insecurity' was a major factor causing the inexperienced teachers to rank the G-L vocabulary more highly in their gradings.

In Chapter 3, I discussed a related experience that Rom Harré had in his upper middle class schooling, where senior level teachers in a prestigious school warned their pupils that too great a use of the G-L vocabulary is pretentious and inconsistent with good style. Instead they urged the students to prefer the Anglo-Saxon to the Latin, following the model of Winston Churchill, and so achieve a plain, meaningful but powerful style of communication deliberately understated by using G-L words sparingly, and so probably with more effect. An over-use of G-L words often gives the impression that the word user is trying too hard, is striking a pose, or is engaged in overkill. Both Labov and Bourdieu make similar observations about this aspect of linguistic style: For a clear indication that people possess high status linguistic capital, look for an easy and relaxed style of communication.

So perhaps the last thing a competent and proficient stylist would want to reveal is the linguistic insecurity offered by too many G-L words. No doubt for Harré's Public School teachers and for Maylath's more experienced professors, a use of plain vocabulary was an important way to avoid appearing tense and forced: as insecure. But whether Maylath's amazingly polarized findings are caused by instructor insecurity or not, there is a practical consequence for students in all this. He points to the plight of students exposed to both types of teacher in consecutive semesters or in adjacent courses. At the very least, as a result of receiving these contradictory teacher valuations, many students would become more insecure themselves about what is appropriate vocabulary for use in academic and literary contexts.

Specialist G-L words are usually literary in their use and this undoubtedly reinforces the bar. Most children begin to encounter these words in quantity in the formal secondary school setting. Their introduction in literature or textbooks, rather than in conversation, also restricts people's access to them. It is certain that exposure to specialist G-L words happens much more often while reading than while talking or watching television. Hayes & Ahrens (1988) counted the proportion of 'rare words' that appear in different kinds of language. These researchers used Carroll, Richman & Davies (1971) as their guide for checking word rarity and the words themselves were overwhelmingly G-L. They found that printed texts provide much more exposure to these words than oral ones. For example, even children's books contain 50% more rare words than either adult prime-time television or the conversations of university graduates; and popular magazines have three times as many rare words as television and informal conversation.

Clearly, then, specialist G-L words appear much more often in formal textual contexts. This is linked, of course, to their historical status as signs located in formal meaning systems, associated with the academic culture of literacy. Taken together, all these things help reinforce their prestige. They are unhelpfully regarded by many people, especially by the insecure and the relatively powerless, as markers of high status cultural capital. This directly influences the rules of use that speakers and writers associate with them.

Young, inexperienced, or insecure writers and speakers, seeking the prestige that comes from the kind of educational success that will allow them to escape from their insecurity and inexperience, often increase their use of these words beyond necessary levels. In this way, they try to associate their own texts with texts that they see as examples of prestigious language in use. By trying too hard to do this, they often overdo it. Instead of creating texts that have just the right selection of specialist words to get their meaning across concisely, they engage in overkill and sometimes smother their meaning as a result.

Added to this, as Maylath's study seems to indicate, assessors doubtful about their status as assessors, project their own search for prestige onto the vocabulary of student texts. By doing this, I believe they reinforce the bar in three overlapping ways: They legitimate the use of G-L words as markers of prestige and formality; they reward students who use them, and so confirm them in their practices; and they recreate the cycle of lexical reproduction that wrongly links excessive use of G-L words with prospects for social success and with the removal of personal insecurity.

## The Genuine Communicative Value of G-L Words

However, when used to serve the meaning of the moment, and not for affect or to gain some sociocultural status or prestige, the communicative advantages of specialist G-L words are undeniable. Specialist G-L words are not highbrow synonyms for ordinary words. Samuels, Bréal, Wittgenstein and Hope, all reject the idea of the widespread existence of synonyms in language (Corson, 1982). It is wrong to suggest that the major part of the vocabulary of English consists largely of synonyms and is therefore redundant.

Speakers with a diverse vocabulary have a capacity in discourse for conveying shades of meaning which adds succinctness and precision, not redundancy, to their vocabularies. Language users with an unrestrained access to the specialist G-L vocabulary of English have a greater capacity for description, definition and nomenclature. A diverse and rich vocabulary is a better tool for dealing with a complex universe, because the speaker or writer need not use the same material over and over, thereby giving an illusory simplicity or meaning connection where there is none. Capacity to deal with expectations and hypotheticals also increases. "It is not difficult to show that more highly differentiated lexical knowledge can facilitate processing in a wide variety of psycholinguistic and cognitive domains" (Stanovich & Cunningham, 1993 p. 211). In other words, in his measured model of prose and oratory, Winston Churchill was hardly going about discarding his acquired G-L vocabulary; he was just being much more discerning in choosing and using that vocabulary, to get his meaning across.

## Sociological and Intrapersonal Factors

Without contradicting what I have already said in this chapter, I do have to qualify it somewhat: In spite of the many linguistic issues that this chapter raises, it is people's lexico-semantic positioning and sociocultural environment that are the more basic factors reinforcing the lexical bar. If people have little or no regular exposure to specialist G-L words, then just modifying the linguistic factors on their own can make little difference. Culture and class together create the conditions of upbringing and the alternative forms of linguistic capital that formal education often discounts. Indeed class systems, based on occupation and income, exist in all modern societies and there is compelling evidence that social class covaries significantly with linguistic and other differences between groups of people (Reid, 1977). Labov's point is a sound one: People who are sociologically similar are linguistically similar.

Chapter 3 points to the distinguishing features in the discursive practices of many upper middle class users of English that orient them towards meaning systems that provide the rules of use for specialist G-L words, and the motivation for that use. These features are clearly represented in the discursive practices of schools and universities, since modern schools and universities are an upper middle class creation, arranged in line with upper middle class habitus and in response to an academic culture of literacy that is itself a class-related product. So these institutions themselves represent and reinforce historic upper middle class cultural interests, values, cultural capital, and language practices. But what are the distinguishing features in the discursive practices of poorer working class people that orient them away from meaning systems that provide the rules of use, and the motivation for use, of specialist G-L words in particular?

*Social Class as a Descriptor*
    I need to distinguish the precise sense for 'upper middle class' in this study from its more ordinary language sense. Specifically by 'upper' I mean members of families in the British 'Registrar General's Classification of Occupations' (1980) grade I/II (professional, semi-professional, managerial, etc.). This is distinct from 'lower' middle class, by which I mean other non-manual workers drawn from grade III. Following the same system, I categorize workers and their families from grades IV/V (semi-skilled, unskilled) as poorer working class. I am acknowledging that a principal factor in social stratification, along with age, ethnicity and sex, is occupation and income. I re-apply these categories to other English-speaking countries like Australia, on the assumption that this is a reasonably accurate way of distinguishing social class using parental occupation. My method for grouping adolescents by social class in Chapter 5 is also based on this criterion. Granting the merits of other methods for judging class membership, this occupation criterion seems the most direct and the most widely used (Goldthorpe, 1980).
    There is significant if not complete overlap between my division of 'upper' and 'lower' middle classes and the distinction between the 'national' and 'native' middle classes made by Jackson & Marsden (1966). They see a national middle class that is metropolitan in interest and fairly mobile, and another middle class that is local and rooted in the milieu of its residence. Of necessity, the 'national' are users and producers of the dominant variety of the language, which has been produced to serve their own purposes by this dominant element of society through a lengthy process involving at least the stages of selection, codification, elaboration of function, and social acceptance of that variety (Hudson, 1980). In contrast, the 'native' middle class may have little need of a vocabulary much different from the vocabulary of the native working class than they themselves are different in social role and world view. Some allowance is made in selecting samples in this study for the existence of these two middle classes, although I do not believe that in lexical orientation, at least in passive vocabulary, there would be much difference between them.
    Wherever I categorize adolescent children by social class, there is a qualification in that categorization. My social class division focuses on two factors: the work of parents; and the family's presumed social class

disposition. Ford's (1969) research suggests that adolescent [British] children may be extremely 'class conscious' and so have at least an incipient disposition towards identifying with one or another class. Nevertheless, the 12 and 15 year olds studied here do not usually 'work'. So in the absence of this criterion for identifying their social class, the children are really class-less. My categorization of them is of course according to their family background, based on the work of their parents, and by presumed social class disposition or habitus. It is a category error to think of children themselves as working class or middle class.

*Sociocultural Influences on Vocabulary*

It is the effect of social stratification upon the lifestyle, experiences, and activities of certain social groups, that is the first-order extralinguistic factor that has produced and maintains the bar. The history of social class relations and their impact on the vocabularies of the poor varies from country to country, and within countries. Elsewhere I review this history as it developed in England (Corson, 1981 pp. 132-151) and was exported to the colonies. Many commentators describe the link between 'the making of the English working class' and various differences in cultural meaning systems between the classes. Prominent among these are Thompson (1968), Nisbet (1967), Klein (1965), and Hoggart (1958).

Durkheim and Gramsci offer seminal insights for understanding how a separation in lifestyle between sociocultural groups shows up in distinct cultural meaning systems, and then in vocabulary differences. Durkheim emphasizes the integrative value of the division of labour for a society, but also its divisive effects in producing isolation among workers who are cut off from the meaning systems of activities associated with the wider social and cultural relevance, importance, and rewards of their work (1893 pp. 357-371). Gramsci looks at the elements of a world view and its cultural meaning systems that are reflected in the language of people from different class positions, whose lifestyles are different because of their work or their area of residence (1948 pp. 4-5 Nota III). It is the division of labour in society that stands out as the key factor in all this. This is the social mechanism that produces social class divisions and differences in lifestyle. So it is also the division of labour that creates and sharpens differences in sociocultural meaning systems, and differential access to the signs that take their rules of use from those systems.

From this literature, and from incidental observations of lifestyle differences between the relatively poor and other social groups in Western societies, I put together a list of six social class-related influences on the language experience and vocabularies of adults in low-income families. These things, and others, impact indirectly but fully on the lexico-semantic positioning of  young members of those families. This list presents factors that keep many poorer working class adults away from high status meaning systems:

the monotonous and enervating nature of physical labour;
the effects of small incomes on life experiences;
the relative absence of outside language contacts;
relatively low levels of education and access to continuing education;
the relative absence of exogenous influences on routine and habit;
the social class-based housing common in English-speaking societies.

When the lifestyle of broad sections of an adult population restricts the experiences, activities, and language contacts available to some children in society, relative to others, and when this re-occurs from generation to generation, then inevitable differences in cultural meaning systems are likely to arise between groups, along with differences in lexico-semantic range.

Other very different language experiences seem to correlate with these differences in sociocultural positioning: differences in the availability of incidental reading materials, especially books and periodicals rich in vocabulary; and different rates of exposure to stimulating and engaging discourse tied to topics in meaning systems that use a differentiated vocabulary drawn from the school's culture of literacy. As a result, many children develop vocabularies very different from those given high status in the school.

Not surprisingly there is much evidence to show that differences in children's vocabularies do correlate with their parents' levels of education and with levels of quality of life generally (Hall, Nagy & Linn, 1984; Mercy & Steelman, 1982; Wells, 1986; West & Stanovich, 1991). Moreover educational research confirms that early achievement disparities increase with age (Walberg & Tsai, 1983) and there is now evidence to show that contemporary schools do little to end or narrow these disparities. Chapter 2 mentioned studies by Hayes & Grether (1983) comparing the vocabulary development of children during the vacation period with their vocabulary development during the school term. Their conclusion is very relevant here: A widening of the 'word knowledge gap' comes from events outside school, not from school itself. The affluent children get the early advantages and keep on getting them. In summary, it is differences in sociocultural positioning that are the key to differences in lexico-semantic range.

I am not suggesting that all poorer working class children are markedly different from upper middle class children in the life experiences that can promote certain kinds of vocabulary development, only that most are. At the same time, children whose families are on the more privileged side of the division of labour, are likely to have broader experiences and wider language contacts that more frequently reveal the rules of use necessary for word learning. The effects of these privileges on active vocabulary range begin to show up most dramatically in the years of middle adolescence.

An adolescent group's vocabulary takes on its character over time, through peer-group contact with sociologically similar people: by imitation, by motivation, and by social-group-specific closed-role pressures. The evidence that these social forces affect language choice continues to grow. As

Milroy notes: "just as there is strong institutional pressure in formal situations to use varieties approximating to the standard, so also effective sanctions are in force to promote 'vernacular' use in non-standard domains" (1992, p. 210). These forces are sufficient to orient a drive within the group as a whole towards cultural meaning systems and their vocabularies that are inevitably different in character, and often markedly different from those of other groups in society.

*Intrapersonal Factors*

Links between the sociological factors and the group lexical dispositions of poorer working class children can be readily inferred from this section's discussion so far. Where adult members of certain social groups have little disposition towards using certain sets of words, it is likely that their children will acquire similar dispositions from them, as only one part of the acquired habitus of which Bourdieu speaks. In addition to the psycholinguistic factors that I take up in Chapter 7, there are four more general psychological factors that help produce this aspect of habitus which is the intrapersonal side of the bar. These four factors are experience, motivation, modelling and habit.

I have already bypassed 'experience' in the absolute sense as a factor. Clearly in modern English-speaking societies, all children experience a very diverse range of words. It is experience in a more limited sense that I mean here. What poorer working class children often miss out on, is wide and regular experience in when, why, and how to use the rules of use of specialist words, both inside specialist meaning systems and in more ordinary language situations. We acquire these rules of use in discursive practice. Once an action is done, the rule becomes the thing that displays the meaning of that action within its own meaning system. Learning words proceeds against a backdrop of rules of this kind that are known only imprecisely at first. Word meanings remain unstable until the network of rules becomes more interlocked and overlapping. But the more words that are encountered, and the more thoroughly they are learned within and across the meaning systems where they are used, the more seamless becomes the fabric of rules that comprise the meaning systems.

Clearly language experiences of these kinds are unequally distributed among the members of societies and cultures. Most of all, many people lack the vital experience of an occasion in their everyday lives for using the word in speech for the very first time. This prime occasion represents that vital experience that acts as a catalyst for further experience and becomes itself a form of motivation. It is the very first tentative use of a word in natural language which is the experience that matters, for first or second language learners.

Motivation as a factor in lexical performance must be resident in the language situation, through absence of stress or cultural constraints, through the presence of interest and other reinforcers, or through a relaxed familiarity with the subject matter of the discourse. It is a dictum of psychology that disadvantaged young people seem to have less motivation for academic learning than those more affluent. This lower motivation applies as well to the use of language forms related to that academic learning: language forms that largely make up the specialist G-L vocabularies of English.

Modelling is the central factor for explaining the intrapersonal side of the lexical bar. Children have little discretion in choosing significant others as models in their early lives. Family members are fixed for them. Among the poorer working class and among minority cultural groups in English-speaking societies, peer groups, neighbours, friends and even teachers may be fixed in the range of models they present for language behaviour. Where the lexical orientation of social groups differs, and where children have limited opportunities for modelling, it is inevitable that vocabulary selection will be constrained to that range of usages manifested by available significant others.

Habit is the final factor. It is the product of the other three: experience, motivation, and modelling. We behave in characteristic ways largely because we have discovered that some responses are more effective than others in the short or long term. If a desire is fortified in the past by adopting certain behaviours, then the same pattern is likely to be repeated in similar circumstances. In this discussion, the pattern is the specialist section of the vocabulary and the sets of complex rules of use that go with it. Many working class children and adults, constrained by various manifestations of the closed role systems and different meaning systems of their social and peer groups, are not disposed towards using specialist words as an habitual part of their language practice, provided they can be avoided, even when these words may suit the meaning of the moment.

Dell Hymes has suggested that the word 'identification' sums up much of the meaning I intend by the four factors discussed above: The young speakers of some social groups do not *identify* with some sets of words. This happens either because of the closed role structures of their social backgrounds, which cause them to perceive their own roles as irrelevant to a use of specialist vocabularies, or because they do not identify with certain semantic or sound or shape characteristics of the vocabularies. Many of the words lodged in people's passive vocabularies seem to fit this category. So this suggestion from Hymes seems a sound integration of the main effect of my four intrapersonal factors.

In other words, closed role arrangements and narratives among some social groups may lead group members to perceive their own roles as irrelevant to a use of certain vocabularies, especially when they are not formally admitted to the relevant meaning systems: to the rules of use that provide the web of word relations within those systems. So, great importance attaches to background knowledge of the relevant cultural meaning systems for words. Not surprisingly, this view is now supported by critiques of diagnostic tests of vocabulary.

Nagy & Herman (1987) cite research in which reading texts were constructed using only words that were known by the subjects. But even when they knew all these fully familiar words, respondents still found the texts incomprehensible without the additional background knowledge needed to make sense of the texts. This background knowledge consists of the rules of use for words within the contexts of relevant language games, rooted in non-linguistic life forms and in material circumstances. So while schools and classrooms, as presently constituted, can certainly introduce words to students, most of the important rules of use are learned elsewhere.

## Conclusion

By reviewing linguistic, sociological and intrapersonal factors related to vocabulary acquisition and use, this chapter explains how factors in the present day maintain and reinforce the lexical bar.

Factors associated with the morphology of specialist G-L words - their shape and length - play an important role. So do phonological factors to do with the unusual sound and aesthetic qualities of G-L words. Their high level of formality and their affected use to gain social advantage, are also factors that influence the rules of use that people associate with them. They do seem to be overused by people seeking social preferment. But because they have a very real role in the communication of difficult ideas, they appear largely in literary contexts rather than on television or even in the conversations of educated people, and this also helps keep them away from the discursive practices of many people.

In particular, children from poorer working class backgrounds tend to receive least exposure to specialist G-L words in use. Because of the absence of modelling opportunities for meeting these words and for experiencing them in use, many children do not develop the habit and motivation needed to use them. But rather than removing this inequality, schools tend to worsen it by basing their standards of achievement on this form of linguistic capital that is unequally distributed across sociocultural groups. Many people do not identify with these specialist G-L words that become increasingly important for formal educational success as children grow older.

# 5

# The Research Studies

Up to this point, by reviewing relevant literature I have put together conceptual and historical evidence about the lexical bar. Although this material allows strong interpretations to be made, it still provides only commonsense inferences of a different sort from those used in deductive logic. Even when commonsense inferences depend upon true premises and correct reasoning, their conclusions are still only probable. Much the same is true of arguments based on quantitative data, since they really allow just another kind of interpretation. But it is evidence that many people give more weight to, and also understand more readily, even in an age when the narrow ideology of positivism is being left behind in social science philosophy and increasingly in research (Bhaskar, 1986; Corson, 1991).

The conceptual arguments presented so far allow me to speculate about the lexical bar in ways that would satisfy many readers in this post-positivist age. But others prefer an interpretation based on the other kind of evidence that quantitative studies produce. This chapter presents a range of empirical studies undertaken between 1980 and 1989.

## Measuring Instruments

The study is limited to the 'content' vocabulary or 'information words' that form the bulk of the vocabulary of English, rather than the relatively few 'pivot', 'function' or 'grammar' words: prepositions, auxiliaries, pronouns, and particles. The content vocabulary is sometimes called 'open-class words', since their number is constantly growing, while the small set of 'closed-class words' rarely increases in number. Nor am I interested, in this study, in that small but important category of words that are neither content nor grammar words (Winter, 1978) unless the words do sometimes have content-like rules of use within specialist areas (e.g. FACT). This third category of words signals the logic of texts or helps build cohesiveness across larger units of discourse. But most of these words have little content meaning within specific fields of knowledge (e.g. words like DIFFER or KIND).

Discussion in Chapter 2's sections titled 'Insights from Philosophy' and 'Insights from Psychology', indicates why earlier vocabulary measures seem inappropriate for these studies of lexico-semantic range. My aim is to explore differences in the active and passive vocabularies of people in line with the use theory: the meaning of a word is its use in a language. To meet this goal, the original instruments developed for this task and used in these studies, are the Measure of Passive Vocabulary and the G-L Instrument.

*The Measure of Passive Vocabulary*

Do the members of some sociocultural groups have a passive vocabulary ranging more widely over certain semantic fields or meaning systems than others? The knowledge categories of the formal educational curriculum provide the universe of meaning systems for this study. As a result, the Measure of Passive Vocabulary draws its target vocabulary from those knowledge categories in the ways described below.

While passive or unmotivated vocabulary, by definition, is not usually uttered, it is still available for certain aspects of language performance, depending on how much time the language user has to activate words in the mental lexicon and the type of activation received. Evidence in Chapter 7 in this book, suggests that passive words are probably more available for reading and for writing than for speaking or listening, because the reader or writer can usually slow themselves down and increase the activation time needed to access a low frequency word in the mental lexicon. But in this application of the Measure, my aim is to promote that word's motivated use in speech.

So the Measure of Passive Vocabulary encourages a use of words, whether they are usually available for active use or not. As an instrument, its structure is simple. In each of its 49 items, there are two words: the target word itself and a keyword. The keyword suggests the semantic field or meaning system from which the target word comes. Although many English words have many different meanings, I am looking at only one specific meaning of the target word in each item. So that meaning informs selection of a keyword to go with it.

Administration

After hearing each target word and its keyword, the interviewee then uses both words in an original sentence. Practice examples that are graded in difficulty, lessen any tension or strangeness in the task (e.g. DOG-BONE; HURRY-DRIVER; SPEECH-MEETING). I also used several techniques to motivate the children, especially when working with the 12 year olds. I encouraged them to attempt all items, rather than leave them out. When they missed some items, I returned to them later, and often this worked. Standard prompts were useful (e.g. 'you're good at this' or 'take your time' or 'think of mathematics') especially with the 12 year olds. In a pilot test, I found that children genuinely enjoyed the task, often describing it as 'fun'. This evident pleasure carried over into the formal studies. All the children were able to do what the task required and none took longer than 15 minutes for the 49 items. As they gave their sentences, I wrote each one on a record sheet in a shorthand. Inflected variations for target words and keywords were accepted in sentences. If the sentence was meaningful, and the rules of use for the target word were at all displayed by the collocation of the word with its keyword, the sentence confirmed the interviewee's grasp of the target word within its specialist meaning system. The word's use gave a test of its meaning that was minimally consistent with the 'use' theory of meaning. Extensive examples of sentences from 12 and 15 year old children appear elsewhere (Corson, 1983a). These suggest the adequacy of the Measure as a test of word meaning.

This Measure lessens the effects of extralinguistic context on vocabulary use. If there is rapport between the interviewer and the children, and also no time limit within reason, they can retrieve words without pressure from their passive vocabularies. Each item asks for an original sentence using two words already spoken by the researcher, and this provides a high level of activation for any words not usually used in speech. So even if the target word is only passively held, the context encourages its use, since the instrument does the retrieving. The words are spoken by another person; their use is appropriate to the context of situation; the topic is left to the interviewed themselves to choose, yet controlled by the meaning system suggested by the collocation of the target word and keyword; and there is moderate encouragement to offer original sentences in the rather interesting experience of making up sentences from discrete words.

Semantemes: words with two or more meanings

In this original application of the Measure, 'semantemes' were the special category of target words. According to convention, a 'semanteme' is a polysemantic word (see Chapter 2). Each semanteme listed in Table 1, has an ordinary language meaning as well as a specialist meaning within one or more of the meaning systems examined. A secondary aim of the study was to see if there were differences in access to the different meanings of some semantemes across meaning systems. For example, among the meanings of the semanteme OBSERVE are its ordinary language sense of 'watch' or 'examine', which carries over into the meaning system of the physical sciences without much change; second, its specialist sense of 'celebrate' or 'honour', when used within the meaning system of religious knowledge; and third, its specialist sense of 'obey' in the meaning system of ethics or moral knowledge. I summarize the lengthy method for selecting and abridging the list of semantemes elsewhere (Corson, 1983a). This involved reducing the

120,000 entries arranged by semantic field in the index of a conceptual dictionary (Chapman, 1979), to provide seven target words for each of the seven meaning systems used in the study.

### Advantages

This Measure's approach to word use has several advantages over the common alternative of asking the interviewee for a sentence using the target word on its own. The new approach requires the interviewee to focus on a specific meaning of the word and assesses grasp of that meaning and no other. For example, an item using only the word OBSERVE as a sentence stimulus, is an inadequate and inefficient instrument for recording passive access to OBSERVE in any of its more specialized senses.

Also this new approach explores meaning systems, and compares a fuller range of meanings for each semanteme in ways that are missed by a one-word approach. For example, I compared the frequency of errors made by 12 and 15 year olds using 39 distinct meanings of the semantemes tested (e.g. there were three distinct meanings for OBSERVE). At 12 years, children had a mean of 8.41 errors, but at 15 years a mean of only 5.05 errors ($p = <.001$). This suggests, in line with expectation, that the range of fields in which these words have their meanings, is narrower for younger children than for older, and that children add meanings to words in their passive vocabularies in an increasing number of meaning systems as they pass through adolescence. Later I mention differences in this that appeared across sociocultural groups. Inferences like these would not be possible had I not used the keyword approach to assess different meanings for each word.

For several reasons, I bypassed another approach to getting the same responses: saying the target word along with the name of a specific semantic field. First, knowledge of the superordinate term for a particular domain is not a necessary condition for having access to the semantic field itself; and so the use of the superordinate head in the item could disguise the item's purpose rather than make it clear. Second, because the names for the semantic fields used are uncommon and rather intimidating words (e.g. 'aesthetics', 'ethics', 'physical sciences'), their mention might lessen children's motivation and confidence. Finally, the keyword rather than the head often collocates in ordinary language contexts with the target word, and this leads to much quicker responses. All this increases motivation and allows for a more searching instrument design.

### Knowledge categories as meaning systems

In applying the Measure within educational research, curriculum meaning systems seem appropriate as heads for semantic fields. As mentioned, the secondary school curriculum is a collection of meaning systems which comes close to covering the whole field of the academic culture of literacy that is given high status in Western education. I adopted the mapping system developed by Hirst (1974), an educational epistemologist. For him, there are seven 'modes of knowledge and experience'. This schema depends for its rationale on the different ways that statements are formulated in each mode: Each has its own logic for testing out statements made within it. Hirst argues that while these seven modes are not constant or eternal, they do provide a mapping system of curricular knowledge as presently perceived. His names for each of these seven modes, in slightly modified form, provide the headings for the seven semantic fields into which target words are grouped. Table 1 shows these seven cultural meaning systems, and their seven semantemes and keywords.

TABLE 1
*Semantemes and Keywords by Semantic Fields*
(keywords are in brackets; bracketed numerals show order of presentation of items to students)

1

(1)   Divide (fifty)
(8)   Define (problem)
(15) Product (multiply)
(22) Code (message)
(29) Solution (problem)
(36) Account (figures)
(43) Unequal (section)

2

(2)   Observe (experiment)
(9)   Solution (mixed)
(16) Image (mirror)
(23) Composition (substance)
(30) Relation (parent)
(37) Instrument (measuring)
(44) Distinct (noises)

3

(3)   Fact (witness)
(10) Harmony (war)
(17) Account (events)
(24) Product (market)
(31) Divide (loyalty)
(38) Judgment (courtroom)
(45) Designer (proposal)

4

(4)   Duty (ought)
(11) Unequal (treatment)
(18) Action (unjust)
(25) Judgment (moral)
(32) Code (conduct)
(39) Develop (honesty)
(46) Observe (laws)

5

(5)   Instrument (music)
(12) Designer (building)
(19) Craft (skill)
(26) Harmony (music)
(33) Image (carve)
(40) Key (music)
(47) Composition (art work)

6

(6)   Spirit (evil)
(13) Bless (priest)
(20) Convért (religion)
(27) Fellowship (church)
(34) Observe (rituals)
(41) Absolute (god)
(48) Faith (religion)

7

(7)   Absolute (truth)
(14) Distinct (facts)
(21) Reason (mind)
(28) Define (meaning)
(35) Fact (untrue)
(42) Relation (statements)
(49) Key (mystery)

1.   *formal logic and mathematics*
2.   *the physical sciences*
3.   *the human sciences*
4.   *ethics*
5.   *aesthetics*
6.   *religion*
7.   *philosophy*

Relevant to later discussion, the range of semantemes in English that span specialist meaning systems, is overwhelmingly G-L in origin and 90% of the semantemes in Table 1 are G-L. Although this was not a factor in their selection, it happened because words of G-L origin are between 65% and 100% of the total specialist vocabularies used as heads for the semantic fields in the Measure of Passive Vocabulary. To reach these estimates, I examined some 8000 words, in proportion to the number of words in each field (Corson, 1983b). In fact, a count of G-L words that disregarded slang expressions and foreign phrases would return percentages in all these fields close to 100%.

*The Graeco-Latin (G-L) Instrument*

This provides a count of specialist G-L words in English oral and written texts. Its use is also a simple matter, since most G-L words are unambiguous. Their origin is clear from their form, showing little change from the original except a modification of the suffix. Using operational rules, I removed non-specialist G-L words whose antiquity and prevalence in English make them part of all child language (Corson, 1982: Rule One excludes numerals, units of time, pivot words, everyday nouns, verbs, adjectives and adverbs. Rule Two excludes conventional intensifiers and expletives. Rules Three to Eleven give the criteria for identifying G-L words, covering affixes, proper nouns, and bases).

The excluded words are mainly pre-Renaissance additions to the language that are chosen for equal use in speech, regardless of any of the sociocultural variables. They include words like TABLE and CHAIR whose original Anglo-Saxon synonyms (BOARD and STOOL) have become obsolete or changed in meaning. I compared the numbers of these non-specialist G-L words that were excluded from the count. Children used these words uniformly across ages, sociocultural groups, and regions, with very high inter-judge reliability. The percentages below from the London and Yorkshire studies, show the consistency with which these non-specialist G-L words were used, proportionate to total words produced (for a key to abbreviations see Figure 1 on page 113).

TABLE 2
*Percentages of Non-Specialist G-L Words Excluded from the Counts in England*

| Yorkshire | | | | London | | | |
|---|---|---|---|---|---|---|---|
| WC12 | 2.3% | WC15 | 3.4% | WC12 | 3.1% | WC15 | 3.2% |
| MC12 | 2.9% | MC15 | 3.6% | MC12 | 3.3% | MC15 | 3.2% |
| | | | | WI12 | 2.9% | WI15 | 3.4% |

Preliminary studies

Before designing the Instrument, I conducted several preliminary studies. In the first, I counted the frequency of G-L words in different types of written English. Table 3 shows the high correlation that exists between the level of 'difficulty' of subject matter and the G-L percentage in that subject matter. To do this I identified a representative text for each type of writing.

For the academic texts, I followed the Dewey call numbers for each academic subject in the University of London Institute of Education library and took the twentieth book on the shelves under that call number. I analyzed the G-L content of three random passages of one hundred consecutive words from each book, and averaged the counts. This content is expressed as a percentage.

TABLE 3
*Literary Areas Ranked According to G-L Content*
(based on random passages of 100 consecutive words)

| | | |
|---|---|---|
| (1) | Philosophy of Education | 40 percent |
| (2) | Linguistic Philosophy | 40 percent |
| (3) | Sociology | 38 percent |
| (4) | History of Religion | 37 percent |
| (5) | Theology | 36 percent |
| (6) | Social Science Methodology | 34 percent |
| (7) | Science Education | 33 percent |
| (8) | Psychology | 32 percent |
| (9) | Ethics | 32 percent |
| (10) | History of Philosophy | 31 percent |
| (11) | Physics | 31 percent |
| (12) | Logic | 30 percent |
| (13) | Music | 29 percent |
| (14) | Mathematics (i) | 29 percent |
| (15) | Mathematics (ii) | 28 percent |
| (16) | Non-Western Religion | 26 percent |
| (17) | English Literature (i) | 26 percent |
| (18) | Human Science | 25 percent |
| (19) | English Literature (ii) | 25 percent |
| (20) | Analytical Philosophy | 24 percent |
| (21) | Newspaper (A) editorial (economics) | 24 percent |
| (22) | Newspaper (A) economics story | 24 percent |
| (23) | Newspaper (A) politics story | 23 percent |
| (24) | Newspaper (A) sports story | 21 percent |
| (25) | Newspaper (A) courtroom story | 19 percent |
| (26) | Newspaper (B) editorial (foreign affairs) | 18 percent |
| (27) | English literature (iii) | 16 percent |
| (28) | Newspaper (B) fuel crisis story | 13 percent |
| (29) | Newspaper (B) theatre review | 12 percent |
| (30) | Newspaper (C) editorial (economics) | 12 percent |
| (31) | Newspaper (B) sports story | 11 percent |
| (32) | Children's fiction 12 years R. A. | 10 percent |
| (33) | Newspaper (C) sports story | 9 percent |
| (34) | Newspaper (C) courtroom story | 7 percent |
| (35) | Children's fiction 9-11 years R. A. | 7 percent |
| (36) | Newspaper (C) economics story | 5 percent |
| (37) | Children's fiction 10-11 years R. A. | 4 percent |
| (38) | Children's fiction 9-12 years R. A. | 4 percent |
| (39) | Newspaper (C) courtroom story | 4 percent |
| (40) | Newspaper (B) air crash story | 3 percent |
| (41) | Children's fiction 7-8 years R. A. | 3 percent |
| (42) | Children's fiction 7-11 years R. A. | 2 percent |
| (43) | Children's fiction 5-6 years R. A. | 0 percent |

I also analyzed passages of 100 words each, taken from children's fiction books written for various reading ages. These books were pulled at random from the children's shelves of the Chalk Farm Library in London. The newspaper extracts were also based on three random passages from an article, or the entire story if it was less than 300 words in length. The papers were all London editions from the same day. The day was chosen at random. The three newspapers are popularly characterized as (A) 'high-brow', (B) 'middle-brow', and (C) 'low-brow'. These peculiarly English terms suggest the relative 'levels of seriousness' of the newspapers concerned, levels matched by a descending incidence of G-L words as revealed in Table 3. The table also confirms the consistently high percentage level of G-L words that appears in English texts from the conventional disciplines and knowledge areas. It shows a descending percentage of G-L words in children's fiction that matches the descending 'reading age' of that literature.

These findings are consistent with the socio-historical study in Chapter 3, tracing the events that allowed the G-L vocabulary of the language to establish the technical vocabularies of those knowledge areas that are generally held to be the more complex. Most G-L words were introduced into the language to meet the needs of these knowledge areas. As mentioned, there is a very low incidence of Anglo-Saxon words within these knowledge categories.

In a second study, I looked at *all* G-L words in a thesaurus of common and uncommon words in English. Percentage counts of these specialist and non-specialist G-L words ranged from only 11% of the most common English words to 65% of the least common words, with a continuum of increase between common and uncommon categories. In writing *Using English Words*, I also looked at another word list: the Birmingham Corpus of words. These are words that the compilers believe should be introduced into an all-purpose program for teaching ESL to adults and children for general everyday purposes (Sinclair & Renouf, 1988). Of the top-ranking 200 words in this list, only two (COURSE and PART) are G-L in origin. On the other hand, the 'University Word List' consisting of 836 word families that provide a broad coverage of academic texts for use by ESL learners (Nation, 1990), is quite simply a Latinate vocabulary.

Lexical difficulty

As well as their relative uncommonness, the specialist words counted by the Instrument have a number of features that make them lexically 'difficult': They have a connotative meaning that is not extensional; they are often without suitable synonyms and may be defined only by the use of a number of other words, and even then perhaps poorly; they give precision to texts and these may convey meaning more effectively than texts that lack them; they are not readily inserted in an abstraction ladder of superordinacy; they may allow their users to order thought within specialist meaning systems where such an ordering of thought might not occur without the words themselves; and they may be culturally determined in sense, in that they represent meanings which are rarely readily translated word for word into the languages of other cultures. Throughout this discussion, the term 'lexically difficult' represents this syndrome of features of specialist words in English extracted by the Instrument (see Chapter 8).

Below is a sample list of specialist G-L words. Clearly they are words that we can hardly do without in educated discourse. These come directly from the many used in the speech of the 15 year olds in these studies:

| | | |
|---|---|---|
| intelligence | sympathy | interested |
| attention | qualifies | vicious |
| scandal | concerned | considerate |
| attitude | physical | disobey |
| ideas | civilization | treason |
| tactless | society | discipline |
| ambition | criticizing | accommodation |
| situation | similar | deteriorated |
| facts | community | permanently |
| depends | preserve | personally |
| advantage | system | exploiting |
| confidence | emotions | personality |
| humane | introduce | nervous |
| necessarily | atmosphere | caution |
| competent | circumstances | complicated |
| contact | drastic | maliciously |
| important | consisted | alternative |
| instance | facilities | examples |

When applying the G-L Instrument to the transcripts of children's speech and writing, I counted all the words produced by the children, not just random samples of 100 words each. The length of transcripts was very similar and there were only slight differences between groups in the number of words produced. For example, in the studies in England, 12 year olds averaged 693 words in total, while 15 year olds averaged 670. The West Indian 12 year olds were the only cohort who strayed from around these figures, averaging 853 words, mainly because of one rather talkative child. The corpus of oral and written data was about 120,000 words.

## Research Contexts

### The Schools

Studies took place in school settings in Yorkshire, England (Y); London, England (L); Sydney, Australia (S); and Wollongong, Australia (W). With the exception of the boys from School S, all the cohorts were of mixed sexes and were matched for educational background at both primary and secondary levels. Also with the exception of the boys from School S, all were students of secondary comprehensive schools of similar size and status. All children had experienced common curricula without a Classics component. Great care was taken, then, in choosing subjects whose experiences in formal education had been relatively homogeneous, so that any variations in scores between cohorts on the instruments would not be significantly due to overt educational inequalities produced by the institution of education itself. The children in all the schools had spent all their formal education in the close company of the children from the other sociocultural groups studied in their school.

School Y stands near a small country town which itself is between six and thirteen miles from three large south Yorkshire cities. Its student population of about 1500 children is drawn one-third from the town itself and two-thirds from the many small villages within a five-mile radius. None of these feeder schools is more working class than middle class in population. The sampling process produced representative groups from both village and town feeder schools. The area includes light industrial works, some mining industry, small farming, and agriculture. Following the aims of the study, School Y has a strong mixture of children from middle class and working class backgrounds. There are no children of non-indigenous descent. From School Y the following sociocultural groups were drawn: upper middle class and poorer working class Yorkshire comprehensive school indigenous 12 and 15 year olds.

School L is a neighbourhood school in north London. Its 1100 children include a strong mixture of children from indigenous social groups. It also has a large student body of Afro-Asian and Indian sub-continent Asian descent (25%) and a large proportion of children of West Indian descent (15-20%). These West Indian children had a homogeneity in background that was of great value to the study: The parents of these children arrived in Britain, from Jamaica only, mainly between 1960 and 1964. They were brought in groups to take up positions in London Transport. Many remained as transport employees, while others moved to work on assembly lines in light industry or to semi-skilled positions. Again the sampling process produced representative groups from three junior school backgrounds. From School L the following sociocultural groups were drawn: upper middle class; poorer working class; and West Indian descent, London comprehensive school 12 and 15 year olds.

School S is a prestigious but 'non-selective' private school for boys, set among the wealthiest of Sydney's northern suburbs. Because of its high fees, its location, its reputation, its long waiting list for entrants, and its favouring of the sons and brothers of old boys, School S is very selective. It attracts students who are exclusively upper middle class by family background, although in the cosmopolitan Sydney population this does not exclude the children of well-off immigrant families, who are well represented among the senior school's 1100 pupils. The school has a nominal religious bias, but its chief ideology is academic success. The content of its curriculum is similar in most respects to State comprehensive schools. I included it in the studies because of interest in differences that might arise in vocabulary use if educational contrasts were sharpened. From School S the following age groups were drawn: upper middle class Sydney private school Anglo-Australian 12 and 15 year old boys.

*School W* is on the fringes of the iron and steel foundries which provide direct or indirect employment for much of Wollongong's population. In the post-war period, Wollongong became a boom town with the regional population passing 200,000 with the highest immigrant inflow of any Australian city. In the immediate region of School W, 32% of the population were born in non-English-speaking countries. The 1000 students at the school included a small group of middle class Anglo-Australian children, many children of Macedonian parentage, many children of Italian, Spanish, or Portuguese parentage and about 40 percent poorer working class Anglo-Australians. All the children had attended one of two local primary schools. Their student bodies are as diverse socioculturally as School W. Most children had been classmates with one another through all their years of formal schooling. The children from non-English-speaking families were themselves poorer working class by occupational background, both in Australia and in their home countries. The children used their parents' native tongue as the language of the home in early childhood. They all entered their primary schools in the 1970s as ESL students. From School W the following sociocultural groups were drawn: upper middle class Anglo-Australian; poorer working class Anglo-Australian; poorer working class Macedonian-descent; and poorer working class Romance-language descent, Wollongong comprehensive school 12 and 15 year olds.

*The Sampling Process: Non-Verbal Reasoning and Sociocultural Group*

The closest approximation to the vernacular, or local community variety of a language, is found most consistently in adolescents younger than about 17 years (Labov, 1972a). Also Piaget's stage of formal operational thought tends to appear in language use in late adolescence, if at all (Britton, 1970; Vygotsky, 1962). So I compared children at 12 and 15 years, to measure changes in vocabulary use by subjects whose ages fell on either side of the onset of this developmental stage. The sampling process followed three steps.

Step 1 began with all 12 and 15 year old children present in the four schools ($N = 1597$) who completed a group-administered test. This served as a guide to their motivation levels when working in their school in my company. I reduced the beginning N by about 60% through excluding children whose scores fell below the 50th and above the 90th percentile for their age on this test of non-verbal reasoning (Heim, 1974). This AH4-P includes 20 items that are diagrammatic and 20 that are pictorial, all aimed at assessing 'reasoning' skills. Britain's National Foundation for Educational Research advised that this test was suitable for 12 and 15 year olds. They also said that they had carefully inspected it for cultural bias, and had established national norms through its wide use. The mean score on these norms (the 50th percentile) was the low point of the range for including children. I also used the same test in the Australian schools, assuming that if national norms for the test were established in Australia, they would be very close to the British ones. Mean scores for each cohort of children on the 40 items of the AH4-P, were all within three points of means for all other cohorts of the same age. They ranged from 24.0 to 26.4 for the 12 year olds, and from 25.3 to 28.5 for the 15 year olds.

Step 2 reduced the groups further and established sociocultural profiles. I used three sources of information about all the children's ages and sociocultural backgrounds: school record cards, showing their ages and parents' occupations; advice from the children's pastoral teachers and heads of house, either cross-checking the accuracy of details on the record cards, or confirming the culture/language origin of the children; and confirmation from each child in an informal discussion after the interview session, on the topic of their future career interests and planned specialization in school. The British *Registrar General's Classification of Occupations* (1980) provided criteria for matching social class by parental occupation. This classification divides the complete range of contemporary occupations into five grades. Within these five, there are three bands of occupational types: grades I/II taken together include professional and semi-professional non-manual workers, administrators, managers, and supervisors; grade III includes other non-manual workers, manual, skilled workers, and unskilled supervisors; and grades IV/V together include semi-skilled and unskilled manual workers. I used grades I/II to designate children as 'upper middle class', and grades IV/V to designate children as 'poorer working class'. Both parents' occupations were used as factors: children whose fathers' occupations fell within I/II, were classified as 'upper middle class' (MC) if their mothers' occupations fell within the same range, or if the mothers were not formally employed; children whose fathers' occupations fell within IV/V, were classified as 'poorer working class' (WC) if their mothers' occupations were also IV/V, or if they were not formally employed and had not held positions at III or above. I omitted children from single parent families, children of fathers who were known to be unemployed, and all those who fell within the Registrar General's grade III. To create the groups of immigrant children in Schools L and W, I included only children whose parents had arrived together as immigrants from the same country. After Step 2, about 15% of the original N remained.

In Step 3, I used the technique of 'systematic sampling' to draw final cohorts from these groups that were now matched by age, motivation and non-verbal reasoning level, and sociocultural background. The final groups were consistent in size with accepted sociolinguistic cell sizes (Lawton, 1968; Hudson, 1980),

*Controlling for Non-Verbal Reasoning and Motivation Levels*
A wide range of researchers studying the relationships between language and other sociocultural variables, insist on use of a measure of non-verbal reasoning and matching their sample by ability through keeping non-verbal test scores as a constant. Dittmar (1976) cites these researchers and

offers reasons why non-verbal tests in this situation are preferable to verbal. I decided against a test of verbal reasoning for this study because the instruments used could themselves measure abilities rather similar to those measured by a test of verbal reasoning. A test of non-verbal reasoning helped control the wide range of variables that tests of language performance measure: not just complex acts of perception, comprehension, and memory, but also important attributes such as skills in attending, listening, interpreting, comparing and abstracting (Ginsburg, 1972).

More important here was the matter of controlling motivation levels. The test of non-verbal reasoning seemed a reasonable way of ensuring some measure of motivational homogeneity, in the context of the school, across sociocultural groups, provided that the range of scores on the test used as a standard for selecting sample members, was itself sufficiently high. By administering a far-from-easy non-verbal reasoning instrument and by using a nationally normed mean score as the minimum score for inclusion in the larger samples, I ensured that the children had reasonably high motivation levels in the school setting and in my company. I gave the test to all first year and fourth year children present on the test days in the high schools.

*Problems of Interviewer Presentation of Self*

A number of studies raise problems of speech and accent that might inhibit interviewees, depending on their sociocultural background (Cook-Gumperz, 1973; Labov, 1972b; Hodges, 1971; Brah *et al.*, 1977). In School Y and School L, where the tester and interviewer was an Australian working with White or Black English children, the effects of these speech and accent problems appeared to be generalized rather than confined to one group. This in itself acted as a measure of control for the study. Considerable care was taken to become a familiar figure for children in all the schools used in the studies. Taking part in playground games during recess breaks helped in the process, especially with the West Indian 15 year old boys in School L, where nationality provided a bridge to interaction because of traditional cricketing rivalries between Australia and the West Indies.

Labov reports on the cultural divergence in interview settings between African Americans and European Americans in the United States. This seems so inhibiting for African American children as to necessitate elaborate counter-measures in the interview situation, and so prompted my interest in the similar effects in the British context. Watson's research in England, reported by Brah et al., (1977), found a sharp drop in West Indian performance with a White experimenter. But he recorded only a slight drop in a semi-formal situation (such as a one-to-one interview). Brah et al. themselves were more concerned with differential presentation of self to interviewers of different ethnic origins. Their paper supports the trends found in other research, but only for respondents who identify strongly with their own group. I return to this conclusion later when interpreting certain findings in this study. Here I should mention that strong Creole accent and syntax were present in the speech of six of the seven West Indian 15 year olds, with no trace of Creole in the speech of the 12 year olds. As dialect is a central construct of culture and accent is a cultural trait, it is possible that these six 15 year olds possessed a strong group and cultural identification, which the younger group did not.

*The Interview Setting and the Questionnaire*
In each school, the room for the one-to-one interviews was private and free from interruption. In all cases, the children found their own way to the room where I met them for the second time. We had a short discussion on what class they had left, and about my purpose ("to find out something about the language used here in . . . "). Then the interview process began with the Measure of Passive Vocabulary. This interesting task seemed to prepare all the children and relax them for the interview questionnaire.

Discussing ways of obtaining valid speech data, Dittmar quotes Labov's "methodological axioms" for linguistic research. The last of these, which fills the requirement of obtaining good data, relates to interviews:

> In spite of objections and granting the merits of other methods (group sessions, anonymous observation), the individual, tape-recorded interview must be said to offer the most reliable method for systematically obtaining speech data (1976, p. 193).

Labov mentions an 'Observer's Paradox': to find out how people talk when they are not being observed systematically, we can only obtain this data by systematic observation. My purpose was not to counter this paradox, but to examine speech produced within the formal educational context in order to detect differences that might relate to differential educational success. Elsewhere Labov describes the type of speech obtained in an interview situation as "careful speech (semi-formal; normal case in interviews)" (1966, p. 90). This is also a good description of pupil-to-teacher speech in classrooms, where the teacher elicits, the pupil replies, but where (unlike me) the teacher also makes an on-the-spot evaluation (Sinclair & Coulthard, 1975; Milroy, 1987; Young, 1992). I conclude from this that the interview situation created in this research is a good example of a 'formal educational context'.

After responding to the Measure of Passive Vocabulary, the children interacted with me around the speech performance questionnaire. This was presented to them in as uniform a way as possible. Many examples of questions and answers appear in Chapter 6. I tape-recorded responses to this questionnaire and this gave me speech transcripts for the G-L Instrument. In the Australian studies, I collected written responses to a written version of this questionnaire in whole group settings. The questionnaire aimed at a high degree of context control, across ages and sociocultural groups, and context neutrality.

What may be said in any given context obviously varies according to the age or sociocultural background of individuals. So the subject matter of this questionnaire was limited in the descriptive task (G-L-D), to experiences that all secondary school children share and remember well: their junior or primary schools. The children determined the details and subject matter of their descriptions according to their own interests and memories. This gave them the opportunity to make word selections according to the meaning requirements of their own commentaries. Lawton (1968) used this subject with success in a similar interview questionnaire.

In the explanatory task (G-L-E) I selected a number of unambiguous moral questions and dilemmas that children have thought about by the age of 12 years: things to do with truth and lying, killing, what makes a 'good' person for them, what things are always 'wrong' to do, and what new laws would be helpful (Corson, 1989). I asked the children to create theoretical points of view and arguments based on examples. Questions around these issues presented the children with moral issues suited to public discussion without embarrassment or censure. But the task also channelled the children's responses towards making vocabulary choices that were different from the purely descriptive first half of the questionnaire.

To ensure accuracy, transcripts of the interviews were made by hand on the same day as the tapes were made. These were later typed and the typescripts checked back to the original tapes. In London and Yorkshire, the G-L Instrument was applied only to the oral language texts of interviewees.

As mentioned, in the Australian studies, I looked at oral and written language in the two contexts, expecting to find some differences in specialist G-L use, since there is agreement that certain vocabulary differences separate edited writing from spontaneous speech (see Chapter 2). The written texts were collected in group sessions without time limits, some weeks after the oral interviews, in response to written questionnaires using the same questions as those given orally.

# Research Findings

Chapter 6 presents many extracts from the transcripts and some complete transcripts. It compares differences in the children's word use in response to the same questions. It also presents a replica of a text answering the written questionnaire. Several complete oral texts also appear elsewhere (Corson, 1987).

### Passive Vocabulary

Figure 1 indicates that, with one exception, there is a monotonic development by age for all sociocultural groups in their passive vocabulary. An independent re-analysis of the data, conducted in New Zealand, found no significant differences by sex of students in passive vocabulary (Anderson & Soler, 1989). Regardless of their sex, the middle class children begin ahead of the rest and maintain that lead. For example, comparing only the Australian groups, the middle class Sydney group at 15 years outscore in group mean the working class Wollongong group with very high significance on total scores on the measure, and also in the fields of ethics and aesthetics ($p = <.001$) and with high significance in the remaining fields ($p = <.05$).

Again the middle class Wollongong group, who have shared the same school experiences as their working class mates, outscore the latter at 15 years with high significance on total scores and also in the semantic fields of logic and maths, aesthetics, and philosophy ($p = <.05$). Combining the results from the two schools in England (N = 59), the middle class 15 year olds, who have shared the same school experiences as their working class peers, outscore them with high significance on total scores ($p = <.02$) and also in the semantic field of ethics ($p = <.05$).

An analysis of variance performed on the Australian samples (N = 80) returns a highly significant source of variation by age on total scores ($p = <.001$), and by sociocultural group on total scores ($p = <.002$). Two-way interactions are not significant ($p = >.800$). Examining the samples as a whole (N = 139), differences by age on all seven semantic fields and on total scores for the Measure, are all highly significant ($p = <.001$) as they are by age for each individual sociocultural group, with the exception of the West Indian cohorts. This exception needs explanation, as do the performances of the Australian groups from immigrant families who are poorer working class themselves, yet whose mean scores significantly exceed their poorer working class Anglo-Australian classmates ($p = <.05$).

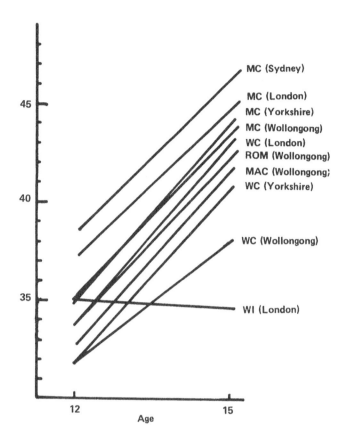

FIG. 1. *Line graph illustrating group means recorded on the Measure by age and sociocultural group (N = 139) (overall significance level by age: p = < .001)*

*Key:*

| | |
|---|---|
| *MC (Sydney)* | = *upper middle class Sydney (private school) (boys):* |
| *MC (London)* | = *upper middle class London (comprehensive):* |
| *MC (Yorkshire)* | = *upper middle class Yorkshire (comprehensive):* |
| *MC (Wollongong)* | = *upper middle class Wollongong (comprehensive):* |
| *WC (London)* | = *poorer working class London (comprehensive)* |
| *WC (Yorkshire)* | = *poorer working class Yorkshire (comprehensive)* |
| *WC (Wollongong)* | = *poorer working class Wollongong(comprehensive)* |
| *ROM (Wollongong)* | = *Romance Language background, Wollongong, (comprehensive):* |
| *MAC (Wollongong)* | = *Macedonian Language background, Wollongong, (comprehensive):* |
| *WI (London)* | = *West Indian immigrant London (comprehensive).* |

Why was there no difference in the mean scores of the two West Indian age groups? While the 12 year olds scored at the same level as the 12 year old British-born children, so did the 15 year olds, contrasting with all other 15 year old groups. It seems that the two West Indian age cohorts were different in some other important respect. While designing the study at School L, I had carefully considered the matter of motivation that Labov raises (1972a). I tried to head off any negative interviewer effects by becoming a familiar part of the West Indian pupils' school day. Also the non-verbal reasoning test was mainly included in the study to ensure that students had a high level of motivation towards school activities and towards me as a co-participant in those activities. Finally, I have to say that the West Indian 15 year olds gave no evidence of low motivation in the interview sessions. The opposite seemed to be the case.

Since the families of all the Jamaican children had arrived in Britain at around the same time (about 15 years prior to the research), and because most of the 15 year olds had Creole features in their spoken English (which the 12 year olds did not), I conclude that the 15 year olds were at a relative disadvantage when compared with the 12 year olds in a test of this kind, firmly rooted as it was in the cultural meaning systems of an English school system. I acknowledge that the older group's use of Creole features in their speech could have been adopted to mark in-group identity, a phenomenon common among older adolescents. But I still conclude that the more unsettled nature of their early life experiences, the greater influence of their very different Jamaican lexico-semantic positioning on their English, and their greater reasons for group identity, partly as a result perhaps of their language homogeneity, are all factors which offer some explanation for the 15 year olds' singular performance on the Measure.

In the Wollongong study, why do the children of non-English speaking working class family backgrounds outscore their Anglo-Australian working class peers so conclusively at 15 years? The answer to this is more complex. There may be considerable positive transfer effects from their Latinate first languages for the Romance language speakers (since nearly all the semantemes are Latinate in origin) and also for the Macedonian children, since, like Czech, Russian and other Slavonic languages, Macedonian has borrowed extensively from Greek and Latin sources this century (often via English) to augment its vocabulary. On the other hand, evidence from studies of word recall and recognition in Italian at least, discussed in Chapter 7, suggests that the processing of Italian and English G-L words in the mental lexicon is rather different, although they seem morphologically similar.

These immigrant children may also be manifesting the effects of a deliberately heavy concentration on spoken English, probably offered by local 'middle class' ESL teachers, in their primary and secondary education to date. This would promote use of a more 'formal' vocabulary, which would orient them towards greater use of the G-L. This could also explain why they are almost identical in specialist G-L use to their middle class classmates in three of the four tasks. Also in their results on this G-L Instrument, they may be reflecting an observable school achievement rate above their Anglo-Australian working class peers which is due, in part at least, to strong parental influence towards success in school, common among closely-knit immigrant communities and observed among Wollongong's immigrant iron and steel foundry workers (Jakubowicz and Wolf, 1980). As Ogbu (1987) notes, immigrant minorities know what they have to do to succeed in their new culture, while native-born non-dominant groups tend to accept their own status as largely their lot in life. As Bourdieu suggests, most people wrongly believe that school assessment processes are impartial, and that their failure is their own fault.

*Summary of the Passive Vocabulary Findings*
It is clear that there are important and educationally serious differences in the passive vocabularies of some adolescent sociocultural group members relative to others. The fact that the *15 year old* working class Wollongong group mean, for instance, is below the *12 year old* middle class Sydney group mean, suggests limited long-term exposure of the former to the meaning systems of the high school's culture of literacy. In their final stages of schooling, their passive access to these meaning systems and to a culture of literacy in which they have presumably had eleven years exposure in school, is less than middle class children who are just beginning their secondary education. But there is still development with age in passive access to these meaning systems for all but the West Indian groups.

While accepting that serious differences in lexico-semantic orientation exist, it is clear that working class children at 15 years show considerable development in their passive access to the cultural meaning systems examined. They show that they are skilled in using a range of words in one sense at least: They know 'how to use them' in their passive vocabulary and in a measure designed to elicit that vocabulary. So they are able to receive many messages framed in the language of the school, provided those messages give adequate levels of activation for low frequency words. But this tells us little about their disposition to make up their own messages in the school context, and to participate actively in the school's culture of literacy, which is the key language feat for secondary school success. A measure of active vocabulary is a guide in this area.

**Active Vocabulary**
I present sociocultural group G-L percentages for all the studies in Table 4 and represent the data in line graphs at Figures 2, 3, 4 and 5.

| Group and test | MC (Syd) | MC (Lond) | MC (York) | MC (Woll) | WC (Lond) | WC (York) | WC (Woll) | ROM (Woll) | MAC (Woll) | WI (Lond) |
|---|---|---|---|---|---|---|---|---|---|---|
| *Oral Language* | | | | | | | | | | |
| Twelve years | | | | | | | | | | |
| GL-D | 1.10 | 1.01 | 0.44 | 1.36 | 0.76 | 0.38 | 0.86 | 0.87 | 1.30 | 0.77 |
| GL-E | 1.99 | 2.02 | 1.46 | 1.96 | 2.16 | 0.91 | 2.09 | 2.25 | 2.07 | 1.84 |
| fifteen years | | | | | | | | | | |
| GL-D | 3.09 | 3.11 | 2.44 | 3.22 | 0.82 | 1.27 | 1.70 | 2.52 | 2.31 | 0.84 |
| GL-E | 5.28 | 6.24 | 5.05 | 4.02 | 2.06 | 1.52 | 3.18 | 4.21 | 4.03 | 2.38 |
| *Written Language* | | | | | | | | | | |
| Twelve years | | | | | | | | | | |
| GL-D | 2.07 | | | 1.54 | | | 2.01 | 2.21 | 1.69 | |
| GL-E | 3.77 | | | 2.69 | | | 3.94 | 4.08 | 3.21 | |
| fifteen years | | | | | | | | | | |
| GL-D | 5.16 | | | 6.71 | | | 2.25 | 5.66 | 4.38 | |
| GL-E | 9.86 | | | 8.07 | | | 4.67 | 6.20 | 6.17 | |

TABLE 4

*Mean Percentages recorded on the G-L Instrument by Age and Sociocultural Group showing Percentages on the Descriptive Task (G-L-D) and on the Explanatory Task (G-L-E) in Oral and Written Language (N = 139)*
*Key: as for Figure 1*

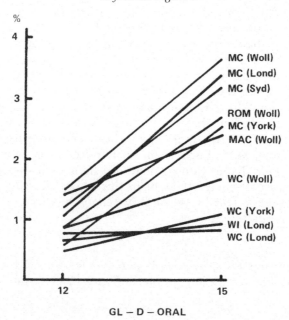

FIG. 2. *Line Graph illustrating group percentage means recorded on the G-L instrument by age and sociocultural group. Descriptive task — oral language (N = 139).*

*Key:* as for Figure 1

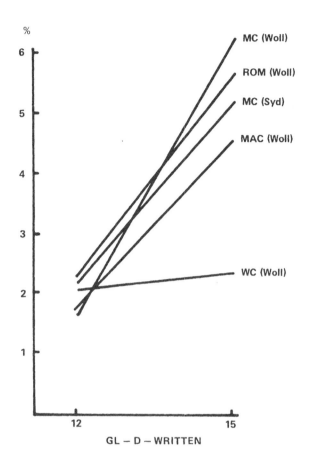

FIG. 3. *Line Graph illustrating group percentage means recorded on the G-L instrument by age and sociocultural group. Descriptive task — written language (N = 80).*

*Key:*

| | |
|---|---|
| *MC (Sydney)* | = *upper middle class Sydney (private school) (boys):* |
| *MC (London)* | = *upper middle class London (comprehensive):* |
| *MC (Yorkshire)* | = *upper middle class Yorkshire (comprehensive):* |
| *MC (Wollongong)* | = *upper middle class Wollongong (comprehensive):* |
| *WC (London)* | = *poorer working class London (comprehensive)* |
| *WC (Yorkshire)* | = *poorer working class Yorkshire (comprehensive)* |
| *WC (Wollongong)* | = *poorer working class Wollongong(comprehensive)* |
| *ROM (Wollongong)* | = *Romance Language background, Wollongong, (comprehensive):* |
| *MAC (Wollongong)* | = *Macedonian Language background, Wollongong, (comprehensive):* |
| *WI (London)* | = *West Indian immigrant London (comprehensive).* |

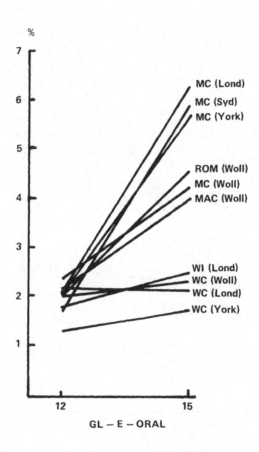

FIG. 4. *Line Graph illustrating group percentage means recorded on the G-L instrument by age and sociocultural group. Explanatory task — oral language (N = 139).*

Key:
| | |
|---|---|
| MC (Sydney) | = *upper middle class Sydney (private school) (boys):* |
| MC (London) | = *upper middle class London (comprehensive):* |
| MC (Yorkshire) | = *upper middle class Yorkshire (comprehensive):* |
| MC (Wollongong) | = *upper middle class Wollongong (comprehensive):* |
| WC (London) | = *poorer working class London (comprehensive)* |
| WC (Yorkshire) | = *poorer working class Yorkshire (comprehensive)* |
| WC (Wollongong) | = *poorer working class Wollongong(comprehensive)* |
| ROM (Wollongong) | = *Romance Language background, Wollongong, (comprehensive):* |
| MAC (Wollongong) | = *Macedonian Language background, Wollongong, (comprehensive):* |
| WI (London) | = *West Indian immigrant London (comprehensive).* |

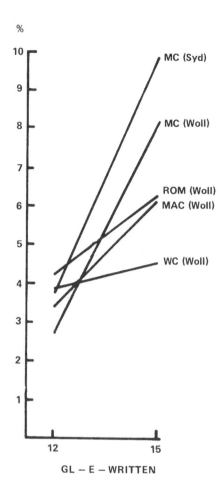

FIG. 5. *Line Graph illustrating group percentage means recorded on the G-L instrument by age and sociocultural group. Explanatory task — written language (N = 80).*

*Key:*

| | |
|---|---|
| MC (Sydney) | = *upper middle class Sydney (private school) (boys):* |
| MC (London) | = *upper middle class London (comprehensive):* |
| MC (Yorkshire) | = *upper middle class Yorkshire (comprehensive):* |
| MC (Wollongong) | = *upper middle class Wollongong (comprehensive):* |
| WC (London) | = *poorer working class London (comprehensive)* |
| WC (Yorkshire) | = *poorer working class Yorkshire (comprehensive)* |
| WC (Wollongong) | = *poorer working class Wollongong(comprehensive)* |
| ROM (Wollongong) | = *Romance Language background, Wollongong, (comprehensive):* |
| MAC (Wollongong) | = *Macedonian Language background, Wollongong, (comprehensive):* |
| WI (London) | = *West Indian immigrant London (comprehensive).* |

Such a complex set of data needs precise interpretation. So I discuss the findings in point form:

(1) At 12 years in none of the four contexts (G-L-D, oral and written; or G-L-E, oral and written) is there significant difference in active use of specialist words between sociocultural groups (see Figures 2, 3, 4 & 5).

(2) By 15 years, the differences become pronounced and very highly significant statistically (see Figures 2, 3, 4 & 5). While again there are no significant differences by sex (Anderson & Soler, 1989), the middle class children consistently reveal high levels of access to the G-L specialist vocabulary while the working class indigenous and West Indian children reveal little development over their 12 year old peers. Analyses of variance, performed on the data from the Anglo-Australian cohorts (Figures 3 & 5), return sources of variation by age and sociocultural group that are highly significant ($p = < .005$). In all four contexts of task, there is strong interaction between age and sociocultural group ($p = < .01$). These interactions are clearly revealed in all the line graphs of Figures 2 to 5.

(3) Large and important differences exist for 15 year old middle class and working class children on all four tasks (see Figures 2, 3, 4 & 5). In the written tasks (Figures 3 & 5), the middle class children increase their use of specialist G-L words to levels of high semantic significance relative to 12 year old percentages (when set against the G-L percentages in English literary texts, in newspapers, and in children's books ranked by reading age [see Table 3]). But working class 15 year olds use very much the same percentages of specialist G-L words as do 12 year olds as a group.

(4) At 15 years, the Macedonian and Romance children, drawn from poorer working class immigrant families, use many more specialist G-L words than the Anglo-Australian working class groups. They are almost indistinguishable from their middle class Wollongong classmates in their oral use of specialist G-L words (see Figure 4). Similar explanations to those offered under 'Passive Vocabulary' may account for the wide active vocabulary range of these ESL children. Their example in these studies lends strong encouragement to the belief that formal education can promote significant language development among marginal groups and give wide access to the specialist vocabulary of the language. Mainly through extra-familial exposure to English, much of it in the intense and standard language-oriented setting which ESL courses promote, these children have become well-placed lexically to succeed in schooling.[1]

---

[1]   I have little detail about the type of ESL primary education received in the mid 1970s by immigrant Wollongong children. But perhaps almost any form of education that concentrates on 'language in use', as ESL classes and classes in other second language learning often do, would be better suited to vocabulary development than is the language atmosphere commonly provided for all in ordinary classrooms.

This discussion also overturns the claims of some interpreters of my work who have argued from it that instruction in the Classics is essential for providing children with an unrestrained vocabulary competence in English. The point needs to be made clearly: none of the children in these studies had an education in the Classics, and with the exception of the School S boys, they all came from common programs in unexceptional comprehensive schools.

(5) For the total sample (N=139) there is an approximate doubling in percentage use of specialist G-L words as the context task is switched from descriptive to explanatory, or from an oral task presentation to its written counterpart. So the constraints of context provided by the four tasks operate with great uniformity, regardless of sociocultural group. But only the 15 year old middle class groups, among the non-immigrant children, use specialist G-L words in their texts at levels far above the 12 year old cohorts, and reach levels of use approaching those found in 'serious' writing (see Table 3).

(6) There is much internal consistency among the scores of individual sociocultural groups across the four tasks. Analyzing only the Australian groups, correlations of .49, .57 and .62 are returned respectively when percentage scores on GL-D oral and GL-D written, on GL-E oral and GL-E written, and on GL-D written and GL-E written, are compared. These correlations confirm that the disposition to use or not to use the specialist G-L vocabulary of English is a consistent one for sociocultural group members regardless of context of task or language mode.

*Effects of Extralinguistic Context*

The fact that the same patterns of G-L use occurred in the private language mode of writing as it did in speech, seems a strong refutation of the idea that extralinguistic context has much control on sociocultural group vocabulary selection in academic contexts. It seems unreasonable to believe that the same effects of extralinguistic context would be at work in the distinct language activities of speaking and writing when wedded respectively to the distinct functions of describing and explaining. It also seems unreasonable to conclude that these effects of extralinguistic context would make the vocabulary selections of children the same across different tasks and modes.

So the word selections of these adolescent groups seem to be a fairly accurate indication of their academic lexico-semantic range, regardless of context of situation. In short, working class 15 year olds relative to their middle class peers, are not disposed to use specialist G-L words widely in any of the four contexts examined in these studies, contexts very close to the semi-formal contexts created by ordinary classroom events in present-day education.

*Extralinguistic Context and Sex Differences*

As mentioned, a re-analysis of the data found no significant group differences by sex, in active (or passive) access to the specialist G-L vocabulary. In Chapter 6, I look at representative individual texts, produced in response to the interview schedule by many different girls and boys. I pay some attention in that discussion to individual differences in rules of use. But I make no reference in that chapter to individual differences in rules of use that might have a sex dimension, since none was evident in the transcripts. This prompted me to think about what changes might produce differences between boys and girls in their rules of use for words.

Perhaps making some major change in the extralinguistic context would lead to sex differences in the ways that children use individual words. For example, the adult-to-child, face-to-face interview used here as a context of interaction to gather the oral data, is very different from a group discussion activity. Also a group discussion can be mixed-sex or single sex. Boys' and girls' discourse norms do vary when contexts are changed in this way, and they change too when an adult is not present (Corson, 1993; Edwards & Westgate, 1994). Again, changing the functions of language being used might produce sex differences. For instance, changing the tasks from 'describing' and 'explaining', to 'speculating' or 'interacting', should produce a different use of discourse norms by sex, and perhaps different vocabulary rules of use as well. Perhaps older boys and girls, in particular, would use mental state words to do with intentions and feelings rather differently, even in the same context, since men and women often seem to mean different things when they use emotion words even in the same context. For example, the rules of use for words that appear in controversial debates about gender issues, like ASSERT, ATTACK, or HARASS, often differ depending on the sex of the word user. These differences in rules of use for words can be a cause of miscommunication between the sexes. The degree of difference might also increase or decrease from context to context, and from function to function, since the rules of use for words change as these things change.

These modifications in research focus would no doubt move the inquiry away from contexts very close to the semi-formal contexts created by ordinary classroom events in present-day education. Nevertheless more research along these lines would provide very helpful data for studying gendered communication differences more generally. Similarly, changing the settings from the school's contexts of interaction in this way, would be useful for looking at other sociocultural differences that occur in the rules of use for words, differences that lead to miscommunication between class and culture groups. But by saying all this, I am not suggesting that this change in research focus would uncover new differences in G-L vocabulary use by different sociocultural groups, only differences in the rules of use for the same words that they already seem to have. As mentioned, the evidence strongly suggests that the word selections of these adolescent groups are a fairly accurate indication of their lexico-semantic range, regardless of context of situation.

*Lexical Diversity and Cloze Procedure*

In the Yorkshire and London studies, I used a conventional measure of lexical diversity (the 'corrected' TTR [type/token ratio]: Carroll, 1964b) to examine the transcripts from the two speech tasks. There were no large arithmetic differences between groups in lexical diversity, apart from trends in the same direction as the passive and active measures, and a strong trend which suggested that the 15 year old middle class London and Yorkshire children had a much more diverse active vocabulary than all other English groups. This is consistent with their greater use of specialist G-L words.

In the Australian studies, I used a 'pilot Cloze analysis' which the children completed with the other written tasks. In this Cloze test, I asked them to 'fill in the gaps' in written passages. These passages were edited oral responses taken from those previously given by the English children to parts of the general questionnaire. In the 30 blank spaces, only a specialist G-L word fitted the sense conveyed by the language context. Results were consistent enough with the other measures to suggest that some similar Cloze test might be a reasonably good predictor of active access to specialist G-L words in oral language and especially in literacy. Correlations of the Cloze Test with oral G-L-D and G-L-E, were .46 and .60. With written G-L-D and G-L-E they were .66 and .72. The Cloze Test also correlated with total passive vocabulary scores at .49 and with age at .51.

## Educational Success and Failure: The End-of-Year Examinations

Earlier chapters argue that having an extensive English vocabulary inevitably means knowing more specialist G-L words. I also argue that introduction into certain lexico-semantic systems is more open to some sociocultural groups than to others, because the discursive practices of some groups outside schools are closer to the culture of literacy of the school than others. This chapter extends that conclusion: On the evidence of their vocabulary use in these studies, middle class adolescents are better positioned by their discursive experiences to move within those academic meaning systems, even when their reasoning ability and their school histories are the same as other children's. In this section, I try to make the link between vocabulary and educational success a tighter one, by showing that children who do do well at school seem to have a more extensive G-L vocabulary.

In a follow-up study, I looked at the end-of-year examination results of the four School W 15 year old groups (N = 30). This series of exams marked the end-point of the school careers of many of these children. The teaching staff at School W had not been advised of the results of their students on the measures used in this study. Although the school examinations were in no formal way measuring the students' specialist G-L vocabulary, the results of the study suggest that *this is largely what the exams were about.*

Correlations of the 15 year olds' total scores on the Measure of Passive Vocabulary with their examination results, returned coefficients of .57 for English, .58 for Maths and .38 for Science. Correlations of the 15 year olds' total G-L written percentages with their examination results, returned coefficients of .64 for English, .42 for Maths and .58 for Science. Similar correlations resulted when specialist G-L scores on the oral and written tasks were combined, averaged, and used as variables.

Coefficients of correlation, even at these levels, may suggest but not confirm a cause and effect relationship between factors. However the conclusion seems inescapable: The same children who performed least well as a group on a battery of instruments measuring specialist G-L vocabulary access, also performed least well on the most important and fundamental measures of school performance most of them will ever experience. This confirms that the link between active written and oral access to the specialist G-L vocabulary of English and educational success or failure, is a very strong one. Specialist G-L word usage stands as a mediating factor between sociocultural group background and educational success or failure. Other research should examine the question of whether or not students do really do better because they have a more wideranging vocabulary.

## Conclusion

Hamlyn concludes that "if there is a way of establishing the abstractness and complexity of a subject, this is 'eo ipso' a way of establishing that people normally find it difficult, and vice versa" (1967, pp. 41-42). So texts judged as 'difficult' are also more complex and abstract. There is much evidence in these studies to support the claim that people usually find texts high in specialist G-L words to be more 'difficult' than texts low in G-L.

There is much empirical evidence for this in this chapter: An increase in G-L frequency occurs in children's fiction as the reading age/difficulty of the material increases. An increase in G-L usage accompanies increase in the 'level of seriousness' of newspaper articles. Texts from academic knowledge areas are consistently high in G-L frequency, compared to other texts. And an almost uniform increase in specialist G-L occurs in texts as adolescent speech changes from a descriptive to a more abstract explanatory task.

The fact that a similar increase in specialist G-L use occurs as adolescent texts change from oral to written mode, also points to the relative difficulty and complexity levels of uncontrived texts produced in the two modes of language. Word selection itself seems an important variable when attempts are made to move children's language from oral utterance to written text, a task regarded by Olson (1977) as the critical process associated with schooling.

Moreover the fact that different scores in specialist G-L usage are the essential difference between 15 year old middle class and other indigenous children in their lexico-semantic range, invites other questions about whether or not this difference changes the complexity or difficulty level of adolescent texts, or just their formality levels. How does readiness to display this kind of difference in spoken and written texts, actually show up in individual children's language and affect the meanings that they put to use? Chapter 6 examines this question.

# 6

# Using Words in Educational Performance and for Sociocultural Reproduction

> I dunno, there's times when I think there are a few laws I'd like to stop but . . . don't know any I'd like to bring in (London working class 15 year old boy).[2]

> I don't think I'd *introduce* many new ones but I would *abolish* quite a few (London middle class 15 year old boy).

The surface-level differences in word use between these two spoken statements are plain. These boys, who have spent all of their school years together as classmates, are both saying much the same thing and saying it clearly, but in different words. From an evaluative point of view, the differences in the choice of words may be significant or they may be trivial, depending upon the evaluator's perspective and purpose. Later in this chapter I will say more about surface-level differences in word usage and their sociocultural and evaluative implications. But these studies offer more fundamental insights about language usage than just superficial comparisons of word usage. This chapter uses the data from the studies reported in Chapter 5, to look at links between the lexical bar and issues central to education: access to knowledge; school performance and assessment; access to

---

[2] The three dots in extracts (. . .) throughout this chapter, indicate a pause in the speech flow, not an edited deletion. Specialist G-L words are italicized.

meaning systems; and the communication of meaning. From this analysis, I offer conjectures linking the bar with inequality of educational opportunity and with questions about the school's role in social and cultural reproduction.

## Knowledge On Display

The 12 year olds in general, and the working class 12 year olds in particular, are not familiar with many of the words commonly used in the academic meaning systems of secondary schooling, nor do they have the range of meanings for individual words that older children have. One message that these studies offer about the language readiness of many 12 year old children for school learning, is that the specialist vocabulary of the secondary school is not a familiar one for many secondary school beginners, even as a passive vocabulary. So on entry to secondary schools, some children are probably unable to understand messages fully that use this vocabulary. This finding corroborates Barnes, Britton & Rosen's assessment that "a lesson largely couched in such language will be beyond many pupils' comprehension" and that "children whose home life does not support such language learning may feel themselves to be excluded from the conversation in the classroom" (1971, pp. 54-55).

Linking this with Peel's conclusion (1972), that conceptual learning just from the verbal context is not easily achieved by children before fifteen years, it is easy to see why children who start out in secondary school well behind their peers in passive vocabulary, may stay there or fall further behind. The experience that matters is not just the input of words into a passive vocabulary. For vocabulary development, it is quality output that matters: the very first tentative and motivated use of words in speech to serve some real world function (Swain, 1985; Peirce, 1995). This is the experience that first allows a word user to reach into the life forms in which words are grounded: to apply the rules of use that give meaning to words. This is also the experience that provides habit and motivation for further use. Although children before 15 years acquire complex meanings through talking about them in a setting where the words become a natural part of the talk, oral language work that centres on the vocabulary of the school is still rare. The scarcity of this opportunity in schools almost guarantees that children who are behind in vocabulary development and who do not have similar opportunities for vocabulary development outside the school, will stay well behind others who do.

But in language performance, it is active vocabulary that matters. This is where the most public face of the lexical bar is revealed. Achievement in schools is highly dependent on the students' ability to express what they know clearly: to 'display' knowledge. In later sections I discuss the legitimacy of this conventional form of assessment by asking whether knowledge 'displayed' is a reasonable indicator of knowledge possessed and of access to meaning systems. At this point I am concerned with the display itself and what it *seems* to say about access to knowledge. The reality and pressures of school systems everywhere, are that teachers seem more concerned with children's language performance - in examinations, tests, reviews, informal assessments, reports, essays, assignments, seminars, public presentations, and tutorials - than they can be with how accurately these displays reflect the knowledge and intellectual state of their students.

This knowledge on 'display' is usually in spoken or written language. The vital trait for teachers in these performances is the communication of meanings. The more insightful and diverse these meanings are, within the meaning systems given high status by the school, the more impressed teachers will be. The chief factor that influences the communication of meanings is the content of the language: the use of words. Clearly children with a broad access to the vocabulary of those meaning systems, are going to impress with their language more readily than others. If they are able to apply this readiness to use specialist words appropriately in their written work, then they are hugely advantaged in formal education.

Much of the work of schools prepares children to succeed in the final level of schooling. Often this endpoint is marked by a series of written examinations or other written assessments, often anonymously judged by independent assessors. When these assessors come across written answers that make wide use of specialist vocabularies drawn from the meaning systems of their subjects, they are more impressed than they are by answers that lack precise and specialist terminology. The absence of these words in written work may not always disadvantage students directly, but an indirect disadvantage results when their presence advantages other students.

The written transcript in the student's own writing that is reproduced in Figure 6, indicates the 'display' and communicative advantage in a discourse about values that a diverse and available vocabulary offers. This extract has a specialist G-L count of about 13 percent. It is from a 15 year old School S boy who is responding to these questions: (8) What sort of person is a 'good person'? (9) Is it ever all right to lie? (10) Is it ever all right to kill? (11) Are there any other things it's always wrong to do? (12) Which new laws would you choose, if you could?

This extract has about the same percentage of G-L words as most of the articles in a 'middle brow' newspaper written for adults (see Table 3 in Chapter 5). Since the underlined G-L words are used appropriately in this unedited piece, an assessor using the criterion of word choice would rate the boy's use of vocabulary very highly. He introduces a number of words specific to the meaning system of the task, which is ethics (RESPECT, AFFECT, DISADVANTAGE, INNOCENT etc.). More importantly, in his argument he shows clear familiarity with the rules for using them within that meaning system. An assessor would probably have little difficulty in judging the quality of the writing.

At the same time, judgments by teachers about oral language use are much more haphazard affairs. Children's oral language will often be the first contact that teachers have to base an opinion about potential on. The quality of this display can become an imprecise indicator of educational potential, especially if there are other indicators that reinforce teacher prejudices, such as children's dislike of schoolwork, lack of parental interest in the school, or evidence of disadvantage in the children's dress or appearance.  Teacher expectations often adjust accordingly. The evidence of language is vital in confirming stereotypes and activating prejudices.

8.    A good person is a person that <u>respects</u> other people and puts a lot of <u>effort</u> into the things that he does. He also shouldn't do things that hurt other people or <u>affect</u> their lives. A good person should be able to <u>decide</u> when and where to make <u>certain</u> <u>actions</u> and know how to learn from his mistakes. He also shouldn't knock other people for their <u>abnormalities</u>, and try to <u>respect</u> them for their good <u>points</u>.

9.    Telling a lie is usually wrong but can sometimes be right. A person should tell a lie only if it doesn't <u>affect</u> other people or his <u>surroundings</u>. If a person tells a lie, then it will mostly just be <u>disadvantage</u> for him, as well as other people. If a person tells a lie once, then he will be <u>encouraged</u> to tell more in <u>future</u>, no <u>matter</u> how he feels.

10.    Killing a person is usually wrong but can be right. If someone is killed as an act of pure self <u>defence</u> when their is no other way out, then the person is <u>innocent</u>. Otherwise, nobody has the right to take the life of another person, only that person has the right. Therefore, <u>committing</u> <u>suicide</u> should be <u>legal</u>, because any person should have the right to take their own life. However, under some <u>circumstances</u> this doesn't <u>apply</u>, as the person may be <u>influenced</u> by alcohol or drugs.

11.    It is always to <u>vandalise</u> other peoples <u>property</u>, unless it's for their own good. This usually doesn't <u>apply</u>, so <u>vandalism</u> should, and is, <u>illegal</u>. This rule also applies to <u>theft</u>.

12.    I wouldn't <u>introduce</u> any new laws, because I feel that the behaviour of people <u>depends</u> <u>purely</u> on them, although <u>punishment</u> for <u>crimes</u> can help a great deal.

FIG 6. *Written transcript from 15 year old School S boy*
(specialist G-L words are underlined).

*Teacher Stereotypes of Vocabulary Use*

Although a general and long-standing finding of research is that teachers' perceptions of culturally and socially different children's non-standard speech, produce negative expectations about personalities, social backgrounds, and academic abilities (Rosenthal & Jacobson, 1968; Verma & Bagley, 1975; J. Edwards, 1989), in practice this has not lessened the injustice very much. For example in Britain in the 1990s, there are still grave doubts about teachers' abilities to be objective when formally assessing oral language ability at senior school level. Findings there reveal that the standard language variety rates much more favourably than non-standard varieties, and this routinely discriminates against working class and minority group non-standard speakers (see Corson, 1993). In fact, it seems that teachers bring these stereotypes with them into the profession.

V. Edwards (1986) reports student-teacher evaluations of anonymous children's speech, where both the academic and the interest level of speakers of minority and other non-standard language varieties was viewed less favourably. Remarkably, there is now much evidence too that teacher attitudes to children's non-standard language use are more critical in judging the quality of language use than the children's language itself. There is even evidence to suggest that the stereotypes that beginning teachers from the majority culture hold about children from minority backgrounds, causes them to 'hear' those children as non-standard in their language, regardless of how standard their speech actually is (Fasold, 1984).

What role does vocabulary have in all this? Probably the frequent presence of high status specialist G-L words in the oral language of some schoolchildren will improve the reputations of those children in many contexts of use, while their absence for other children may have the opposite effect. The two speech extracts that opened this chapter give an example of these differences. Clearly the boys are both saying the same thing, but one chooses the specialist G-L words appropriate to the meaning system (INTRODUCE and ABOLISH) while the other extends words from ordinary language to do the same job (BRING IN and STOP). It is true that we usually do not speak of 'stopping' laws. Depending on the task for which the language was used, many assessors would grade this kind of text below the more specialist text, since the latter is firmly linked to the rules of use of the specialist meaning system and the speaker seems to be more at home within it. So these texts could create stereotypes about the two boys' educational potential. But if I had to assess them as they stand, I would rate them equally and look for more evidence. I return to the issue of bias and stereotyping later in the chapter.

*Contrasts by Age, Region and Sociocultural Group*

Evaluating the 'plain Saxon' vocabulary of the following oral transcript may be a little easier. I present the interview in full:

**Would you tell me all about that last school of yours?**
Well, there were only 'bout 'undred pupils what went and it were very little. All school would just fit into, all school would fit into [this block], like. 'Cause it were so little. And were only four classrooms and . . . this school starts at nine o'clock I think in the morning, don't it? Anyway used to start quarter and finish at quarter past three. Used to be different like that: And we used to play football, same as this school like that, and play rounders, cricket . . .

**What about the children?**
We . . . They were most different sizes were . . . little ones when they started and the big ones they were lots of different sizes in them. And that's about it. I can't think of ought else.

**What about the teachers?**
Were . . . were four teachers like I said didn't I? They were . . . two male and two female and. . . they were all good teachers, like, they didn't used to shout at you much. We used to get on with them very well.

**about the classrooms?.**
They were a lot littler. And . . . they just be about . . . just a bit bigger than this room here like . . . and we had all sinks . . . we all had sinks in . . .

**What did it look like?**
From the outside . . . It looked, used to look so bad and that, it were clean and used to have a fence up at out-side, in the front playground to stop the infants trying to climb over. We used to have a big fence up. And it were fairly tidyish school, like not many crisp packets lying about, 'cause teachers used to get right mad. Make us all pick 'em up.

**anything else?**
Most of me friends is come to this school now, but there are still one or two what will be moving up next year.

**What did you like about that school?**
I used to like football. And . . . cricket, different games like that. And . . . I used to like Maths as well. I used to do.

**What did you dislike?**
Oh . . . dislike, nought much. But I didn't used to like Assemblies very much. That's when you got to sit on floor and get clothes mucky and that.

**Could you tell me about one day at that school?**
I can't think of one . . . No . . . were so many . . . so many days to . . . well, last day I think were best day because it seemed to go right quick before 'e came up here. Just got there in morning. We did a bit of Maths I think and some English. And went down to Assembly. And that were before dinner. Then I think we played rounders then most afternoon. And when we came in after break went down to 'all and sung songs, like we used to do every Friday. We used to go down, we used to sing different songs like. Headmaster and everybody. All teachers and everybody used to go down there.

**Was it a good school?**
Yeah . . .

**What makes a good person?**
My . . . a good person, oh honest, cleanly dressed, well spoken, and . . . didn't lie.

**What does a good person do?**
. . . go to church . . . and *well-mannered*   like I said afore. Only thing I can really think
of

**Is telling a lie always wrong?**
Not always wrong but it can be sometimes, like if you . . . can't think of one now, but it is.
Sometimes it's right to tell a lie I think  . . . Like if any robbers came into your house
said "where's all your money?" like I'd tell 'm wrong place so I could ring like police up
so they could get here while they're trying to find it.

**What about killing . . . is that always wrong?**
Yeah. I *expect*  . . . I think it will be but . . . if you killed somebody in first place like . . .
and somebody else kills them it isn't like wrong then 'cause they've killed in first place,
haven't they?

**Are there other things that are always wrong to do?**
If you're told not to do something at school and you go and do it, that's wrong, then isn't
it?

**If you could choose the laws by which we live, which new ones would you choose?**
Laws . . . what I'd do, I'd . . . let everybody go out of gaol like and if he killed or did
ought like that I'd make 'em come back into gaol again for about ten years. And if he did
ought else I'd have 'em 'anged, and that'd sort country out, wouldn't it like.  Yeah, it'd
stop all these killings and stuff, wouldn't it?  all these *ambushes* and what they do. I'd
stop their old age pensioners going on bus fares, just with their passes. I'd make 'em pay
as much as children, like, because what two pence is nought really, is it? 'Cause they
get away with far too much, don't they? They get these, what, so much a week, well I'd
cut that down a bit 'cause they're getting between twenty five thirty pound a week aren't
they. Just for doing nought. Cut it down a bit because they taking it off other people to
give it to them, aren't they? Taking off your wages just to give it to other people.

(Yorkshire working class 12 year old boy)
(805 Word Oral Interview. Specialist G-L :  0.25% )

In vocabulary, this boy's fluent flow of language is at the other extreme from
the 15 year old written text reproduced in Figure 6. While his rural Yorkshire
dialect comes strongly through in the transcription, he illustrates another
strong trend that appeared among the Yorkshire students in general: using
fewer G-L words overall than the London students. In fact regardless of class
background, the 12 year old Yorkshire students were almost identical in their
low level of G-L usage and this interaction by age and region, when compared
with the London 12 year olds, was highly significant. This is consistent with
the fact that the children come from a region a little removed historically
from the dominant central variety of English. It also highlights the fact that
before adolescence, children model their vocabulary usage increasingly on
their peers. Indeed my reason for including a Yorkshire school in the study
was to examine any contrast that there may be across regions within England.

It seems that the 12 year old Yorkshire children's lexico-semantic range
was a direct reflection of their deep and regular immersion in the discursive
practices of their peer group, interactions not discriminating much by social
class background. This makes all the more remarkable the sharp differences

in active vocabulary use between the 15 year old Yorkshire social class groups, since the only general discursive change that happens in these groups of Yorkshire children's lives, between 12 and 15 years, is that they are exposed to the academic meaning systems of secondary education and to the rules of word use operating within those discourses.

While the above 12 year old boy's spoken text might send some strong messages about his class background to someone familiar with non-standard varieties in England, he is little different from most of the other 12 year olds in his range of interests and in his view of the world. There is no great need for this boy to use specialist G-L words, since he is not very far into the kind of academic meaning systems that exercise their use. But there are embryonic ideas in the text that might link up later with more complex concepts, like 'retribution' (i.e. when killing someone who has already killed) and 'justified deception' (i.e. when misleading robbers). But this kind of immersion in specialist meaning systems is still in this boy's future. So is the kind of vocabulary that goes with it. His present range of interests does not call for it.

Compare the above spoken text with this written text, from a 15 year old working class Wollongong girl. I also present this in full, using her spelling:

**Would you tell me all about that last school of yours?**
The last school I was at before this one was a lot smaller than this. There wasn't many children at the school because it was only a small town. The teachers were easy to get on with, they were a bit hard at times but you always knew it was for your own good. The classrooms were a pretty good size and they weren't all dirty e.t.c. The school looked neat everybody used the bins and there were alot of plants and bark gardens in the school.

**What did you like most about it?**
At primary school you had a lot of friends but you only hung around your best friend. I had a couple of best freinds but I like to *associate* with every one and not just one person.

**What did you dislike?**
I didn't dislike anything about the school except maths, and I used the like the athletics carnivals.

**Could you tell me about one day at that school?**
One day at school I had a fight with this girl that thought she was just great. All the girls used to be scared of her and they used to buy her things so that she wouldn't bash them up. Until one day I got sick of it so I bashed her. After that I got the cane so I will never forget it.

**Was it a good school?**
Yes, because it wasn't a rough school and because you didn't just learn maths, english and science all the time you could do pottery, art, crafts and *developing* in dark rooms, make plays e.t.c.

**What sort of person is a 'good person'?**
A good person is one who is nice and will help you when your in trouble. A good person should help people in need instead of stabbing them in the back.

**Is it ever all right to lie?**
Telling a lie is wrong if it is going to hurt someone. But if you've done something wrong and you know you'd get in big trouble for it I *surpose* you would have to lie to save yourself.

**Is it ever all right to kill?**
Killing a person is only right when it is in *self defence*. Otherwise killing is stupid.

**Are there any other things it's always wrong to do?**
It is always wrong to breaking or entery because you can get put in jail or in a home and plus the things you steal are not yours and somebody worked very hard to get them.

**Which new laws would you choose, if you could?**
I would choose one and change 2. I would make it that you couldn't be murdered on any charge and that there was no life in prisonment. And I would choose that marijuana should be *legalized* because it has just the safe *effect* as alchol and plus it keeps *cancer* away from your heart.

(Wollongong working class 15 year old girl)
(424 Word Written Interview. Specialist G-L : 1.65%)

In its G-L range, this girl's vocabulary is very like the Yorkshire 12 year old boy's spoken text, even though hers is a written text, and she is a 15 year old.

As a rough pattern, written texts seem to double in their specialist G-L content when compared with spoken ones. Probably this occurs because language users have more time, while writing, to activate low frequency G-L words in the store of words in their mental lexicons. As they strive to create better collocational relations in their texts, relevant to specific meaning systems, and to tap into the appropriate rules of use, motivated writers give themselves more time to access the 'right' word, and it often takes more time if the words are low in frequency. Chapter 7 discusses factors that influence word activation levels in the mental lexicon. Several factors seem influential in speeding or slowing the activation process: the time available in context to access words, when creating or receiving a spoken or written message; the frequency of lifetime encounters that the word user has had with the specific words; and, perhaps also, any 'language awareness' that the word user has acquired that would make the specific word more transparent. In creating written texts, for example, the more time that writers have to access words, the more likely they are to access words that get their meaning across with precision and conciseness. Compared with writers, speakers usually do not have the luxury of pausing and applying the same activation time needed to access low frequency words. The link between the frequency of exposure that people have to words, and their readiness to use them, seems very tight.

Returning to the above text, this 15 year old girl has little precision and conciseness in her writing. In its lexical diversity, the text is very like her spoken interview, given some weeks earlier. Contrary to the norms of use found across most of the texts received from the children, her specialist G-L percentage use was very similar in both spoken and written modes. She does introduce the difficult concept of 'killing in self-defence' and she uses it to construct an argument by implication. But in general she does not seem to have a relaxed familiarity with the meaning systems that the questions draw her into, nor with the discursive practices that flow through those systems. In fact, she has only a vague sort of acquaintance with the relevant modes of discursive practice. Her written language is not very different from the 12 year old's spoken language in the previous transcript. Her lexico-semantic experiences have not drawn her into the language games in such a way as to make her a participant, so she displays little evidence of having the rules of use that obtain in any of these circles.

The Macedonian immigrant girl in the next transcript has spent most of her school days sitting near or alongside the previous girl. Not only have these girls had very similar school experiences, except in respect to ESL exposure, but they are also matched in non-verbal reasoning level and come from poorer working class family backgrounds. The two texts were both written on the same morning, at the same time, in the same place:

**Would you tell me all about that last school of yours?**
My last school that I went to was K. Public school. This also was the only other school that I've been to, besides [this one]. It was a small school but I enjoyed it there. When I first began there, it wasn't very well *furnished*, however, throughout my years there, I watched it grow and *develop* into a *modern, comfortable* school.

**What did you like most about it?**
What I liked the most was the warm and friendly *atmosphere*. It was as though we were one big, happy family. Of course, I must *admit* that there were a few teachers and children who wouldn't *exactly* fit in the above *category* as "friendly and warm".

**What did you dislike?**
One of the few things that I disliked were some of the *ridiculous* rules that we had to follow.

**Can you tell me about one day at that school?**
I can still recall the day when all of the sixth class girls, *including* me, *decided* to *protest*. It was as though we all went on strike. Until that day, for the whole of our recess and second-half of lunch we used to play a game called "stumball". This game was very *similar* to "softball", however there were no bases and it *permitted* all of the girls to play, as there was no *certain* number of teams needed, as in "softball". We got into *serious* trouble and even the Principal came out of his office to give us a *lecture*.

**Was it a good school?**
I *suppose* it was a fairly good school. As much as I hate school now, I must *admit* that there were more good *points* about it than bad. To begin with, as I *mentioned* earlier, it was a friendly school and there always seemed to be something *interesting* or should I say *exciting* going on.

**What sort of person is a 'good person'?**
I would *describe* a good person as someone who has feelings towards other "*humans*". A person who tries not to do what is mostly *considered* as wrong. Of course, one cannot

really say what is right or wrong, for every *single* person has a different *opinion* of these two *matters*.

### Is it ever all right to lie?

I feel that telling a lie is not always wrong. There are many *reasons* for the way I feel. One *example* would be if someone is really pleased with something that they have made or bought and if they ask for your *opinion* which happens to be the *opposite*, you can't just come straight out with it for you would hurt them terribly. Also if one small, white lie can save a lot of hassle for a lot of people, then it isn't really "that" wrong. However, telling a lie could never really be right either.

### Is it ever all right to kill?

Killing a person is not always wrong in my *opinion*. If a person is in a great deal of pain and is in one *sense* "rotting away" then I feel that you would be doing them a *favour*.

### Are there any other things it's always wrong to do?

I don't think one can say what is wrong or right. Everyone has a different *definition* of those two *matters*. I cannot think of anything that is always wrong for there is always a *case* where it could be *considered* as right.

### Which new laws would you choose, if you could?

I'm not sure that I would choose any new ones for there already are too many. So many, in fact that I'm not sure of half of them. I do know, however, that there are quite a few I would wipe out *completely*.

(Wollongong Macedonian 15 year old girl)
(560 Word Written Interview. Specialist G-L : 7.32%)

This girl's comments overall suggest she has had deep engagement with the meaning systems touched on by the questionnaire and with the rules of use that link to words used within those systems. It is hard to accept that she has had near-identical school experiences to the previous girl, since their overall differences in vocabulary use suggest the immigrant girl has had years of English language development that the former has not had.

Even in the descriptive section of the questionnaire, her responses about her school are insightful and also explanatory. Her use of ATMOSPHERE, DEVELOP, MODERN and COMFORTABLE in answer to the first two questions, reveals a striking command of the rules of use for these words and the relationships that they contract for people inside the language game. She wields the words compellingly, making original statements that have more than mere descriptive power. Her written response to the questionnaire is about one-third longer than her classmate's. So she may reveal a greater willingness to elaborate on her responses: to say more; to add details and to qualify without prompting. But her longer responses do not mean that she adds words unnecessarily. Instead she goes further into her topics than her classmate does, implying that she has a much greater familiarity with the topics. In fact, her apt use of G-L word collocation, in later questions, suggests someone very much at home in the relevant systems of use. For example, she brings together ADMIT with POINTS; INTERESTING with EXCITING; REASON with EXAMPLE; OPPOSITE with OPINION; and

CASE with CONSIDERED. Clearly this girl has been through a very different lexico-semantic positioning. What brought about these differences?

The answer is not a simple one. Perhaps there is some transfer for this girl's English lexical diversity from the Macedonian that was her first language, since Macedonian has borrowed extensively from Greek and Latin sources. Overlaying this remote but motivated connection with the G-L roots of English, are the effects of a deliberately heavy concentration on English word skills in her primary and secondary education through ESL classes. She may also be choosing more 'formal' vocabulary, which would orient her towards a greater use of the G-L (although a piece of writing in school is about as formal as any 15 year old's language ever gets). She may be reflecting strong parental influence towards success in schooling that is common among closely-knit immigrant communities. No doubt, too, throughout her life in Australia, her parents and extended family have recognised that she has greater language fluency than older members of the family, and put her skills to use as an interpreter in their daily rounds in the new culture. Perhaps this would giving her an active language maturity, early in life, that is beyond her years.

All of these discursive practices and events would separate her from her Australian-born classmate, who fluently speaks the mother tongue English of a working class Australian girl, but who has received no greater language stimulation than any other native-born Australian. Taken together, these factors have great power in explaining the differences uncovered between all the immigrant Wollongong children and their native-born working class peers.

*Difficulty in Active Access to G-L Words*

The first extract below is from an Italian-Australian 15 year old boy, and the second is from a working class Australian 15 year old girl. Again these children have spent most of their school lives in one another's company, they come from the same social class position, and they are matched in reasoning ability. Yet teachers listening to their oral responses to the same question, would have little difficulty in deciding which student got the message across more readily:

**Would you lie to save a friend's life? When else would it be all right to lie?**

Yes I would. Oh yeah, it might be sort of *futuristic* whatever, but if a *dictatorship* or *militaristic sort* of outlook came upon Australia and people were going around *collecting* friends of mine because of the *religion* or *race* that they came from and if they asked me if they were of a *particular* race, I would say that they weren't from the race they were collecting prisoners for or whatever (Wollongong Romance-descent 15 year old boy).

Well . . . if somebody was going to get . . . someone was going to get bashed up or something and you said, and they, they didn't want to come because they knew they wouldn't be able to win and they'd just get hurt, well then, you'd tell the other person that they're sick or something and they couldn't come. So then they . . . you'd be saving both people from being . . . *embarrassed*, you know. And that'd be all right (Wollongong working class 15 year old girl).

Listeners assessing these two responses, on the run as it were, might judge the two students as very different in reasoning ability. Yet they are not. Perhaps again the first student's experiences of formal ESL exposure and informal contact with two languages, one almost totally Latinate, help explain these differences. The contribution of the specialist G-L words to the first extract is vital in adding to the 'display' value, whereas the plain text of the second lacks precision, explicitness, and that subtle quality of 'colour'. It also lacks the cohesion of the first. Even though she has a real and worthwhile point to make, it is hard to pick it out from the redundant words. This might suggest that she is searching for suitable word meanings as real content for her message. It might also suggest that the words are not available to her, because she is unfamiliar with the rules for applying them within that language game. It probably suggests both, along with other things that later discussion should highlight.

Notice with what difficulty the single specialist G-L word comes into the speech of the second student above, even while that word is the point of her argument (i.e. avoiding embarrassment). This is a rare case where a working class indigenous adolescent hinges an argument on a single specialist word. The extract below provides another rare case of this usage. Notice again with what difficulty the word comes into the student's speech. This is a common feature of working class specialist usage in the oral transcripts:

**Why is stealing always wrong?**
Because if you steal, if everyone else stelt, you know, did steal an' there'd be no, no . . . *civilization* really . . . 'cause people would be stealin' all the time and takin', and that would lead to wars. So you shouldn't really steal (London working class 15 year old boy).

Chapters 7 & 8 explore the effect of regular or irregular exposure to words of different frequency levels on the ease of activating words in the mental lexicon. Low frequency words, or words that a user has only rarely encountered, need greater levels of activation in the mental lexicon. When there is plenty of time for this activation, verbal memory is jogged. So when we slow down our speech, as the girl and boy in the last two extracts are doing, low frequency words become more available. They also become more available when we 'prime' the word by hearing its first letter, or its first syllable, or a semantically similar word.

At this point, I draw attention to these last two extracts as powerful examples of word users struggling to access specialist G-L words in speech which they hold passively, but whose low frequency in their past discursive experiences means that they need more and longer activation to access them in the mental lexicon than higher frequency words. As Chapter 7 argues, this is a very important factor maintaining the lexical bar in contemporary society, and reproducing it across generations. When people find that words are hard to recall, they rarely use them. As a result, others who share the same discursive arrangements, especially young people or people trying to learn the words in a second language, hear them less often: As a further direct result, similar patterns of vocabulary activation get reproduced from one generation of speakers to another.

### Differences in G-L Form Class Usage

The use of adverbs, as a form class, stands out in texts that have a high percentage of specialist G-L words. Comparing middle class and working class oral texts, the ratio of specialist adverbial usage is more than seven to one. The following spoken extract shows this high adverb usage at work:

> **What other things is it always wrong to do?**
> *Influence* people into making bad *decisions*. That's always wrong. Because . . . *especially* if you're doing it *deliberately* to make him do it. *Possibly* what you're doing, you know, you're going to put him in the wrong *circumstances* and you're not doing anything about it. You're just leading him on (Sydney middle class 15 year old boy).

Middle class children also use three to four times more specialist G-L nouns, verbs, and adjectives than working class children. The effect of this display on school assessments can be readily gauged. I discuss its actual communicative value in a later section. Below is an extract from a written text that uses all of these form classes. It puts specialist G-L words together in the same ratio as do academic texts in the areas of English literature and other areas of the humanities (see Chapter 5). Although it does not do this with the same eloquence as mature language users might, this boy has not had much chance to edit his text before giving it to me:

> **Which new laws would you choose, if you could?**
> Laws are made to *benefit* the *average citizen*. The only laws I <u>might</u> change are some traffic laws. Some of these laws give a *certain* car *involved* in an *accident* a biggest *advantage*. Speaking very *seriously* I would change the *prostitution* laws. I would not make it straight out *legal* (the outcome would be *obvious*) - but I might make *certain licenses available* in *limited* numbers. (Sydney middle class 15 year old boy).

### Effects on Reading and the Re-Application of Specialist G-L Vocabulary

High school teachers rarely assess performance in reading by listening to children read, in the way that teachers in primary schools do. Secondary teacher assessments are more indirect; they are made on the basis of children's ability to reformulate and recommunicate what they have read. But as mentioned, until children are 15 at least, they have difficulty acquiring new concepts from their reading alone. Words met in books for the first time are often lost on young children who are unfamiliar with them.

I took the three extracts below from school textbooks in a curriculum resources library. They show the type of increase in percentage G-L that often occurs as the reading age of the material increases. Extract A is written to suit children with a reading age of 8 to 8.5 years.  Extract B is written for students of 11 to 12 years.  Extract C is written for intermediate secondary school students of about 15 years:

<u>Extract A</u>: Reading age 8-8.5 years, 2% specialist G-L

Where is Water?

Everyone knows the answer to that question.

When rain falls, we see water in puddles.  Sometimes water rushes down the side of a mountain, carrying rocks with it.  In a quiet lake, water is like a mirror.  You can see the sky *reflected* in it.

Water floats leaves and little sticks in a running river.  Sometimes there is so much water that it floods the land.  At the seashore, great waves of water come in from the *ocean*.  They rise in a tower of foam and fall back into the *ocean* again.

© Longman Cheshire Pty Ltd.  From *Time to Wonder*.  Reading 360 Australia Level 8, Book 5. 1976, p. 22.  All rights reserved.  Reprinted with permission of the publisher.

<u>Extract B</u>: Student level 12 years, 20% specialist G-L

When *objects* made of the same *material* have the same kind of *electric* charge, they *tend* to *repel* each other.  This seems always to be true.  The *objects* may be *positively* charged or *negatively* charged.  It makes no difference — so long as they have the same kind of charge.  On the *basis* of thousands of *tests*, then, *scientists* can make this *general statement*: *Objects* with like *electric* charges *tend* to *repel* each other.

© Addison Wesley.  From *Addison Wesley Science* by V. N. Rockcastle. 1980, p. 147.  All rights reserved.  Reprinted with permission of the publisher.

<u>Extract C</u>: Student level 15 years, 25% specialist G-L

Because of your brother's *experience, iodine* meant "hurt".  That was his *perception*.  As a *result*, he *perceived* your behaviour as unfriendly.  He then *inferred* that your feelings toward him must be unfriendly and he also *inferred* that your *intention* was to hurt him.  You can easily see that your *perception* of the *situation* was *entirely* different from his.

Feelings, *intentions*, behaviour, and *perception* are all *involved* in friendliness and unfriendliness.  How a person *perceives* a *situation* helps him *decide* whether a behaviour is friendly or unfriendly.  His *perception* then *causes* him to make *inferences* about feelings and *intentions*.  It also *causes* him to behave in a *certain* way.

© Science Research Associates, Inc.  From *Social Sciences Resource Book* by Ronald Lippitt, Robert Fox, and Lucille Schaible. 1969, p. 97.  All rights reserved.  Reprinted with permission of the publisher.

The publication of *The Lexical Bar* was a factor in changing some publishers' practices.  Policies for placing high G-L texts, like Extract C above, in textbooks for adolescents were modified somewhat.  Incidentally too, the generic male pronoun used in Text C has largely disappeared from published materials for children.

Most of the vocabulary in Extracts B and C above would probably be available in the passive vocabularies of all the 15 year olds interviewed in these studies. Although 15 year olds from some sociocultural groups score much lower in their passive access to specialist G-L words, there is no clear barrier at work in passive vocabulary as there seems to be for the active use of these words. This is probably because, in every instance, the children heard the target words first: The Measure of Passive Vocabulary 'primed' their use. So the difficult words in Extracts B and C would be interpretable in principle. In other words, an encounter with the words would locate word entries stored in the children's mental lexicons. But in practice, many children would obviously baulk at reading these passages. Even if they did plough their way through them, their reading would be slowed by many of the accessing factors that I have hinted at already and which I discuss more fully in Chapters 7 & 8. As a result, the meanings of the passages would also be hard for many children to establish. Moreover, because of the constraints on many children's active use of specialist G-L words, this vocabulary would not be readily available for application in original oral and written messages of the children's own devising.

*Ideas on Display*

In reading and listening to the oral utterances of the many children who took part in these studies, it became clear to me that the 12 year old children from all social groups displayed greater ease, in getting their '12 year old-type' messages across, than did the working class Australian and English 15 year old children, with their '15 year old-type' messages. As earlier extracts confirm, the working class 15 year olds often seemed to struggle to say what they meant, especially in the explanatory context. In their speech, this struggle often ended with some phrase of resignation: a statement which the students' non-verbal manner suggested was not an ideal statement of what they really wanted to say. Unlike the middle class 15 year olds, the words did not come as readily, if at all. The desire was there; the knowledge and ideas were probably there; but the language on display was not.

In contrast, the vocabulary of the 15 year old middle class children allowed them a range of expression that matched their apparent logical development. The following precise and concise written response displays this ready communication of active meaning, unequally available it seems to some groups of 15 year olds:

> **Which new laws would you choose, if you could?**
> I would *completely abolish capital punishment* because nobody has the right to put anyone to death, no *matter* how *serious* the *crime* was which he has *committed*. In a lot of murder trials, for *example*, it can't be *proved* that the *defendant* was guilty (Sydney middle class 15 year old).

At the same time, this ready communication of meaning, through active use of specialist G-L words, is not solely a characteristic of 15 year old middle class children. The following oral extract is good evidence that 12 year olds can 'do things with words' that are often associated only with a much later level of development:

> **Are there other things it's always wrong to do?**
> You say, well, they're wrong now but perhaps in another *instance* they'd be right to do. If you were, if you were greedy for some *reason* and everybody thought you were being greedy, you know, but if you were really hungry and you hadn't eaten for a fortnight, it's right almost to be greedy  (Yorkshire middle class 12 year old girl).

The intellectual elegance of this girl's argument suggests that she is already well into formal, analytical reasoning in complex areas. Her compelling argument rebuts the commonsense dogma that moral rules are universalizable. Clearly the two specialist G-L words provide the hinge to her argument: the ethics of doing one thing rather than another varies across contexts, from instance to instance, depending on the justifiable reasons that are available. There seems a form of language development here that few of the 15 year old working class children achieve in the spoken task. The latter have many of the words in a passive sense, as Chapter 5 confirms, but apparently not a deep enough acquaintance with the rules for their active deployment within a relevant system of meaning.

### Cultural Meaning Systems and the Lexical Bar

As Harré & Gillett imply, it is difficult to be sure that people are 'inside' cultural meaning systems if they do not use the words and show themselves to be skilled users of these sign systems. When we think in complex areas, especially in the specialist meaning systems given high status in education, we organize our thought and communicate it in the special signs of those systems, provided we have learned the rules for applying that vocabulary in a given context. But when we do not have active access to the words, communication in these complex areas becomes difficult.

For precise communication to take place in the explanatory task used in these studies, that task solicits an active use of specialist words. In this case, the specialist words come mainly from the fields of ethics and jurisprudence. To get a given meaning across in specialist fields, one alternative to using specialist G-L words would be to express the same ideas in other ways: either by paraphrasing them, or by extending the meanings of other words drawn from everyday language. The speaker in the first extract cited at the beginning of this chapter, does the latter: He uses the everyday words STOP and BRING IN in place of the specialist G-L words ABOLISH and INTRODUCE.  But looking over the transcripts from these studies, there is no evidence that 15 year olds are using paraphrases as substitutes for specialist G-L words. Paraphrasing is not a common alternative to specialist G-L usage by adolescent speakers or writers. Nevertheless, extending the meanings of the more everyday words can provide a good alternative to specialist G-L words, at least in some contexts of use. But in other contexts, precision inevitably falls away when synonyms are fabricated in this way, since most specialist words are without adequate synonyms and often lack even distant synonyms (see Chapter 4). At the same time, even the use of paraphrase can lead to longer messages, which interferes with communication since they ask the recipient to juggle many more words and also more transformations of syntax.

For Vygotsky, the greatest intellectual difficulty is the application of a concept that has been finally grasped and formulated on the abstract level, to new concrete situations that must be viewed in an abstract way. This is "a kind of transfer usually mastered only toward the end of the adolescent period" (1962, p. 80). Britton reflects this view, arguing that "it is an achievement of late adolescence to theorize objectively, to handle highly abstract concepts with due regard for their logical relationships, their interrelatedness within a system, and their implications downwards, that is to say at a concrete or empirical level" (1970, p. 262). Now clearly the development associated with this adolescent achievement covers a long time-span. Its flowering in late adolescence is only the finishing touch added to an assembly of cultural meaning systems established by life experiences and relationships contracted since infancy. Although many adolescents do achieve great range and precision in the vocabulary available to them, we need to conclude, with Chomsky (1980), that the conceptual system associated with their active word use is already substantially in place.

These studies suggest that a demand for a widespread active use of specialist G-L words begins to occur during the stages of middle to late adolescence. But it is the availability of life experiences, including rich language contacts, long before this adolescent stage of growth that provides the important foundation. The first school years, spanning pre-school and infant schools in some educational systems, are certainly an important period of great language development. Also important are the years around the onset of adolescence, when children's minds seem very flexible and when word shapes, sounds, and meanings hold a special fascination. But to succeed in contemporary education, all children throughout childhood need a steadily developing immersion in discursive practices centred on the meaning systems of the culture of literacy that is valued in education. Clearly, as studies cited in Chapter 2 confirm, social inequalities in income and life chances, linked to the division of labour in modern capitalist societies, mean that the home and wider community cannot be expected to give all children this immersion. Quite clearly, the school wrongly presumes that its modes of accreditation are fairly based.

The life experiences, the sociocultural backgrounds, and the habitus of some people admit them at critical periods to contact with academic meaning systems, so that they become familiar with the life forms and conventions of use in which specialist G-L words are grounded. When adolescent interest in analytical reasoning develops and invokes an increasing use of specialist concepts, immersion in the systems that embed those concepts supports a ready and widespread active use of specialist G-L words. But many people have life histories that do not admit them very much at all to academic meaning systems, and so they do not readily identify with the vocabularies of those meaning systems. Even when formal education manages to arouse their interest in those systems, they may effectively stay outside the systems, because schools often deny children opportunities to put themselves inside the conventions of use of specialist G-L words. They deny them occasions to use specialist G-L words in motivated and purposeful dialogue.

What the lexical bar partly represents is a gulf between the everyday meaning systems and the high status meaning systems created over time by the introduction of an academic culture of literacy. This part of the bar exists in all languages, not just in English. It is a barrier that everyone has to cross at some stage of their lives if they are to become 'successful candidates' in conventional schooling. But what reinforces this barrier in English, and probably in some other languages too (see Chapter 9), is the unique series of events that created the G-L and Anglo-Saxon divide in English, and then through their unequal access to education placed the poor and the privileged on either side of that lexical divide. Access to academic meaning systems is difficult enough in any language. In English the lexical bar increases that difficulty.

### High Status Cultural Capital, Formality, and Specialist G-L Words

Specialist G-L words appear more often in formal texts. This helps to reinforce their prestige. They are seen by many as markers of high status cultural capital and this affects the rules of use that speakers and writers associate with them. Inexperienced or insecure writers and speakers, seeking linguistic prestige as an escape from their insecurity and inexperience, often increase their use of these words beyond necessary levels. More than this, as Maylath's studies indicate, assessors doubtful about their own status seem to project their own search for prestige onto student texts. By doing this, they reinforce the use of G-L words as markers of prestige and formality. So by rewarding students who over-use them, these assessors contribute to a cycle of reproduction that links excessive use of G-L words with social success, with possession of high status cultural capital, and with an end to insecurity.

Specialist G-L words fill up meaning systems that are the most difficult and the most abstract. For these reasons alone, the words will attract high regard among certain influential sectors of society. So, inevitably, this vocabulary is a high status one that is favoured in education. Its possession and use confers sociocultural prestige on the person who uses it well and at the 'right' time. While on the one hand, possession and appropriate use of a diverse vocabulary improves educational performance by allowing the creation of texts at higher levels of abstraction, on the other, affected use of specialist G-L words adds little to meaning. Indeed, it can easily diminish it and say something negative about the user at the same time.

Wittgenstein's famous piece of advice, that we look not for the meaning but for the use of a word, is as important in choosing words for our own use as it is in judging words used by others: By looking at a word's use in a given context, we find out something insightful about the speaker or the writer; and very often that speaker or writer is ourselves! At the same time, every new context is a new setting for judging the use of a word. So in judging whether or not a word is well used, we need to consider all the sociocultural factors that can vary across contexts, including especially the age and the experience of the word user.

Consider the following written extract, which seems affected on first reading. Yet a close look suggests there are few italicized words that the boy could leave out of his text and still say what he wants to. Could he replace many of these words with near synonyms or suitable paraphrases, and still get his meaning across?

> **Is it ever all right to lie?**
> Telling a lie can be *profitable*, but it can also *destroy* your *conscience*. In *rare cases* lies are *accepted*. For *example*, when *protecting* friends, *relatives* and people you love. It is *unjustified* when trying to *escape responsibility* (Wollongong middle class 15 year old boy).

On inspection, most of this writer's specialist G-L words seem essential to saying what he means. It is hard to think of an adequate paraphrase for CONSCIENCE; while words like RESPONSIBILITY and UNJUSTIFIED link with rules of use that penetrate this meaning system: They are important in a discourse about ethical reasoning. He could rewrite his text without the words, but it would probably be longer and more discursive. Above all, it would not be natural language, since it would be rewritten just to show that it could be said another way. Although the extract does seem very formal, are there good contextual reasons for this?

Most assessors would see the above text as stilted and too formal if it came from an experienced adult writer. But we know that this piece comes from a 15 year old who is struggling to 'get it right' and also struggling to impress the institution of education. Most teachers of 15 year olds accept an over-use of polysyllabic words for what it really is: an unintentional parody of prestige language, but a parody that most of us have to go through to learn to use language well. As Balester notes about 'hyperfluent writers': They "stand in a subordinate or relatively powerless relation to the audience" and desperately try to appeal to it (1991 p. 81). I agree too with Rose's observation about novice university students who struggle to use vocabulary in new and difficult areas, also at the boundaries of their ability:

> trying to move into the unfamiliar, to approximate a kind of writing they can't yet command. And as they try, they'll make all the blunders in word choice . . . that regularly get held up for ridicule . . . Before we shake our heads at these errors, we should also consider the possibility that many such linguistic bungles are signs of growth . . . we should welcome certain kinds of error, make allowance for them in the curricula we develop, analyze rather than simply criticize them. Error marks the place where education begins (cited in Maylath, 1994 p. 184).

This seems to me a sensible and entirely welcome way to think about infelicitous uses of vocabulary by students still developing their written language proficiency.

But outside halls of learning, very few people are impressed by excessive formality in vocabulary, especially if its aim seems only to impress or dominate. Even inside education, changes are now under way. For instance, what Bourdieu calls 'magisterial language' - the impressive but rather empty language that sometimes passes for academic eloquence - is at last getting the critical treatment it deserves; and this book is part of that critique. At the same time, to learn how to get inside appropriate usage, the novice word user still has to try out the uses of new words: to use them for the very first time in motivated discourse, even if they are never used again.

This is also true of oral texts, where the specialist G-L vocabulary has a similar role in developing spoken proficiency. For example, these two extracts answer the same question:

**What sort of person would you describe as a good person?**

Person who helps, like. Who'll give, not who'll give but not too much that will make them . . . put them out too much. Person that listens and doesn't just say anything, but don't really do anything (Wollongong working class 15 year old boy).

He, he's gotta be, he's gotta suit your *personality*. He's gotta have *similar interests* . . . he can't be too noisy 'cause they can get *annoying*. He's got to know what to say, when to say it and he's gotta *respect* you. If he *treats* you as an *equal* and if he's *considerate* and *polite* then he's gotta be fairly nice (Sydney middle class 15 year old boy).

The first text is certainly filled with meaning for the speaker, but that meaning is very difficult for the listener to grasp. This is because there is little content vocabulary, drawn from an appropriate meaning system, for the pivot words and the syntax to point to, and so lift the message to a higher level of coherence and meaning. The first text suggests that the speaker is someone who has not talked very much about this sort of topic before, certainly not enough to assimilate the sort of concepts that might be useful in displaying an ability to tell good from bad in relation to someone else's behaviour.

In contrast, the second text has many of these concepts, almost to an abundance: PERSONALITY; [not] ANNOYING; SIMILAR and INTERESTS; RESPECT [you]; TREATS and EQUAL; CONSIDERATE and POLITE. All of these words reach deep into the actual meaning system that users of English associate with the topic of 'being an agreeable person'. Sometimes the words can appear singly, to make a single point. Sometimes they appear in close collocational relations, linking distinct concepts to give original meaning and cohesive power. Sometimes, as here, they come together in a more extended collocation, over a larger fragment of discourse, to help create a descriptive chain or an explanatory argument. But there is no question of formality in the second text: only a direct expression of descriptive and explanatory meaning.

Again in the two oral texts that follow, one text clearly goes further than the other in what it has to say:

**When would it not be wrong to lie?**

If somebody's going to kill you, you'll have to kill him first to save yourself. Killing is wrong most of time when people do it (Yorkshire working class 15 year old girl).

It *depends*, if killing another person means *survival* for oneself then of course it's *correct* in one's own mind . . . killing for *advantage* is wrong . . . killing *unnecessarily* (London middle class 15 year old boy).

Both are saying very much the same thing in relation to 'killing in self-defence'. But the first asserts a position without any verbal recourse to arguing it. In contrast, without using complex premises, the second introduces the Latinate ADVANTAGE and UNNECESSARILY which adds more to his similar assertion, by qualifying it and by offering an argument entailed by those words.

On other occasions, by the conciseness they allow to texts, specialist G-L words offer a summation and a signal that further debate is unnecessary. They add formal verbal authority to a statement. These three responses answer the same question:

**When would it not be wrong to lie?**

It's helpful. It can stop other people from gettin' hurt if you lie to them (London working class 15 year old girl).

Not so much if you get in trouble you shouldn't really lie, but sometimes you 'ave to (London working class 15 year old boy).

When the *consequences* of knowing it will *cause* trouble (Yorkshire middle class 15 year old boy).

The first two 15 year olds offer no more in support of their stances than 12 year olds might offer. In contrast, the authoritative message of the third response draws its force from its Latinate components. In an important way, they control the sentence's structure, enhancing meaning by providing a focus for a complex use of syntactic structure: in the gerund form that follows CONSEQUENCES; and in the abstract noun that the verb TO CAUSE often has as its object. Unusual uses of syntax like these often accompany a broad use of specialist G-L words. Learning the words as signs means learning the rules of use for them, and some of those rules are syntactic.

While most rules of use are outside language itself, having to do with the logic of life forms and non-linguistic relationships that obtain within language games, the complex use of syntax certainly adds to the formality of texts that contain these words. It also increases the difficulty in using the words well. So this tends to reinforce their formality and also increases their status as items of linguistic capital, since they are linked in people's minds with the kinds of relaxed eloquence that many experienced and dominant language users achieve, and which the inexperienced and insecure would often like for themselves.

It seems, then, that specialist G-L words are used in many ways to create formality and to enhance personal status. Speakers of English need to be aware that these are common functions that G-L words can serve. They need to distinguish these rather negative functions from the more positive and genuine communicative function that the words can have, if they are used appropriately within specialist meaning systems or to point to those systems. When people use them deliberately in the pursuit of formality or prestige, this is often an attempt to exercise power over others. In formal situations, people opt for more formal word use to help establish solidarity with significant others. They do this to make some people feel part of the process, but also to exclude others. When people use high status words in another way, to impress, this is an attempt to exercise dominance over others, or to escape from insecurity, or both.

So it seems important to make sure that novice users of these words know that sometimes they can be used as instruments of power. But novices also need to know that when a specialist G-L word suits the meaning of the moment, then its use really does help communication. There is plenty of evidence of this in these studies. In almost every use of specialist G-L words observed in these studies, the 15 year old children applied them in ways that suited the words' rules of use: The words really helped create meaning and smoothed its communication.

In all four contexts, the oral and the written, the descriptive and the explanatory, the 12 year old children in general and the 15 year old working class children select specialist G-L words at a similar rate to the percentage in children's fiction written for a reading age of 7 to 9 years.[3] In contrast, middle class 15 year olds, in the explanatory task, select specialist G-L words at a percentage rate comparable with fiction written for a reading age of 12 years, or comparable with serious newspaper stories, or comparable with some adult English literature. This remarkable variation in favour of middle class 15 year olds confirms that the specialist G-L vocabulary is lending high performance level support to communication by some groups of children. In summary, that communication is appropriate to the semi-formal context of use that the school represents, with little evidence of excessive formality.

---

[3]　In specialist G-L counts performed on transcripts in these studies, I counted a word repeated in the same context of utterance only once (Corson, 1982). In G-L counts done on public texts (see Table 3 in Chapter 5), all words were counted whenever they occurred. Also I excluded any G-L words in the transcripts repeated verbatim from the interview question. As a result there is some small imprecision in comparing the two types of text.

## High Status Linguistic Capital and Sociocultural Reproduction

> In becoming people, human beings appropriate structure from the social Umwelt [environment] and, so structured, produce an Umwelt that realizes structures akin to those from which the individual's organization arose in the first place (Harré, 1990 p. 350).

A central point of early reproduction theorists, was that education systems reproduce social arrangements necessary to maintain societies in their traditional forms. Schools were said to perform this function by constructing subjectivities and dispositions that are amenable to their students' learning the skills needed to fill their class-specific places in the society's division of labour. Standard formulations of these ideas come from Althusser (1971) and Bowles and Gintis (1976). Clearly these were rather imprecise formulations since they attributed too much influence in reproduction to formal education itself, and too little to historical, political, and cultural forces outside the school. They also tended to discount processes of resistance within schools, like those examined by Willis (1977: see Chapter 2). In short, they were rather fatalistic formulations, suggesting an inevitable reproduction of social arrangements through education that would continue as long as societies tolerate the maintenance of education in its conventional forms.

Later theories go beyond this. They consider the universe of cultural influences in which the school is lodged. But they still argue that educational systems act in the interests of the dominant classes in society by lending approval to an 'official' culture that matches the dominant classes' world views, tastes, and interests. Apple (1982) lists some of the major social functions that schools have: They select and certify a workforce; they maintain privilege by taking the form and content of the dominant culture and defining it as legitimate knowledge to be passed on; they are agents in the creation and the re-creation of an effectively dominant culture; they legitimate new knowledge, new classes, and strata of social personnel. In short, for Apple, schools allocate people and legitimate knowledge, or legitimate people and allocate knowledge. So in many of its practices, formal education looks after the interests of some sociocultural groups much better than the interests of some other groups.

Language is the chief vehicle for this routine activity of unjust power distribution through education (Corson, 1993). As I argue in early chapters of this book, Bourdieu's analysis (1977; 1981) is a critical one in understanding how this reproductive process operates, and its link with the lexical bar. His ideas have much to do with the lexico-semantic positioning that people receive from their upbringing and from their sociocultural contacts. His concept of cultural capital includes those sets of meanings, styles, cultural systems, and dispositions which children mainly receive from their families, communities, and peer groups. This cultural capital receives a certain social value. Schools tend to render legitimate or illegitimate certain elements in the student's cultural capital. Since by tradition schools act in the interests of the dominant classes, then it is the cultural capital of ruling groups that is legitimized by schools. As mentioned already in Chapter 2, the dominant sociocultural groups' cultural capital is an 'academic' one, when compared with the culture of working class people and of many minority groups:

> Those whose 'culture' . . . is academic culture conveyed by the school have a system of categories of perception, language, thought and appreciation that sets them apart from those whose only training has been through their work and their social contacts with people of their own kind (Bourdieu, 1971, p. 200).

This academic culture receives public expression in language forms whose rules of use are more readily available to those who share the legitimated cultural capital than to those individuals whose systems of meaning are markedly different ones, that do not support a wide and ready use of these language forms. Language, specifically its vocabulary, provides evidence of entry into those meaning systems that emerged as part of the academic culture of literacy. Specialist G-L words help communication within those meaning systems, since their rules of use are essentially what those academic meaning systems comprise. By their use, these signs ease the process of communication for some people in schools and universities, which are the places where the academic systems of meaning are highly valued. But also by their use, they make communication in those systems more difficult for others.

In English-speaking societies, coincidences of social and linguistic history have combined to create a lexical situation that is unique among languages: Most of the specialist and high status vocabulary of English is Graeco-Latin in origin and most of its more ordinary vocabulary is Anglo-Saxon in origin. English in this respect, relative to other languages (see Chapter 9), has a fairly clear boundary drawn between its everyday and its high status vocabularies. But this boundary is only contingent upon and reinforced by the etymological provenance of words. It is not erected by it.

## Conclusion

The presence of specialist G-L words in active vocabulary directly helps educational performance by allowing users to put their knowledge 'on display' in speech and writing. While their absence from texts may not always directly disadvantage people, they get an indirect disadvantage because others are advantaged by their presence. Their absence from texts may also reinforce harmful stereotypes that prevent people revealing their true potential. But on the evidence of these studies, older adolescents from different sociocultural positions have a very different lexico-semantic relationship with academic meaning systems, even when they have spent all of their school lives in the company of one another: in the company of children from backgrounds more favourably positioned.

Some groups of children are very unequally positioned by their lifetime discursive experiences to show that they can operate within meaning systems associated with the school's culture of literacy. This inequality cannot be put down solely or even largely to the formality or prestige of the vocabulary that they do not use. There is a lexical bar here that all students will always need to cross, if schools remain largely as they are, but some are much better placed by their sociocultural positioning to do so than others. This is a result of the unequal distribution of society's rewards and the associated life chances that come from that unequal distribution of rewards. This inequality is ultimately brought about by the division of labour that exists in societies that are themselves unjustly ordered.

This aspect of the lexical bar operates as an instrument of sociocultural reproduction in this way: The bar is partly a function of the historically induced and social class-based orderings of society associated with the division of labour. It separates the vocabularies of the members of some sociocultural groups from the dominant and high status specialist vocabulary of the language, mainly because their discursive positioning gives them little access to rules of use within the relevant meaning systems. Because educational selection processes are based upon a long-term display of access to that vocabulary, since its use signals immersion in the meaning systems valued in education, the bar reproduces differential attainment rates in education and then helps to reproduce the same stratified orderings of society across generations.

A matter closely related to all of this, is the effect that different lexico-semantic positioning has on the human brain itself. If, as seems certain, the human brain is physically shaped by the experiences that its owner has, especially, in this context, by the narratives, the stories, and the other discursive events that people participate in, then the mental lexicon or store of words in the brain will also be differently organized by the different life experiences of people who come from different backgrounds. At the same time, people who are similar in life experiences and in discursive positioning, will have brains that are similar in all those aspects that relate to cultural and social similarities. The next chapter explores these issues more fully.

# 7

# Morphology and the Mental Lexicon

How does the brain process vocabulary? Does exposure to discourses of different types, create different mental structures and processes in the brain? Until recent years, answers to these questions were little more than guesswork. But since the late 1970s, psycholinguistic studies into the processing of words in the brain have progressed to the point where some firmer conclusions can be drawn, especially about the role of morphology in processing complex words in the mental lexicon.

This chapter works from the very recent but well attested claim that the brain's neurobiological mechanisms will alter as a result of different social environments and discursive practices. The brain is physically shaped by the experiences that its owner has, especially by the narratives, the stories, and the other discursive events that people participate in. In this chapter, I assemble evidence suggesting that the physical arrangement of the mental lexicon itself adapts in this way too, as the brain changes in response to different language experiences, especially the words and other signs that it encounters. Since differences in sociocultural positioning produce very different language experiences, then discursive practices encountered over a lifetime will arrange different people's mental lexicons very differently, so that they come to process words very differently as well.

The state-of-the-art review attempted in this chapter is very relevant to my theme, since it is differences in morphology that are basic to the differences that exist between the two main word types in English, the G-L and the Anglo-Saxon. Again the chapter also argues that the various ways in which different languages process morphology in the brain, strongly suggest that exposure to discourses of different types lays down different word processing mechanisms in the brain. A related factor of great importance in sustaining the lexical bar, is the role that the morphological and semantic transparency of words plays in facilitating word processing, since for most speakers of English, specialist G-L words have lost their transparency.

Later sections in this chapter explore the role of semantic factors in word processing. They suggest how language experience and language awareness can position language users in ways that improve their readiness to put words to work, along with the rules of use that are their meanings.

## Psycholinguistics and Discursive Psychology

Discursive psychology is also very concerned with discourse and the brain. In particular, it asks how discursive practices and encounters with language change the brain. For people interested in improving the human condition, learning about this basic question also allows us to think about how the brain changes discursive practices, including the social and cultural conditions that those practices reinforce, and how the cycle of discursive practices reproduces itself in societies, cultures, and other human groups.

Everyone's brain is a repository of meanings accumulated throughout life; it provides the physical medium in which mental content is realized (Gillett, 1992). In this respect "it is no different than the neuromuscular system, which is 'shaped' by learning to play tennis and is thereby rendered available as the appropriate instrument for the minded agent to play a match with" (Harré & Gillett, 1994: 81). When people select meanings for use, in responding to events in the world around them, they draw on rules that are shaped by the many discursive practices that they have experienced.

Discursive practices, and the rules they create, are very similar within the language games of similar sociocultural communities. But they differ across different communities. These degrees of sameness and difference lead to diversity in human behaviour while also producing much commonality within groups. The vocabulary of a language is the key vehicle for laying down these discursively-created rules. "In fact, the role of words in forming and refining our thoughts is becoming increasingly clear from theoretical, clinical, and experimental work in cognitive psychology" (Harré & Gillett, 1994: 82).

Psycholinguistics differs from discursive psychology in the same way as other branches of experimental psychology differ from it. Psycholinguists look for invariants in the way language is organized in the brain. They work from the belief that human mental processes are much the same for everyone and that the way to understand these invariant processes is by experimentation and induction. But as this chapter argues, the very important evidence that psycholinguists have turned up about morphology and the mental lexicon, now tends to argue against the basic belief that they operate from. Instead the evidence strongly suggests that apart from a few broadly similar patterns that apply to everyone, the arrangement of the mental lexicon is highly idiosyncratic. In other words, that arrangement depends on the lexico-semantic positioning and the language experience that any given individual receives as a result of the discursive relations in which he or she is placed.

## Seminal Studies of Morphology and the Mental Lexicon

In *The Lexical Bar*, I examined the rapidly expanding research that looks at the relationship between word structuring patterns and verbal storage systems in the brain: the link between morphology and the mental lexicon. As Sandra (1994) notes, the numbers of polymorphemic words in many languages is a striking fact, matched by the fact that language users coin and understand morphologically complex words without much difficulty. This point raises the profile of morphology in understanding word use: Morphology clearly serves an important purpose in human communication.

### *The Work of Bruner, Forster, and Taft*

Most of the research examining morphological processing in word recognition arose from a non-linguistic background. Well before the stress fell on morphology, Bruner and Postman's early series of studies, in the late 1940s, had looked at variations in word reaction times according to different evaluative characteristics of words. That work reported significant differences in reaction times between words of several different evaluative types (Bruner, 1983); this offered a clear demonstration that word recognition times require semantic explanations. Elsewhere, prior to 1975, the issue of word access and especially the use of the lexical decision task (see below), mainly looked at various questions about phonological recoding, word frequency, and word associations, bypassing semantic issues. The morphological work reviewed in this chapter grew out of this cognitive literature. It simply asked whether the complex morphological structure of a word plays a role in lexical access.

Forster's search model of lexical access was the first prominent account of lexical processing. His work with Taft (1975) remains the source theory for all of the later work. Sandra (1994) describes it as 'seminal' in establishing the study of morphology as an independent line of research in psycholinguistics. Later evidence favouring a more interactive framework for understanding word processing in the brain, has led to a decline in support for the 'search' model. But Forster's model is still useful for understanding later work in the area, and because all later research derives from that model.

Forster divided the mental lexicon into an input system and a separate storage of all the 'information' about every word. This model of the lexicon was more like a library reference system than a dictionary. A master file of lexical entries was consulted through an ordered search of an access file: an orthographic access file dealing with the spelling and shape of words, for decoding written messages; and a phonological access file dealing with the sounds of words, for decoding aural messages. There was also a semantic file, but this was only vestigial and for production purposes only. Each piece of word information in the access file, when contacted, indicated the address of a corresponding word entry in the master file. The analogy was with the books of a library: These were the word entries in the master file; the library's catalogues were access files; and the catalogue reference numbers guided the search.

## The Absence of Semantic Factors

In *The Lexical Bar*, in 1985, I argued that the relevant component missing from the search model was some strong recognition of word meanings as factors in word processing, especially recognition of semantic transparency and the linguistic motivation of words more generally. Bruner & Postman's early studies certainly pointed in that direction. Forster admitted a bias in his studies towards mechanisms of retrieval, rather than towards the information itself that was being retrieved (Taft, personal note). His lack of concern with meaning and linguistic context was common in this early psycholinguistic literature which argued that the interesting lexicosemantic questions must be deferred until more is known about the mechanisms and about access efficiency itself. In this and other respects, Taft and Forster were partners in the experimental psychology world view, already alluded to.

But if we are to allow semantic factors to play a role in processing, either at the pre-access level considered by Taft and Forster or at other levels, then clearly the way that an individual's brain is organized lexico-semantically will depend on the life experiences that the individual has received: the sociocultural position in which the range of human discourses has placed that person. So factors to do with social background, cultural background, type of experience with a given language, language awareness, and depth and breadth of immersion in cultural meaning systems generally, will all combine to shape brain function. My review of research on the arrangement of the mental lexicon has these kinds of points as its subtext.

In fact, the history of research in these areas since the mid-1980s, has been one of conceding a greater role to semantic factors in lexical access itself. But how could word entries be stored semantically?

A logical analysis suggests that words in the brain could conceivably be stored ready for activation and according to their semantic attributes, in a number of possible ways: first, word class (nouns, verbs etc.) is one possible set of storage categories. Second, meaning relations within semantic fields of many different kinds, is another. Third, the different meanings of single 'semantemes', could provide another abstract relationship for storage purposes. Fourth, within their word classes, words could also be stored in 'paradigmatic' fields, depending on their shared semantic features (Aitchison, 1987). Fifth, they could be stored too according to their 'syntagmatic' relations (Taylor, 1990). Chapter 2 describes these technical categories: semantemes; and syntagmatic and paradigmatic fields - all borrowed from field theory.

The question of where meaning appears exactly as a functional force in the mental lexicon, seems very important in a book like this that explores meaning systems. Although cognitive representations in the brain may be functionally disassociated from language (Allport, 1983), many questions still arise about the role of meaning in activating word entries themselves. For example, how much does meaning affect efficiency of access itself? Do phonosemantic and morphosemantic features of words help us locate and use them? My review of morphological studies below suggests that aspects of words, linked to the strength of their 'motivation' or their 'conventionality', provide distinct cues that affect word recognition. These cues relate to the sound or form of words, including their 'embedded morphemes'. I also argue that language experience and acquired language awareness itself, are key variable factors that produce individual and group differences in processing words in the brain.

### Orthographic Processing: Reading and Writing

As late as 1979 a review of research in English morphology concluded that "work has scarcely begun on the problem of the 'psychological reality of the morpheme', and a great deal of thoughtful analysis is still required, even on the data already available" (Derwing and Baker, 1979, p. 223). This section interprets work from 1979, when the pace of analysis quickened. Much of this work on the morphographic approach to lexical access has examined the act of receiving messages in print, rather than sending original messages in speech or writing. But significant reciprocity is likely to exist, on one plane between the two processes of receiving and sending messages, and on another plane between phonological and orthographic processing.

Taft (1985) concludes that words are recognized in print on the basis of their orthographic representation and not on the basis of any rule-generated phonological representation. Phonological recoding may come into play when the visual information is inadequate to access a lexical entry, however it seems that contact is established mainly through a word's orthographic features. What is the nature of these orthographic features? What parts of the word in print help in its processing?

### The Lexical Decision Task

A regular logic of inquiry in these studies is the lexical decision task. Using this lexical decision task, a word's frequency in the language is linked with retrieval time by subjects in milliseconds. Sometimes too the frequency of a word's stem is used. This word 'stem' in relevant psycholinguistic research, refers to that part of a word that remains after all affixes have been removed. This differs from the word's use in linguistics (Bauer, 1983).

In the lexical decision task, subjects press a response key if the stimulus item is a word or not. Latency of response to a word is seen to reflect time taken to activate that word in the mental lexicon and to decide that the activated entry is the correct one. Latency of response to non-words reflects time taken to decide that there are no entries that match the stimulus item.

In this kind of research, words and nonwords are presented out of context, as single words. For example, Taft (1979) showed that Latinate words like REPROACH, with a high-frequency stem (-PROACH as in APPROACH) were recognized faster than words like DISSUADE which have a lower frequency stem (-SUADE as also in PERSUADE), although the actual words presented are matched in frequency. Burani et al. (1984) report a similar result for Italian words. In these studies, word 'frequency' in the language is based on a computational analysis of frequency in written language (in Taft's case: Kucera and Francis, 1967). From the computed word frequencies, stem frequencies can be determined. For example, the frequency of the stem -PROACH is higher than -SUADE because -PROACH as a stem occurs in words which have a combined higher frequency than do words in which -SUADE appears.

One problem in judging the reliability of the lexical decision task is that it measures words in isolation from a context which displays the conventions for their use. Does this artificial kind of reaction-time test, really reflect usage in context? It may do in fact. Treiman, Freyd & Baron (1983) examine lexical processing in the reading of sentences. They conclude that effects attributed to spelling-sound rule use found in lexical decision tasks with single words, also appear in sentence-reading tasks, and that this spelling-sound factor, along with phonological recoding, is important even for fluent readers.

*The Interactive Activation Model: Prefixed Words and Word Stems*

In his early work, Taft discarded letters and letter groupings as possible access codes. He settled on a code based mainly on the word's stem morpheme. His main interest was words with bound stems (i.e. stems that are not words in their own right). In English, these words with bound stems are usually prefixed G-L words. The early evidence supported the view that the (first) stem of a word with two or more morphemes is its access code, and any prefix (or inflected suffix) is 'stripped off' prior to coding (Taft and Forster, 1975; Stanners Neiser & Painton, 1979; Taft, Hambly & Kinoshita, 1986). For example, the seven Latinate words IMPRESS, COMPRESS, REPRESS, OPPRESS, SUPPRESS, EXPRESS, DEPRESS will all have the same access code -PRESS.

The most important finding from Taft & Forster (1975) came from reactions to non-words compared with reactions to real bound stems (i.e. not words in their own right: e.g. -PROACH and -SUADE). Real stems took longer to classify as non-words, suggesting that bound stems have separate lexical entries which delays the process of making a non-word reaction to a real stem item. Following later criticism made of the materials used in the 1975 study, Taft (1994) repeated the experiment with better controlled stimuli. His results upheld the conclusions of the original study.

Early evidence questioned the view that affixed words are also stored in the access file in their whole word forms (Stanners *et al.*, 1979), although it was Taft's conclusion that until a person becomes aware of a word's morphological structure through development, then it is logical to conclude that the affixed word is stored as a whole word. While Taft (1991) still prefers to drop the idea that the whole word routinely has an entry of its own, later work tends to strengthen the view that words are not only stored by their stems (Bergman, Hudson & Eling, 1988) but also as whole word entries (Sandra, 1994). This view, that morphologically complex words have several entries, including their stems, their affixes, and their graphemes, forms the basis for the 'interactive-activation model'.

In this model of the mental lexicon, activation level is mainly determined by the degree of overlap between the several input entries and the target word. The better and more complete the match between the various inputs, the higher the level of activation. This model accounts for the results of previous research on bound stem words and non-words, on stem frequency, on pseudoprefixed words, and on non-prefixed stem non-words. These same results had also been used to support the 'search' model.

For the purposes of my discussion here at least, the interactive-activation model seems consistent with a very similar model, called the 'augmented addressed morphology' model (the AAM). The 'augmented' part of the model's name indicates that it includes a procedure for accessing novel words (Caramazza et al., 1988; Laudanna et al 1994). In this AAM, the stem and the whole word are both represented, and there is a race in activation to see which will be first in facilitating access to the word, with the winner determined according to the intensity of past experience of the stem or the whole word. Again in the AAM, most lexical entries are morphologically decomposed (Burani & Laudanna, 1992).

Returning to the multi-level interactive-activation model, here a range of different sub-word segments is at work in word processing, including the whole word itself. One of these levels contains morphemic units, if the word has two or more morphemes. This change in emphasis from the 'search' model came about as problems appeared in that earlier model. For example, some studies gave conflicting evidence about stem-frequency effects (Bradley, 1979; Andrews, 1986). Also, an increased role for semantic factors in processing argued against the semantic-free access system that Taft and Forster were advancing (Sandra, 1990; Marslen-Wilson et al., 1994), depending on the localization of the semantic effects. As well, the excessively serial nature of the search process seemed too rigid for a process like word recognition. Finally the need for an independent 'prefix store' in the 'search' model was a complication, since what counts as a prefix is not easily decided, especially by readers assimilating large numbers of words. Taft (1994) has now followed many other researchers towards favouring the interactive-activation model.

In this model, there is no formal prefix stripping, but prefixes still provide independent activation units (McClelland & Rumelhart, 1981; McClelland, 1987). The interactive-activation model also allows phonology to play a role in processing words appearing in print. Associated with each orthographic node is a set of phonological nodes related to the pronunciation of words and their parts. What sequence does the activation process follow in this model?

At the top of the process, concept units provide the meeting point between the representation of a word's form and its meaning. "When activated through the lower level units, these units make available the semantic characteristics of the word" (Taft, 1994 p. 280). Different morpheme units may or may not cue concept units. So activation enters the lexicon at grapheme level and proceeds up to the concept level, "though during this process increased activation at higher levels can feed back down to enhance the activation of promising lower level units" (280). Frequency of word or of morpheme use is a factor in this model, since pathways that are used more often will lead to stronger activation in the unit to which they lead. So a unit for a high-frequency word gets more stimulation than a low-frequency word unit.

In this model, the lexical decision response-time depends on how much activation occurs at whole word level. On reading a word, many variations in activation pathway are possible. For example, Taft (1992) reports studies showing that the body of the word is an important unit of lexical processing. This is usually the vowel of a word's first syllable plus its terminal consonants. For example, in processing the word INVENT, the body -VENT will activate INVENT, -VENT and any other cognate G-L words (CONVENT, PREVENT etc.). At the same time, the graphemes I and N activate IN- at morpheme level, raising the activation of INVENT above its competing cognates. Like many prefixes when used by many people, IN- may have direct semantic impact at the concept level, since it can convey a vague sense of 'inwardness'. But the morpheme -VENT is rarely transparent in this way for readers. The words that contain it have no motivated meaning for most people that comes from -VENT on its own, although it can still have a motivated meaning for some people, deriving from its origin in Latin (see below).

*The Interactive Activation Model: Suffixed Words and the Priming Effect*

Suffixed words are studied using lexical decision times with non-word stems, pseudo-suffixed words, and suffixed nonwords. Researchers manipulate the frequency of the stems of suffixed words, and measure the facilitation gained by 'priming' a suffixed word with its stem. Priming is also used with other types of words. For example, response times to HAPPY improve when it is primed with UNHAPPY (Stanners, Neisor & Painton, 1979). Response times usually improve when words are primed with morphologically related words in this way (see below). Using the interactive-activation model, Taft (1994) explains the priming effect as follows: The lingering activation of a node provides an advantage over other nodes not recently activated. But since these facilitatory effects often seem to linger beyond the time expected by a simple maintenance of activation, other factors seem to be at work, as well as the morphological.

Inflected suffixed whole words may not be represented at all in the mental lexicon (e.g. WALKS, WALKING, WALKED) if their inflections are regular. If this is the case, it might reduce memory load considerably in some languages; although there is no evidence to suggest that 'memory economy' is a necessary factor in how the mental lexicon works, since human brain capacity is vast. But perhaps only the stem form appears (WALK), while inflected information about the word class of the stem is activated in some other way. This may be relevant to processing in a language like Turkish, with its millions of inflected forms. These would not all be separately represented in the lexicon, although a Turkish speaker's frequent exposure to some of the inflected forms might lead to separate entries. Every experience of a word, whether inflected or not, increases its memory trace (Sandra, 1994), so if an inflected form of a word is used often enough, it may come to be re-presented as a separate word in the mental lexicon along with its stem form.

The evidence for a stem representation of suffixed derived words is not as strong as the evidence for a stem representation of prefixed words. This suggests that derivational suffixes are not stripped off in all cases (e.g. the -ION from ATTENTION). Sandra (1994) suggests that the same mode of representation may not apply to all derived words, whether suffixed or prefixed. For example, a good case can be made that Anglo-Saxon words in -NESS, like HAPPINESS have no representation separate from their stem, but that Latinate words in -ITY must have separate representation, since adding that suffix changes the pronunciation or the phonological representation of the word (e.g. AUTHOR and AUTHORITY).

## Phonological Processing: Speaking and Listening

Less work has been done on phonological processing. Most of that has looked at aural word recognition, not word production in speech. The emphasis seems to be on studies of components in speech processing that match patterns appearing in the acoustic input against patterns stored in the mental lexicon (Altmann & Shillcock, 1994).

Most of the reading studies that I already reviewed above, ask subjects to speak by giving a name to the visually presented words. But Marslen-Wilson et al. caution that "what holds for the access of lexical representations of written words may not hold for access from the speech signal (and vice versa)" (1994 p. 4). Yet, as I have suggested, even written words may eventually contact a phonological representation in the access process, since for much of the time we hear language as we read it, and beginning readers hear it all of the time. Obviously too some kind of interaction between the sound and the shape of words, even in orthographic processing, is implied by the interactive-activation model.

### *Phonological Processing in Reading*

Early studies by Lima and Pollatsek (1983) suggest that syllabic units defined orthographically as well as syllabic units defined phonologically, may be involved in lexical access. Some partial confounding at least of sound and orthography is clearly at work in the four systems: reading, writing, speaking and listening. So language users who have a broad mastery of all the systems are probably better prepared to access their mental lexicon through any individual mode than those who are not. But does the sound of a morpheme affect its processing, or only the sound of a whole word?

At whole word level, phonological factors are clearly important for recognition, since we pronounce many G-L words differently as whole words than as separate morphemes (e.g. ASCERTAIN and CERTAIN). Taft (1994) concludes that phonology is a factor at morpheme level in visual word recognition, but only for prefix units. But the role of phonology seems even less clearly definable if we reduce it to linguistic terms: regular phonological alternations may not cause problems in lexical access because the underlying phoneme has no value on the feature dimension involved in the alternation (Lahiri & Marslen-Wilson, in Sandra, 1994 p. 234).

In other words, the mental lexicon can sometimes register two different sound units as if they were the same sound. This may relate to the ability that most listeners have to process words spoken in a dialect slightly different from their own. For instance, I have found that processing words in a written text, spelled according to the sounds of a very different dialect of English, is difficult for me without sounding out the words first. For me, the strange orthography can get in the way of word recognition and meaning, but the sound exposes the words and their meanings, even if the sound is rather different from what my dialect would predict.

But there may be important differences from word type to word type, not to mention differences from speaker to speaker. In studying recoding in visual word recognition, Seidenberg (1985) finds low-frequency words are accessed phonologically while access to high-frequency words depends on their orthographic representation. Also speech errors occur more often with low-frequency regularly inflected words than with high-frequency ones (Stemberger & MacWhinney, 1986). This suggests that high-frequency inflected forms may be separately stored as whole words ready for prompt access. A corollary of these two results suggests that there are great differences from person to person in the mental lexicon, since exposure to the words of a language (word frequency) is a function of the range of discursive practices a person contracts. Word frequency for individuals cannot be decided finally, or even with much accuracy, by reference to frequency counts based only on written language texts.

*Phonological Processing of Morphologically Complex Spoken Words*

Most researchers agree that aural lexical access occurs in two separate stages: First, some initial part of the signal is used to activate a broad cohort of candidate words. Then the second stage consists of cohort reduction (Dupoux, 1994). Again the most interesting question is whether the sound of a morpheme affects its processing, or only the sound of a whole word.

From their priming studies of derived words and suffixed derived words, Tyler et al. (1994) and Marslen-Wilson et al. (1994) propose that the type of morphological relation that links a prime and a target word affects whether or not priming is obtained. They report that stem-pairs prime each other strongly when they are semantically related, but not when the semantic relationship between them is synchronically opaque. Even prime and target words that are morphologically related do not prime one another reliably if there is no semantic transparency (e.g. SUCCEED and PROCEED). The reason for this is that the listener does not mentally represent words as sharing the same stem, and so as morphologically related, unless there are semantic reasons for doing so. This seems to be a straightforward developmental point, linked to language experience and explicit language awareness.

In the same sets of studies, derived suffixed words do not prime one another, even when semantically related and when sharing the same stem. Hearing a semantically transparent suffixed word like GOVERNMENT, first activates its stem GOVERN-. But then it also inhibits activation of other related words like GOVERNOR by suppressing their suffixes when the suffix -MENT is heard. So hearing a suffix temporarily inhibits combination of the stem with all other suffixes. The stem cannot be simultaneously interpreted as two different words, with different meanings and syntactic properties. This suggests that semantically transparent and morphologically complex suffixed words are represented in decomposed morphemic form, with the same stem shared by a number of related words. Once again, hearers must be aware that words are semantically transparent for them to be stored in this way.

The processing of prefixed spoken words seems to proceed without any recourse to prefix-stripping, on the evidence of studies using the lexical decision task. Both prefixed and non-prefixed words seem to be recognized aurally in much the same way: "by continuously mapping the sensory input onto representations of lexical form and identifying the word at the point at which it becomes unique, relative to its word initial cohort" (Tyler et al., 1988 p. 379). In other words, listeners will identify prefixed words like REMIND or MISCOUNT at the point at which they diverge from all other competing words in a person's mental lexicon, like REMARK or MISCONDUCT. The same researchers also note the vital effect of individual differences between speakers and contexts, on the listing of words in the mental lexicon:

> The specific realization of a word-form will vary radically as a function of differences in speakers, in speech rate, and in the phonological environment in which the item occurs. The representation in the recognition lexicon must abstract away from these sources of variation. It is an urgent question for the study of spoken word-recognition in general to determine just what the nature of this abstract representation might be (p. 379).

In other experiments, Marslen-Wilson et al. (1994) also look at prefixed words, but using a priming task. They borrow the same criteria from their studies of suffixed words. Again semantic transparency has a strong effect. Word pairs like DISOBEY/OBEY prime one another, but pairs like RELEASE/LEASE do not. But even two different derived prefixed words, sharing the same stem, prime each other if they are semantically transparent (e.g. INPUT and OUTPUT). In this respect, prefixed words seem to be different from suffixed words in their processing. This happens probably because the fact that they are different words, is immediately available to the listener on hearing the prefix at word onset: They are not competitors for the same stem in the activation process. This suggests that semantically transparent and morphologically complex prefixed words are also represented in decomposed morphemic form, with the same stem shared by a number of related words.

But again, hearers must be aware that words are semantically transparent for them to be stored in this way.

Marslen-Wilson et al. regard earlier studies that make no allowance for matters of semantic complexity, as questionable. But their own conclusion, underlining the idiosyncratic nature of word interpretation, seems important both for past and for future studies in this area. They ask, what is the basic unit in which the mental lexicon is organized?

> Our answer, for derivational forms in English, is clearly the morpheme. This should be understood, however, as a cognitive, or psycholinguistic concept of the morpheme, developmentally definable for each listener in terms of its synchronic semantic interpretability . . . [This claim] is broadly consistent with a range of psycholinguistic research stretching back over two decades (1994 p. 31).

### Evidence from Languages other than English

Marslen-Wilson et al. (1994) also urge caution in mixing the evidence coming from research in different languages. For them, this evidence can only be interpreted metaphorically, at best, in a theory of English morphology:

> No doubt there are universal properties of morphological representation and access in the mental lexicon, but to find out what they are we have to begin by constructing systematic accounts of individual languages. Crucially what we cannot do is investigate fragments of the morphological system in a number of different languages and then hope to combine the results into a single language-independent theory of morphological processing and representation (1994, p. 4).

There is a growing body of evidence in favour of language specificity in certain areas of language processing, although in principle all the variation can be interpreted within some sort of language universal framework (Cutler, 1994). An important insight for my discussion also comes from Cutler, when she describes language-specific processing as "a property of the listener, not of the input being presented to the system" (p. 118). What does this mean for language processing in general, and morphological processing in particular?

Cutler reports studies of fluent French-English bilinguals, some dominant in one or the other language. These studies show that response patterns by English-dominant listeners, when segmenting verbal input, are stress-based, but French dominant listeners produce a syllabic response pattern. Speakers of Japanese have yet another listening response pattern, which no doubt matches a speech production pattern that is culturally specific. In doing research among the Sámi peoples of Arctic Norway (Corson, 1995c), I observed Sámi speech patterns in their use of Norwegian that are markedly different from those of other Norwegians. These speech patterns appear even when the Sámi speakers are fully bilingual. In the past, other Norwegians have stigmatized these Sámi-specific patterns, but they continue as 'a property' of the Sámi speaker and the Sámi listener.

Again, insights from discursive psychology and the sociology of language would urge extreme caution in comparing evidence, not just from separate languages but even evidence from within languages, taken from people who are socioculturally different in important ways, as the Sámi and other Norwegians are. But if the brain's structures and processes are shaped by the discourses we encounter, as they seem to be, what can we really say about the way the mental lexicon processes words across languages? Perhaps not as much as the early psycholinguistic research might lead us to expect. Although the processing of visual material operates in a left to right manner in those languages that are written left to right, evidence exists that even here a serial process of decomposition from left to right is not mandatory (Beauvillain, 1994). Nevertheless some important, but far from identical role for morphology in word processing is still reported across very different languages and it carries insights relevant to the differences between G-L and Anglo-Saxon word morphology.

Zhou & Marslen-Wilson (1994) study the mental lexicon in Chinese, a language whose vocabulary, like Anglo-Saxon, is dominated by a massive number of compound or monomorphemic words. Indeed compounding is the common way of creating new words in Chinese. A limited number of morphemes (around 6000) is used repeatedly in the compounding process. The research on the mental lexicon in Chinese indicates that the access process is morphological. While disyllabic compound words are represented as wholes in the mental lexicon, their morphological structure is also represented at the word and the morpheme levels, in this way giving greater word motivation to fluent Chinese users because of that dual representation.

Holmes & O'Regan (1992) cite strong evidence to confirm that morphological principles are central to word processing across several European languages. Their own research supports the effect of morphological structure on the recognition of low-frequency words, but it also allows that high-frequency complex words may be stored independently from the family of words stored under their stem. Where a language like Italian makes extensive use of conjugational suffixes, its stem representations are linked to the set of conjugation-appropriate affixes (Caramazza et al., 1988). But evidence from a much more highly inflected language like Serbo-Croatian does not support the idea of a decomposition procedure for words that are regularly inflected  (Lukatela et al., 1980). Also studies of Finnish, another highly inflected language, reveal morphological decomposition at work on inflected nouns, but not on derived nouns (Niemi, Laine & Tuominen, 1994). As a result, the researchers conclude that none of the models so far proposed in the literature would explain all aspects of their findings for Finnish.

Bergman, Hudson & Eling (1988) in the Netherlands use the lexical decision task to examine prefixed and suffixed nouns, and especially the role of the stem. Dutch university students process morphologically complex Latinate words in Dutch much more slowly than morphologically complex Germanic-Dutch words of the same frequency.  They conclude that word origin is compounded with some other factor, such as transparency of morphological structure. This factor advantages Germanic words in Dutch, allowing them to be decomposed quickly. At the same time, because the

Latinate words have stems and affixes that are less frequent and more conventional in meaning, they are decomposed with greater difficulty.

Chapters 2 and 4 linked this conclusion from Dutch with the situation for many speakers of English, who have a highly Anglo-Saxon (Germanic) vocabulary and for whom Latinate words are not motivated in meaning either. Also working with Dutch words, Zwitserlood (1994) studies the role of semantic transparency in the processing and representation of compound words. Using priming experiments, she reports that semantically transparent or partially transparent pairs of words prime one another. But at the same time, opaque compounds prime no better than monomorphemic words that accidentally contain the same morphemes in the language (e.g. CAR and CARPET). Morphological motivation has a clear role in processing.

Other studies from the Netherlands lend strong support to the view that processing is largely stem organized. Looking at the aural decoding of verbs in Dutch, these studies conclude that only a stem-organized lexicon would explain their results (Jarvella & Meijers, 1983). For prefixed words, the stem seems to give the best information for processing a word. But research by Schreuder & Baayen (in Sandra, 1994) suggests that prefix-stripping in Dutch and English would require up to eight times more search steps than a model in which words with the same prefixes are stored together.

Support for the inefficiency of prefix-stripping as a process, also comes from Laudanna et al. (1994) who look at Italian vocabulary. They agree that prefixes may be represented as units of access in the mental lexicon. But they also conclude that not all prefixes are represented in this way; and that the likelihood of the separate storage of a prefix is affected by the ratio of the number of words with that real prefix over the number of words with the same pseudoprefix (i.e. the same letters, but not a real prefix). Sandra summarizes these views by saying that, if Taft's reasoning is correct, reliance on prefix-stripping depends on the efficiency it guarantees. Some prefixes are more helpful than others. I would add that some prefixes are more helpful to some language users than are other prefixes, and that having this advantage is a matter of experience and language awareness: discursive practices that lay down the patterns in the brain ready for later use and ease of access.

Italian words, with few exceptions, have suffixed inflections, and so most Italian vocabulary is morphologically complex. But the bare uninflected root of Italian words never corresponds to an actual word. This is a major difference between Italian and English. Yet the root in Italian still seems to be the unit of representation shared by morphologically related inflected words (Burani & Laudanna, 1992).

In studies of French word processing, there is also conflicting evidence. Some studies conclude that morphological decomposition is not routinely undertaken (Cole, Beauvillain & Segui, 1989). Others provide support for the relevance of the stem in reading both types of affixed words, even when they have only 5 or 6 letters (Beauvillain, 1994). Some conclude that low-frequency prefixed and suffixed words seem to be decomposed for analysis and that lexical access takes place via the stem (Holmes & O'Regan, 1992; Segui & Zubizaretta, 1985).

Psycholinguistic researchers explain these many differences in word processing across languages, by pointing to the different distribution of prefixes, suffixes and other elements that exist in different languages, rather than by seeing them as 'properties of the listener' or of the speaker. Certainly linguistic differences between languages would produce different processing patterns. But I believe that studies that made reference to the sociocultural provenance, the lexico-semantic positioning, and the language awareness of the subjects used in the experiments, would be helpful in explaining many differences in results. Perhaps they would explain the most important differences.

Most of the subjects used in the experiments described in this chapter, are university students who would be very different from other social fractions in their lexico-semantic experience. While there will be similarities among all users of a single language in their processing of vocabulary, and also among users of all languages in their processing of language in general, discursive practices encountered over a lifetime will arrange different people's mental lexicons very differently, so that they process words very differently as well.

## Semantic Factors in Word Processing

As indicated at various points in my discussion so far, evidence is growing to confirm that semantic factors influence word processing in very important ways. The interactive-activation model itself is very flexible about incorporating all kinds of semantic detail, especially possibilities to do with semantic transparency and motivation generally. Perhaps there are always semantic factors at work in the lingering activation of nodes over extended periods that priming studies report (see above). Clearly words that are good primes for other words are semantically related to them in some way. On those occasions when a subject perceives both the morphological and the semantic connection between the prime and the target word, then this would explain in semantic terms the extended activation effect noted in studies. This facility becomes quite directly a property of the language user, with words in the mind themselves only vehicles for activating that property.

Taft (1994) argues that whether a stem is used as an access code for a whole word or not, depends on semantic factors. Whole word transparency or opaqueness is now seen as a much more important factor linking word and concept representations (Sandra, 1990; Marslen-Wilson et al., 1994; Zwitserlood, 1994). Indeed many studies now suggest that morphologically related words will only be linked in the mental lexicon if there is a transparent semantic relationship between a derived word and its free stem (Holmes & O'Regan, 1992; Marslen-Wilson et al., 1994). I should add, that transparency here once again should properly be seen as a property of the word user, whether as listener, reader, speaker or writer. If the semantic relationship between two words appears opaque to a word user, as do the relationships between many G-L words for most word users, there is no facilitatory effect:

> From the point of view of structural decomposition in the lexicon, words like APARTMENT or DISCOVER, despite their morphological decomposability on linguistic, etymological, and phonological grounds [into APART and COVER], appear to be represented in the same way as words like ELBOW or CELERY (Marslen-Wilson et al., 1994 p. 27).

In fact, on the basis of their six experiments, Marslen-Wilson et al. do argue that the structure of the adult lexicon reflects the experience that individuals have had with the language as they learn it. Since most users of English have little or no access to the etymology of words, they will only mentally represent them as morphologically complex if this gives some semantic and memory advantage. The Latinate words DEPARTMENT and PRINCIPAL are examples. These are not usually analyzed into their stems and suffixes when they are first acquired as new words by people, because the stems (DEPART- and PRINC[E]-) are no longer semantically relevant to the whole words. As a result, the whole words are mentally represented, and they are accessed directly during processing, not via their stems.

Prefixes also carry greater activation potential for people who see a transparent meaning in them, although their value in activating words is still probably minimal when they appear as prefixes on a great many words. When the prefix is a very common one and has little activation potential, the stem plays the major role in accessing the concept word. Again Taft (1994) uses the word INVENT as an example: The stem -VENT might be more transparent for users of the language familiar with its Latin origin in the Latin verb 'to come'. This could increase activation for all its derivations (e.g. INVENT, PREVENT, CONVENT, VENTURE, ADVENT etc.), while the IN-prefix might not add much meaning in most uses.

Prefixes are much more informative and helpful in accessing a word when they are less common (e.g. the G-L POLY- or CIRCUM-). Taft suggests that "the amount of overlap between the meaning associated with a prefix and that associated with the word in which it occurs, is also likely to play a role in determining morphological structure" (1994 p. 284). In earlier studies, Smith & Sterling (1982) had suggested that some sort of 'pre-lexical parser' is at work to allow more efficient lexical access by identifying potentially significant units. They found that there is an inevitable slowing down in the processing of affixed and even pseudo-affixed words relative to other words. Smith and Sterling present tables recording their studies of words beginning with the Latinate prefixes PRE- and IM-. These tables suggest that the longer the word in general, the more clearly its meaning is located in its structure: the more available its meaning is through a prior understanding of the sense of its affixes and stem.

All this is not to say that semantic transparency is routinely represented in the mental lexicon. Rather, only those words that carry that sort of information for individual language users will be motivated in this way. By being aware of the information at the time of word acquisition, people then make their mental lexicons receptive to this sort of representation. So the brain will only become receptive to this sort of information when the language users are aware of the transparency of words when putting them into memory, and again when taking them out for use.

### Experience in Word Learning and Use: The Role of Language Awareness

Every experience of a word or of its stem, increases its memory trace and makes it more ready for activation. So exposure to words is a central factor in explaining the effects of the lexical bar. If a regularly inflected form of a complex word is used often enough, it may come to be represented as a separate word in the mental lexicon as well as in its stem and affix forms. These several entries provide much greater activation for its use. As mentioned in Chapter 2, the evidence strongly suggests that the brain's neurobiological mechanisms can alter as a result of different social environments and discursive practices (Harré & Gillett, 1994). No doubt the mental lexicon adapts in this way too, as the brain changes in response to language experience, and provides new and perhaps unique ways to process the words that it encounters and already stores.

Research on the acquisition of morphology points to the importance of developmental differences to do with language experience (Lo Duca, 1990; Tyler & Nagy, 1989). It confirms that the quality and the regularity of word experience allows children to treat words in their mental lexicon on the basis of idiosyncratic criteria derived from that experience, and not just on the basis of morphological rules that usually have many exceptions (Bertinetto, 1994). Relevant to age, Derwing & Baker (1979; 1986) report an increasing capacity for morpheme recognition and that younger children rely more on phonetic considerations than older children. But in general, adults consider both semantic and phonetic similarity in judging morphological relatedness. Derwing & Baker suggest that specific etymological instruction of some kind, received at school, might be a factor in this age effect. Elbro (1990), who confirms that a morphologically mediated route into the mental lexicon has explanatory power in the study of dyslexia, also recommends teaching morphological structure to dyslexic students as an aid in spelling and in reading.

Taft's broadly defined stem may have its best effect, as he suggests, with certain subjects, such as those with a more sophisticated knowledge of the language. He recommends teaching word relationships using the common component that a broadly defined stem provides, allowing them to be broken down into manageable chunks and their morphological relations to be made plain. This proposal is consistent with curriculum studies and evaluations reviewed towards the end of Chapter 2. Taft also sees a flexibility in his stem proposal: Plainly people who are unaware of the morphological relationships that exist between words, are unlikely to use a morphologically based access code. I would add that a morphologically based retrieval code would be of little use to these language users either.

Apart from in *The Lexical Bar*, little attention has been paid to the developmental aspect of morphology in the mental lexicon. But as Sandra agrees, the fact that morphemes occur in an identical or related form and meaning in words, can lead beginning language users to discover the existence of those morphemic units and to use them when encoding morphologically complex words in the mental lexicon. He says that "morphology could be a powerful device for facilitating the acquisition of polymorphemic vocabulary items and improving the retention of such items" to develop a mental lexicon representing this semantic information (1994, p. 261). There is other support for these ideas too.

Freyd and Baron (1982) studied the acquisition of morphologically complex words by adolescents in a nonsense language. They conclude that superior students are especially good at using derivational relations in learning new words:

> by discovering relations between members of a pair of parallel words, a child may begin to consider the members of the pair as derivationally related. This implies an ongoing change in the way words are stored . . . Such [a morphological] analysis might be useful for some language tasks and not for others. For example, it might facilitate retrieval of words, or it might make learning new words easier (p. 283).

They see two extremes in using morphological analysis: children learning their first words, and linguistic scholars with a depth of understanding who are capable of making a diachronic analysis.

Usually, in range of language experience, a second language learner is much closer to the scholar than to the child acquiring language for the first time. So the second language learner has much more language awareness to draw on, in learning and representing words. Indeed Sandra confirms from his own studies of Dutch students learning English vocabulary (1988; 1993) that many older learners spontaneously rely on morphological knowledge to learn new words. Interestingly they are often able to recall only the stems of words correctly, and sometimes only a word semantically related to the stem. Finding a motivation for the presence of the stem in a newly added derived word helps its learning. "Quite possibly" he says, "the effect hinges entirely on the subject's perception of the semantic relatedness between the novel word and its stem (in some cases also its suffix)" and "this is exactly what should be the case. The encoding takes place at the semantic level, where subjects perceive the salience of the properties encoded by the morphemes in the word" (1994 p. 262). This is an act of language awareness. I return to this topic in Chapter 9 when recommending changes for educational practice.

## Conclusion

As mentioned in Chapter 2, the evidence strongly suggests that the brain's neurobiological mechanisms can alter as a result of different social environments and discursive practices. No doubt the mental lexicon adapts in this way too, as the brain changes in response to language experience, and provides new and perhaps unique ways to process the words that it encounters. But psycholinguistic researchers do not explain differences in word processing, either across languages or within them, by pointing to the sociocultural positioning of speakers. Yet this would seem to help explain the great range of findings that are reported in this chapter. In other words, studies referring to the sociocultural provenance, positioning, and language awareness of subjects might explain many of the differences in results and perhaps all the important ones.

While there will be similarities among all users of a single language in their processing of its vocabulary, and also among users of all languages in their processing of language in general, discursive practices encountered over a lifetime will arrange different people's mental lexicons very differently, so that they process words very differently as well. Relevant to English words, the members of sociocultural and language groups who receive more frequent contact with the morphological and semantic features of specialist G-L words, will be very different from other people in their readiness to access this type of word. Not only will they be more familiar with the rules of use for these words, which is a major advantage, they will also have an advantage in physically activating the words in the mental lexicon.

Many studies now suggest that morphologically related words will only be linked in the mental lexicon if there is a transparent semantic relationship between them. If the semantic relationship between two words is opaque for a word user, there is no facilitatory effect. While this means that semantic transparency is not routinely represented in the mental lexicon for everyone, words that do carry that sort of information for a single language user will be motivated, in Ullmann's sense of the word. But people's verbal memories will only become receptive to this sort of motivation when the language user is consciously or perhaps subconsciously aware of a word's transparency, when putting it into memory and when taking it out. Language awareness, relevant to the specific word, seems a desirable acquisition for this purpose.

Specialist G-L words in English are opaque or conventional for most language users. They also have a very low-frequency of use in most people's everyday discourse. I link these two points with the conclusions to this chapter, when setting out the dimensions of the lexical bar in Chapter 8.

# 8

# Difficulty in Lexical Access: The Lexical Bar

What features do some words have that make them more 'difficult' than others? In Chapter 4, I used the phrase 'difficult in access' to refer to specialist words extracted by the G-L Instrument. Chapters 5 and 7 also mentioned features that can make these words 'difficult in access' relative to other words. This chapter looks more closely at some of the features that appear more often in specialist G-L words as a group, features that may make the words more difficult for some language users than for others. None of these features belongs solely to specialist G-L words, but they tend to exhibit these features much more than other words, and this tendency interferes with word learning and use.

In what follows, I am assuming that any attribute of a word that helps its access in the mental lexicon, so that it can be used to express or receive meaning, will reduce that word's difficulty. The discussion begins with the concrete-abstract dimension, but finds it lacking in precision. I explore the idea that words vary in their levels of 'imageability', and I link this idea with high and low levels of word frequency. Then I add conclusions from Chapter 7 about the role of morphological complexity and semantic opaqueness in G-L word difficulty, since, for most language users, most of the Anglo-Saxon section of the vocabulary is much easier to use because of its accessibility in the mental lexicon. The chapter summarizes the impact of all these factors on word learning and use, especially on use of the G-L vocabulary embedded in the high status meaning systems of the academic culture of literacy. It ends by spelling out what the lexical bar is.

## The Concrete - Abstract Continuum

It seems an easy matter to equate 'difficulty' with 'abstractness' but this is not very helpful here. There are many 'abstract' notions named by Anglo-Saxon words in English, yet the words themselves present no special difficulty, even when they are rather low in frequency (e.g. AFTERLIFE, UNDERSTANDING, UNDERWORLD).

The commonly used division of vocabulary into 'concrete' and 'abstract' allows some agreement on words that are more concrete than others, but 'abstract' remains ill-defined. At best, in early psychological studies of word difficulty, 'abstract' roughly equates with 'non-concrete' or 'unpicturable'. But more recent studies see this abstract dimension as much more inscrutable. There are many different levels of abstraction that head off in all directions, not just along the simple plane suggested by the 'picturability-unpicturability' dichotomy. 'Abstract' is hardly an absolute notion. There are different kinds of abstractness, some of which people may label as concrete, using their own criteria of abstractness: their own rules of use within language games.

More recent vocabulary studies in psychology have tried to isolate relevant attributes underlying the abstractness-concreteness continuum. The major psychological attribute is now thought to be 'imagery': the ease with which a word arouses sensory images.

## Low Imagery and Low Frequency

The so-called 'word frequency effect' is one of the most robust and regular findings in visual word recognition studies (Cole, Beauvillain & Segui, 1989). Here high-frequency words are more easily recognized than low-frequency ones. This is not surprising, since the link between the two variables, 'frequency in the language' and 'ease of recognition' seems almost tautological. Although the 'imagery value' of words is less studied, it is as robust a finding. Imagery value involves any sensory modality, not just visual imagery. A word might suggest sights, sounds, smells, strong emotions, other sensations, or all or none of these.

In psychology, the favoured method for determining a word's imagery level is to consult the views of a sample of language users who are asked to locate the word on an imagery differential scale. Early research correlated imagery rating with a number of other word variables, and these are clearly linked to difficulty in access. In spite of this early progress, Postman summarized the findings in this way: "it is far too early to take it for granted that the only important difference between concrete and abstract words is the ease of imaginal encoding" (1975, p. 323). But this summary anticipates conclusions in later research, strengthening the view that the imagery scale represents an attribute similar to the concrete-abstract continuum, but distinct from it.

Paivio et al. (1968) had examined 925 nouns, spread in their frequency of occurrence from common to uncommon. These nouns were rated on a seven-point 'low imagery-high imagery' scale. These researchers correlated their values on that scale with other variables: High imagery correlated with 'concreteness' at a level of .83; and it correlated at a level of .90 with 'meaningfulness' (defined as the mean number of written associations that could be made in 30 seconds). Elsewhere Paivio (1968) had also reported a high factor-analytic correlation between imagery and learning, using paired-associate stimulus-and-response learning. Later, studying imagery in 900 of the same nouns, Christian et al. (1978) concluded that the influence of rated imagery on free recall seems firmly established. They also found that word frequency is positively correlated with free recall at a level similar to the partial correlation of imagery with free recall.

Thorndyke (1975) showed that this attribute of imageability tends to be critical for the recallability of verbs in particular. Berrian et al. (1979) returned a similar finding using 328 adjectives. Thorndyke also identified the importance of imagery ratings as a predictor of comprehension: "high imagery verbs provided better targets for recall ('responses') than low imagery verbs in all cases" (p. 367). In fact, when the researchers controlled imagery levels, they found that the time it took subjects to comprehend vocabulary was not influenced at all by word 'conceptual complexity' (i.e. the structural complexity of the meaning of a word: the number of primitive meaning components or features and their inter-relations). But the same researchers made no reference to morphemic complexity, semantic transparency, or syntactic functions. Kintsch (1972) on the other hand, examined morphemic complexity and found that imagery effects remained, even when that type of complexity was controlled.

Although there is much evidence to suggest the critical importance of 'imageability' as a factor reducing difficulty in access, imagery level is certainly not the only factor. Christian et al. (1978) were baffled by unexplained variations in their study. They concluded that "some other property correlated with imagery is producing the effect and has yet to be identified" (p. 380). Similarly Kintsch (1972) noted the large and unexplained within-group differences. He also claimed that "there may be some as yet unsuspected other factors that deserve further investigation" (p. 64).

I conducted two studies (Corson, 1985) to measure the degree of co-variance that exists between the imagery level of English words and their etymological origin. Using the technique of 'systematic sampling', I randomly took 185 of Paivio's 925 nouns. Of these, 95 were specialist G-L words and 90 were non-G-L words. Coefficients of correlation between imagery rating and etymological origin were .67 and .57 over two mixed samples. These coefficients markedly increased when I removed two types of word from the non-G-L list: words rated as 'low in imagery', but whose transparent form would help their access (AFTERLIFE, UNDERWORLD); and non-G-L words rated as 'low in imagery', whose concrete meanings might help their access (KINE, BLUNDERBUSS). Clearly low imagery level is one feature that distinguishes G-L words, as a group, from other words. Similar studies to correlate low-frequency with G-L origin returned coefficients of .60 and .66, confirming other work (Nation, 1990) that suggests G-L words as a group tend to be much rarer than other words.

Let me bring two factors mentioned elsewhere back into the discussion: the much higher levels of 'formality' that Latinate words have, regardless of their frequency levels (Levin & Novak, 1991: see Chapter 4); and the regular location of G-L words in specialist meaning systems where their use can be compartmentalized by novice language users (Hsia, Chung & Wong, 1995: see Chapter 2). Taking these factors into account, specialist G-L words as a group become even less accessible than the research on word frequency suggests. Low frequency leads to greater inter-individual variation. Indeed for many people these words simply do not appear in day to day discourse with any regularity. So, since G-L words appear largely in formal contexts, in written material, and in specialist meaning systems, they will turn up even less often in everyday language that is removed from formal contexts and from the literate culture of education. It is clear why low imagery, low-frequency, and G-L origin are closely related factors in verbal recallability.

## Morphological Complexity

Kintsch (1972) discusses 'lexical complexity' and matches it against 'imagery'. He argues that many experiments studying imagery are confounded: a word like WISDOM might be hard to learn not because of the difficulty of forming an appropriate image, but because subjects are transforming it first into WISE. This suggestion anticipates later work already reported in Chapter 7 on accessing the mental lexicon. I return to this work in the next section.

Kintsch went on to control for imagery level, for 'meaningfulness', and for frequency (assessed by reference to Thorndike & Lorge, 1944). He found that simple words were indeed learned faster than 'lexically derived words' (words that can be lexically decomposed into a 'root' plus a transformation rule). However this was not the case with lexically complex words of very high-frequency: Words like LEADER or BANKER process like simple lexical entries. It would seem that in learning morphologically complex words of moderate to low-frequency, the effects of their lower frequency are compounded by their morphemic complexity. Elsewhere Freyd & Baron (1982) report that all their subjects had greater difficulty defining morphologically complex words that were matched in frequency with simple words (assessed by reference to Carroll et al. 1971).

So morphological complexity itself seems a contributing factor to lexical difficulty. But the matter is still not straightforward. Cutler (1983) summarizes a range of studies in concluding that morphological complexity does not make the process of word recognition itself more difficult. At the same time, she allows that many types of lexical complexity do lead to greater processing difficulties when the time to construct a representation of an entire sentence is measured. Clearly there is some connection between this kind of complexity and the process of putting words to use beyond the recognition stage. How might this feature hinder access to expressing or receiving meaning?

### The Role of Shape and Sound in Activating Words

In Chapter 2, I reviewed Ullmann's three types of word 'motivation' that lead to transparency. He concludes that between them the three types account for much of the vocabulary of English: "they include all onomatopoeic terms, derivatives, compounds and figurative expressions in the language. Only those words which are not motivated in this way can be put down as conventional [in meaning]" (1962, p. 92). Ullmann also proposes that "the practical test of motivation, as opposed to conventionality, is whether a positive reply can be given to the following question: Is there any intrinsic and synchronously perceptible reason for the word having this particular form and no other?" (1951, pp. 86-87).

Much of the argument that follows in this section, and in the next, comes from the fact that for many language users and for all beginning language learners, there are few 'synchronously perceptible' reasons for specialist G-L words having their particular forms. But as Ullmann also observes, a speaker's level of language development is an important factor in determining levels of word motivation. In other words, a person more aware of the 'synchronously perceptible' features of a word, that give it motivation, will obviously be helped by those features. For someone not aware of these features, the word is only conventional in meaning.

The process of locating words in the mental lexicon varies depending on the morphology of the words: their shape and structure. Psycholinguistic studies of verbal latencies now offer abundant evidence that morphologically complex words contain within their lexical representation in the brain the details of their morphological structure (Cutler 1983; Sandra, 1994). Clearly, if some people are more ready to use all of that detail in activating words than others, then they are better placed to send or receive messages using those words than are other people who are less ready in this way. This point most relates to the stem-and-affix storage of G-L words in the mental lexicon.

Chapter 7 discusses the role that the stem-and-affix storage of words has in activating words. It seems clear that a person's capacity to store words using their stems and affixes, has an effect on the activation level needed in locating a word. If the stem and affixes of a word are not stored separately, then the whole word itself (and probably its graphemes in visual access) provides the only source of activation, making it less likely that the word will be recognised or used. But it is also becoming clearer that 'morphology' does not exist on a linguistic level of its own. This certainly applies to the orthographic storage of words, but also especially to their phonological storage. In *The Lexical Bar*, I cited the following overview of psycholinguistic research made early in the history of morphological studies:

> The view emerging from this work is one in which various types of lexical information, including the meaning, sound and spelling codes of a word, are automatically accessed and passed along for further processing (Seidenberg *et al.*, 1982, p. 531).

But this claim is now consistent with the broad consensus of recent research presented in Chapter 7. Sound, shape, *and* meaning seem to be interrelated and integrated at every point in the mental lexicon. Again, when Marslen-Wilson et al. confirm the place of the morpheme in phonologically activating derivational forms in English, they say:

> This should be understood, however, as a cognitive, or psycholinguistic concept of the morpheme, developmentally definable for each listener in terms of its synchronic semantic interpretability . . . [This claim] is broadly consistent with a range of psycholinguistic research stretching back over two decades (1994 p. 31).

### The Role of Meaning in Activating Words: Semantic Transparency

Access to a word's entry in the mental lexicon is helped by the prior exposure of a semantically related word. It seems clear that the semantic context provided by a sentence fragment does not provide anything like the same priming effect as this semantically related word (Forster, 1976). Clearly in receiving messages, semantic activation of some external kind is very helpful in accessing a complex word entry in the mental lexicon. Also, in sending messages, semantic activation of some kind is very helpful in accessing the word entry to express a given meaning. But for words that are not well primed in either of these ways, this sort of semantic activation will likely come from some meaning resident in the word form itself.

*The Conventionality of English*

If a word has none of the three types of motivation that Ullmann identifies, then it is opaque. In other words, it has a conventional meaning: Its meaning is subject to agreements about its use that users do not necessarily connect to this word rather than to any other. English is much more conventional in this sense than most other languages. For most users, the English vocabulary has followed the French in its movement away from motivation towards conventionality, since the majority of English words, drawn ultimately from Greek and Latin sources, are without any of Ullmann's phonetic, morphological or semantic forms of motivation. The semantic transparency that G-L words offered writers who introduced them into the cultural meaning systems of English, has gone. The readiness of the G-L morphemes "to recapture the concrete image underlying an abstract word" (Ullmann, p. 215), is no longer available to most language users.

So for many, this type of semantic activation in the mental lexicon is now inoperative. Although many mature users of English are able to identify broad derivational relatedness between words (Ohala & Ohala, 1987), many other mature users, including most adult ESL users, are quite unable to perceive reasons for many specialist G-L words having their particular forms and no other. Moreover younger users and other beginning users make relatively little use of this kind of semantic transparency. Derwing & Baker (1979) make this point clearly in their research. They submitted a list of 50 pairs of words to subjects of different ages and asked about the strength of the semantic relationship between the words in each pair (i.e. "does word x derive from word y?"). They found that younger subjects were influenced by word similarity (e.g. CAR, CARPET, PET) much more than adults, who incline strongly towards semantic similarity, if it is at all perceptible.

Chapter 2 introduced the term 'embedded morpheme' to refer to Ullmann's 'concrete image underlying an abstract word' that is 'derivable through etymological probing'. Clearly, on the evidence in Chapter 7, embedded G-L morphemes can provide semantic activation in the mental lexicon, as well as morphological activation through the shape and structure of separately stored stem morphemes and affixes. When a G-L word helps a user in this way, then clearly it is a considerably motivated and activated word. But are there other semantic factors at work that might also be represented in the mental lexicon?

A strong clue could lie in the responses of adolescent children to the Measure of Passive Vocabulary described in Chapter 5. When prompted by a semantically-related keyword, all the children found it easy to express the specialist meanings in original sentences of most of the semantemes presented. This suggests that word activation in the mental lexicon may be facilitated by nodes held in common by words, and vaguely representing meaning relations within semantic fields, rather like the academic meaning systems explored in this study. Perhaps our capacity to say 'intuitively' that words are semantically related 'in some way', comes from the fact that word entries are organized in the mental lexicon according to linked rules of use within specific meaning systems? In fact, it would be remarkable if this were not the case. This would also help explain the tendency of less experienced language users to compartmentalize the meanings of specialist words and so restrict their use.

*Morphological Motivation in the Anglo-Saxon Vocabulary*

If English were a more fully conventional language for all its users, then the opaqueness that specialist G-L words present to many people would not be a factor separating them from the rest of the lexicon. But the Anglo-Saxon half of the lexicon remains a very motivated one. Embedded morphemes, different in kind but similar in function, are a feature that reduces the opaqueness of the majority of polymorphemic Anglo-Saxon words.

To examine this claim, I studied the 38,700 words contained in the index of an English thesaurus (Chapman, 1979). I looked at all listed Anglo-Saxon words of two or more syllables, excluding verbal inflections and proper nouns. Of these 6,370 words, 66% (4,219 words) show unequivocal morphological motivation, coming either from their being compound words or from their embedding some single semantically transparent morpheme from which they are derived. Note, however, that up to 2000 polysyllabic

Anglo-Saxon words, on this count, are without a transparent embedded morpheme and lack this unequivocal motivation.

But many of these words are still not conventional, of course, since they are phonetically motivated to some extent (e.g. WRESTLE, WRIGGLE, WRINKLE and GLIMMER, GLISTEN, GLITTER). Most of the rest represent non-specialist notions learned in our earliest years (HONEY, HUNGRY, KITCHEN, KITTEN) and so these are located as whole word entries in the mental lexicon. But there are enough native Anglo-Saxon words that have become de-motivated with time, to show that the opaqueness of English words for many people is not a unique attribute of the G-L vocabulary.

## Associated Advantages of Anglo-Saxon Words as a Group

On the psycholinguistic evidence, transparent Anglo-Saxon compounds are activated more efficiently than complex G-L words, and this gives them an advantage. The activation of compound words operates with a speed predictable from the frequency of the first word in the compound, rather than the word as a whole (Forster, 1976). So the lexical entry for SEAWEED is activated via the entry SEA. A compound word which has a low-frequency first component, such as LOINCLOTH, is recognized less quickly than a word with a high-frequency first component, such as HEADSTAND, even though the two compounds themselves are of equal frequency (assessed by reference to Kucera and Francis, 1967 [Taft and Forster, 1976]). Possibly the first stem of a compound gives primary activation, while the second and the whole word add activation consistent with the interactive-activation model. No doubt semantic transparency helps as well.

Phonologically transparent Anglo-Saxon derived words are also activated more efficiently than complex G-L words of similar length. Words with derivational suffixes such as -WARD, -NESS, -FUL and agentive suffixes such as -ER, are activated more readily than words with G-L suffixes like -ION. The speed of activation seems to depend on the amount of modification needed to add the suffix to the stem word (Cutler, 1981; Taft, 1985). Also related to these studies, Mackay (1978) asked subjects to utter derived noun nominalizations as rapidly as possible (CONCLUSION, DECISION) after they had heard the respective verb forms. Certain nominalizations took longer than others: The more complicated the process of derivation (the more steps intervening between verb form and noun form) the slower the nominalizations. In general, Anglo-Saxon compounds and derived words need only one step to produce a derived form from its stem.

So for most users of English, Anglo-Saxon polysyllabic forms are doubly advantaged. G-L words are more difficult to activate in two ways: As a group, G-L words lack the semantic transparency that comes from being morphologically motivated. Secondly they seem to process less readily in the mental lexicon, owing to the complexities of their structure. Notice that I am discussing groups of words here. There is no evidence to show that there is anything that distinguishes a random word of G-L origin from a random word of Anglo-Saxon origin. There is only the very strong possibility that differences in processing will exist between them, because of structural, semantic and other differences.

## Processing Difficulties: Patterns of Interference

In summary, the attributes of G-L word difficulty introduced in this chapter are as follows: They are often non-concrete, low in imagery, low in frequency, morphologically unmotivated, and so semantically opaque. When these features and the others mentioned in Chapter 5 combine in words, they interfere with word use and with word learning. Where and when does this interference occur?

There are three ways in which these attributes cause patterns of interference with word learning and use: First, word frequency affects the actual placement of words in passive or active vocabulary. Second, semantic opaqueness affects word motivation. Finally, level of access to the words' rules of use within cultural meaning systems affects a person's readiness to put the words to use. I shall use the review of research on the mental lexicon from Chapter 7 to explain these processing difficulties.

### Word Frequency: Passive and Active Vocabulary

Firstly, their low-frequency in the language will slow the activation of most specialist G-L words for all users who meet them infrequently. This will affect their use in all four modes: in sending or receiving messages, in either the phonological or orthographic mode. As a result, they become available for producing messages more slowly, because they need greater activation. Similarly incoming messages containing these words take longer to process as the need for activation increases. Rapidly incoming messages with words of moderate to low-frequency are more likely to be scrambled (Freebody & Anderson, 1983). In fact, the more low-frequency G-L words that messages contain, the more likely that the messages will be misunderstood.

Moreover for most people, word frequency is a much more severely constraining factor than the psycholinguistic studies would suggest. This is because the studies always decide word frequency in a language by reference to texts based on the print medium (e.g. Kucera & Francis, 1967; Carroll *et al.*, 1971; Dictionnaire des Fréquences, 1971). Yet these recorded frequencies of print usage are not at all generalizable as measures of frequency across language communities. Most first language users of English have relatively few encounters with G-L words in the print medium outside schools. If they are going to come across them, the words have to appear in conversation, or in formal discussion, or in the electronic media. But moderate to low-frequency words are only rarely if ever encountered in these sources, so they are even less available for use than their print ratings suggest. In addition, while large numbers of G-L words are stored in every experienced language user's mental lexicon as passive items, they need longer activation for some people than for others. Why is this?

Lexico-semantic positioning, including immersion in the meaning systems of the academic culture of literacy, is the main factor interacting with word frequency to determine how passive these words are. The results in the two main instruments in these studies tend to confirm this: Sociocultural background clearly discriminates between groups of children at 15 years in their readiness to use G-L words actively that they probably hold passively. Note that all these children had the same school experiences and were matched in reasoning ability. Their different lexico-semantic positioning occurred in spite of their schooling, not because of it.

So while there is always a store of these words in the mental lexicon of every person who has had contact with them, the time that it takes some people to put these words to use can still suggest to others that those people have not learned the words. And in a real sense this is the case, if knowing a word means knowing how to use it.

*Semantic Transparency and Opaqueness: Word Motivation*

In the interactive-activation model, the more nodes or points of activation a word has, the more likely it will be activated in time for use, rather than after the 'communicative moment' has passed. Many of these nodes seem to be based on whatever semantic or morphological features that the word's stem or affixes might offer. If these nodes are not well-established in a person's mental lexicon, by incidental or formal contact with experiences that heighten metacognitive and metalinguistic word awareness, then processing will take place without the supplementary activation provided by these nodes. Once again, words will process more slowly; they will tend to be more passive. To an observer, they may seem not to have been learned at all.

*Meaning Systems and the Academic Culture of Literacy*

Words that are conventional in meaning, low in frequency, and low in imageability often have connotations that vary in subtle ways across contexts. But if used continually within single contexts and meaning systems, they acquire concise and precise uses. They receive lots of support in their meanings within specialist contexts of use: from the collocational relations that they contract with other conventional word meanings within the meaning systems; and from their system-specific rules of use. Unlike concrete and highly imageable words, these words are usually used in culturally determined ways that are specific to some meaning system or other. So using specialist G-L words appropriately will depend on the language user having a relaxed familiarity with the meaning system that embeds them, which means familiarity with the rules of use for that word within the system. Indeed when we have knowledge of any word, we have it according to the rules of use that obtain in a given meaning system. To the extent that we use the word appropriately, we participate in that meaning system and even make propaganda for it.

As earlier chapters have argued, what the lexical bar largely represents is a gulf between the everyday meaning systems and the high status meaning systems created by the introduction of an academic culture of literacy. This is a barrier that everyone has to cross at some stage in their lives, if they are to become 'successful candidates' in conventional forms of education. But for users of English there is something else that reinforces this barrier: the unique series of events that created the G-L and Anglo-Saxon divide in English, which arranged the poor and the privileged through unequal access to education, on either side of that divide.

What is already a difficult enough process of gaining access to academic meaning systems, becomes reinforced for many users of English because of the unique side of the lexical bar in that language. On the one hand, a social group's broadly different conception of the culture and its meaning systems, receives its public expression in a disposition aversive to putting the specialist vocabulary of English to active use, because the meanings of that vocabulary are not embedded, interlocked, and identified with, in that different conception of the culture. But, on the other hand, even when many people do try to make themselves at home within those academic meaning systems, they find their lexico-semantic differences reinforced by the unmotivated morphology of the special vocabulary of the meaning systems. In addition, this morphological strangeness of G-L words is no doubt the single most important attribute that makes them seem excessively formal to people, even when compared with Anglo-Saxon words equal to them in frequency (see Chapter 4).

## The Four Language Modes: Word Learning

When there is interference in all of the ways discussed above, then the bar's effect is at its severest. Speaking, listening, reading, writing and learning specialist G-L words may become difficult in the ways suggested below:

### Reading and Listening

Processing these words is already difficult because of their moderate to low-frequency in the language. If the nodes activated by morphological and semantic criteria are not developed in the mental lexicon, they will offer no help in receiving messages that contain many specialist G-L words. But even if the word entries are activated in time to assist with the incoming message, their meanings will not be clear. The rules of use that they contact within meaning systems may be so vague and so removed from the conventional rules of use within those systems as to provide little additional sense to the incoming message than is provided by the message with its difficult words deleted.

### Speaking and Writing

In trying to send a message within a meaning system using a specialist G-L word, the concept to be expressed will already be vague and rather underdeveloped. Several different words might suit the same vague idea. But the nodes in the lexicon that are activated on morphological and semantic criteria, offer no help in finding the best word, since these nodes are not well developed for that word. So the most suitable and precise word is not processed in time to speak or even to write it. Instead, the speaker or writer activates a high-frequency word that may be less adequate for expressing that concept. Or, the speaker or writer pauses and gives more time to activating the appropriate word (see Chapter 6 pp. 136-38). Or, a morphologically similar but inappropriate word is activated and used in the message (e.g. CONCEPT for CONTEXT).

*Word Learning and Language Awareness*

Words are only fully learned when they are available for active use. When words lodge only in passive vocabulary, with their active use inhibited in the three ways mentioned above, then full word learning has not taken place. Furthermore, difficulties in processing and identifying with strange words will even affect passive vocabulary acquisition.

Listeners or readers meeting specialist G-L words for the first time often ignore them if at all possible. They see them as alien, strange, and forbidding. But this is not just because they are novel words, used to express ideas within unfamiliar meaning systems. It is also because the words are not acquired at the same time as the metacognitive and metalinguistic awareness skills needed to place them appropriately in verbal memory and make them more familiar as English words. Getting language awareness of this kind helps establish nodes in verbal memory, that make the words semantically and morphologically transparent for ease of activation and future use.

By becoming aware of the language's derivational rules, learning specialist G-L words becomes easier. These language awareness skills offer a different level of organization that is supplementary to other ways of analyzing words. It certainly makes learning G-L words easier and there are different ways of going about this: Some suggest new words are best understood by analogy to known words similar in shape (Anglin, 1993). Some propose rule-based models of analysis: giving meanings to each part of a word and combining them (White, Power & White, 1989). I suggest that one technique suits some words, and others suit other words.

At the same time, these ways of discovering laterally-related patterns in order to help the search for words in the brain, may not appear relevant to a person not accustomed to thinking divergently in dealing with vocabulary. Indeed, Anglin (1993) reports that children from some sociocultural backgrounds seem to use these techniques more often than others, and they expand their vocabulary learning as a result. At the same time, he reminds us that there seems to be no difference between sociocultural groups in their ability to use morphological analysis, if they are encouraged to do so. In fact, it can make sense to everyone, if people become aware that helpful patterns do exist to help word learning.

Nevertheless the processing factors discussed in this chapter and in Chapter 7 interfere mainly with the usability of words, not with their learnability. Three factors are said to affect the learning of word meanings, especially in a formal second language learning context:

1.      the *frequency* of occurrence of the words, or the frequency with which the words are presented to the learner;
2.      the *variety* of situations or contexts in which the words occur, or are presented;
3.      the *standards* of performance that are set [in using the words] Eishout-Mohr & van Daalen-Kapteijns, 1987 pp. 65-66).

Learning a word certainly means knowing many linguistic things about it:

> knowing the probability of meeting it;
> knowing other words likely to be collocated with it;
> knowing the limitations on its use, by function and situation;
> knowing its syntactic behaviour;
> knowing its underlying forms and derivations;
> knowing its place in a network of associations with other words;
> knowing its semantic value; and
> knowing its different meanings (after Richards, 1976).

But the key achievement in specialist G-L word learning, is knowing where the word fits within its own meaning system and being able to use it in a motivated way to take part in that particular language game. These rules of use are largely outside language itself and they change for a given word across contexts: They are closely tied to the real world of life forms, material practices, and human interaction. The necessary raw materials for this word learning lie in frequent encounters with words in many contexts displaying the rules for their application, and in regular opportunities to play those language games at a high standard of performance. A language environment that denies word learners these encounters, opportunities, and experiences will deny access to learning the rules for applying the words.

## Conclusion: The Lexical Bar

There are two sides to the lexical bar. One side is the barrier hindering access to academic meaning systems that were created over time through the school's special culture of literacy. The other side is the difficulty of learning and using G-L words as a group when compared with other words in the language. This second side is unique to English. Let me spell these out in a little more detail.

The first side of the lexical bar is a hurdle that all people everywhere have to cross if they are going to succeed in educational institutions that pay high regard to academic meaning systems. Regardless of the language or culture we are in, and regardless of our sociocultural background, we all encounter difficulty at some stage in our lives entering these meaning systems and becoming familiar with the rules of use that provide the meanings of specialist words within those systems. Because of the conceptual complexity of those systems, their specialist words are hard to learn and to use. They are low in imageability, non-concrete, and we encounter them and their rules of use infrequently. Clearly this is not specifically a Graeco-Latin lexical bar in other languages, since most languages lack the second side to the bar that English has. But as I suggest in Chapter 9, in some languages there may be other kinds of differences in word shape, sound, length, or meaning that provide something rather like the second side in English.

The second side of the lexical bar is a creation of sociohistorical events that accompanied the development of English. On the evidence, it seems to affect people differently depending on their sociocultural positioning. Again word frequency in the language is a central factor, since this affects the amount of activation in the mental lexicon that words need for recognition and use. The degree to which specialist G-L words in English are morphologically motivated and semantically transparent depends on the frequency of the encounters that people have with this type of word, and with their morphemes, in contexts that display their rules of use. For people who have only rare encounters with G-L words and their morphemes through the discursive practices made available by their sociocultural positioning, the difficulty of learning and using specialist words within academic meaning systems becomes unusually acute. For these people, the G-L side of the bar reinforces the barrier that everyone has to cross.

# 9

# Changing Practices: Further Research, Equity Matters, and Other Lexical Bars

In *The Lexical Bar*, I made few explicit recommendations about changing discursive practices in schools. There was a reason for this reticence. The results of the studies were so startling that it seemed wrong to argue from them for educational reforms, in case those reforms were seen as the motivation for the studies in the first place. Since the release of that book, the supporting evidence has grown, as set out especially in Chapters 2, 4, 7 and 8 of this book. Other researchers have also taken the ideas further. All this has helped clarify my thinking about what is 'going on' in the lexical bar, and what could be done to remove it.

This chapter offers some recommendations about changing practices in certain areas: relevant to English as a first language education; relevant to valuing students' vocabulary differences; relevant to ESL education; and relevant to the place of language awareness and the study of other languages more generally. It suggests areas for further research and ends by asking about the existence of lexical bars in other languages.

## Words in English as a First Language

Differences between sociocultural groups in active lexico-semantic range are very pronounced at 15 years. In part, they reflect differences in passive vocabulary between groups at the same age. But the active differences are of a much greater order and they clearly affect educational performance

185

and school success: They give some students the kind of high status linguistic capital for use in displaying their knowledge and thought, that formal education tends to value. Occurring as they do in the final years of schooling, these differences clearly discriminate against groups of children from some backgrounds.

How does a person get active lexico-semantic access to the meaning systems of education? I say more about this later in the chapter. But clearly, exposure to the kind of discursive practices that give this access is a lengthy, cumulative process. Those immersed more extensively in these practices and the academic meaning systems, before and outside schooling, are always going to be advantaged to some extent by that greater immersion. The evidence suggests that this kind of lexico-semantic access comes before or during their fifteenth year. But perhaps children from other sociocultural backgrounds just need more time in school to develop this active lexico-semantic range, and to catch up. Perhaps the group differences observed would disappear without further intervention, if another year of compulsory education were routinely available to children, before they were allowed by law to leave most systems of schooling. It may be that many adolescents are being failed in schools, and are legally dropping out, before they are ready to show their ability to succeed. Further research might address this issue by studying older groups of adolescents still in those school systems that retain them longer as a matter of policy, and by comparing the results. Work with school drop-outs could also be very valuable.

The present studies look at the most class-stratified and the most socially mobile countries in the English-speaking world. But other countries, like the United States with its stunning inequalities in life chances based on family wealth and income levels, may offer very different results. Most observers from the United States that I have discussed these matters with, say that the results of studies there would show even greater differences between sociocultural groups. So comparative studies could be helpful for interpreting aspects of the bar and for changing educational practices, so that the extreme effects of lexico-semantic positioning, that are displayed in this book, could be modified a little. At the same time, though, it is still important to remember Bernstein's warning that 'education cannot compensate for society'. The little that education can do in this area would always have to be accompanied by social, political, and economic reforms on a grand scale, to remove unwanted inequities in lexico-semantic positioning that occur before and outside formal education.

Studies of the attitudes of practising teachers of adolescents, whose work centres so much on teaching and assessing specialist G-L word use, could be useful. These would offer a research basis for changing undesirable practices that contribute to the excessive use and valuation of specialist G-L words by teachers who see them as educational status symbols, distorting their rules of use in the process. This might help end the cycle that reinforces the view in some people's minds that these words provide a way into high status cultural capital, and a way out of insecurity and powerlessness.

The studies in this book confirm that specialist G-L word usage stands as an important mediating factor between sociocultural group background and educational success or failure. But other research could turn the issue on its head: do all students really do better in school if they have a more wideranging vocabulary? The case from discursive psychology lends strong support to the claim that successful managers of sign systems are well equipped to operate across a broad range of human activities (Harré & Gillett, 1994). This is in line, of course, with formal education's continuing stress on giving access to the signs of academic meaning systems. But because other factors, to do with class background, race, culture, and gender, have a powerful and often overwhelming influence on educational success and failure, it may be that a great many people succeed in formal education just because of their privileged backgrounds, without ever achieving great and genuine ability to wield the signs and deploy the meanings that specialist words offer. It would be a useful comment on the impartiality of formal education to find that vocabulary range is not always associated with success at higher levels of education.

### Valuing Vocabulary Differences

Elsewhere I have written at length about standard and non-standard varieties, and their valuation in education (Corson, 1993). But the question of standard and non-standard usage is not strictly an issue for *Using English Words*. What this book treats are discontinuities in lexico-semantic orientation between communities and schools. These arise because schools place high status on an academic culture of literacy, including its associated signs, and this culture is relatively removed from the cultural capital of some sociocultural groups, while much closer to others. All this means that there is much more than language differences involved in all this.

Nevertheless, in their valuations of words, many teachers are influenced by what I call 'an ideology of correctness': Because of their own socialization as successful students in schools, many teachers tend to see specialist G-L words as always 'better' or as always 'more correct' forms of word use in academic or formal contexts. When there is a choice between words of similar meaning, they will often prefer the G-L. I call this an ideology, because it can be a distortion of reality that reinforces undesirable imbalances in power linked to the lexical bar. There are a few things that should be said in response to the practice.

Firstly, Maylath's study, reported in Chapter 4, provides a good response to any teachers who prefer student texts to be liberally but needlessly sprinkled with specialist G-L words. On Maylath's evidence, this stylistic preference may be little more than a matter of inexperience on the teachers' part. It may suggest that teachers are rather insecure in their roles as competent 'assessors'. This academic insecurity is not unlike another widely observed form of insecurity in social interactions that Bourdieu talks about. He describes a social trait that is especially common among the bourgeoisie in societies:

the tendency to hyper-correction, a vigilance which overshoots the mark for fear of falling short and pounces on linguistic incorrectness, in oneself and others (1984 p. 331).

Bourdieu sees this tendency as a particular trait of the *petit-bourgeois*, the lower middle classes, as they seek to cement their status within the dominant classes of a society. So it is no accident that schools almost everywhere have always tried to put this 'ideology of correctness' to work, since modern schools were originally staffed with diligent members of the petit-bourgeoisie, and they were created to extend middle class values and preferences to the poor and to the culturally different, in order to 'tame' and 'assimilate' them. Regrettably some teachers in present-day schools and universities have inherited this aim. They still believe that it is their role to stamp out 'error'; and many commentators on education reinforce them in this view.

So what is to be done? There seem to be two sides to the problem of counselling teachers and others on vocabulary valuation. On the one hand, it is easy to know what to say to an assessor who insists that students talk about INTRODUCING LEGISLATION, rather than BRINGING IN LEGISLATION. Briefly, the assessor is unwise to insist on this, because the phrases are synonymous within their specialist meaning system, and should be evaluated as if they were. On the other hand, what are we to say to an assessor who insists that students talk about ABOLISHING LEGISLATION rather than STOPPING IT? Isn't there a qualitative semantic difference here, in most contexts of use, due to the different rules of use for the two verbal actions? In other words, while law-makers do talk of 'stopping legislation', they mean something very different from it when they talk of 'abolishing legislation'.

There are often discontinuities like this between the vocabulary that students bring from outside schools and the peculiar, decontextualized vocabulary demands that specialist meaning systems place upon them. When students are likely to be disadvantaged by this discontinuity (as the students in the second example probably would be), the best policy for valuing vocabulary differences is probably the same as the best policy for valuing non-standard varieties of a language. The problem can be minimized by asking the teachers whose academic subjects elevate G-L words, to adopt and modify the language policy that the Bullock Report in England recommended (DES, 1975): valuing the vocabulary that students bring with them to school, to whatever degree is necessary to treat the students fairly; while adding to it, in every case, those other lexical signs and rules of use that are necessary acquisitions for educated people to make, if they are going to use their vocabulary appropriately within academic meaning systems.

But I would add a rider to the Bullock recommendation: For this 'valuing' to really count, it needs to be carried out in a genuinely *critical* context. In other words, students need to become aware of the social and historical factors that have combined to make the rules of use for one section of the vocabulary more appropriate in contexts resonant with power, prestige, and intellectual complexity, while relegating plain Anglo-Saxon texts to more informal contexts. What I am saying is that in adopting this policy, we would need to provide 'critical vocabulary awareness' as an essential part of the fair treatment we extend to students who do not have wide experience with the academic vocabulary of schools, before and outside formal education.

### Words in English as a Second or Foreign Language

The evidence from studies of ESL students in Hong Kong and of Dutch students working with the Latinate section of their own language, suggests that for many people the special characteristics of G-L words presented in this book are a serious obstacle to ESL word learning and use. Research on adult and adolescent ESL students from different language backgrounds, could explore the difficulties that students have with these words, by matching them in frequency with non-G-L words in English and asking students to learn to use the two types of word in context, for a variety of speaking, reading, writing, or listening tasks.

Research with ESL students on G-L word use could provide many insights into broadly different arrangements of the mental lexicon that may result from lexico-semantic positioning in a language other than English. Are Romance language students better placed in learning English because of the motivation and semantic transparency that Latinate words already have for them? The evidence that students do transfer knowledge from their first language to later languages is now very strong (Gass & Selinker, 1983; Kellerman & Sharwood Smith, 1986; Hancin-Bhatt & Nagy, 1994) especially where the two languages have a high degree of structural similarity. Indeed for Spanish-as-a-first-language bilinguals, low-frequency Latinate words in English may become more transparent semantically because their cognate forms are high-frequency and more everyday words in Spanish (e.g. INFIRM, ENFERMO [Sp. 'sick']: Hancin-Bhatt & Nagy, 1994).

This research on Spanish-speaking bilinguals is quite consistent with the studies of immigrant Romance-language students reported in Chapter 5. But what about those languages that are not very like English? Do Chinese-as-a-first-language ESL students, for example, have special difficulties with G-L words because they are not simple compounds, like the majority of Chinese words? Are they advantaged in other ways, with Anglo-Saxon derived compound words for instance? Do other students have special difficulties if they come from countries remote from the culturally-specific meaning systems of European civilization? This last question could yield insights about both sides of the lexical bar raised in this book: the role of lexico-semantic positioning in gaining discursive access to systems of meaning; and differences in the arrangement of the mental lexicon that might result from those differences in discursive positioning.

Studies of ESL students' difficulties with specialist G-L words might also tell us about the English-relevant cultural meaning systems that immigrant and aboriginal learners of English already have access to. Are the rules of use for words, within the academic meaning systems of English, systematically different from the rules of use for their nearest translatable synonyms in the first-language meaning systems of some ESL students? Should programs that teach students the specialist and the more everyday uses of difficult words, provide more deliberate access to academic meaning systems at the same time? What implications might follow for the curriculum of second and foreign language education? Should the curriculum include more comparative cultural studies, mediated through the learner's mother tongue (Byram, 1989; Buttjes & Byram, 1991) and aimed deliberately at producing intercultural competence in the rules of use of related words in the two languages? All of these issues are important for the practice of ESL and EFL education, since there is much evidence that adult ESL students from some backgrounds give years of concentrated effort to language learning, but get few rewards in English fluency.

### Changing Practices to Extend Vocabulary: Oral Language and Literacy

Clearly there is more to difficult texts than that they include words that are themselves difficult in access. But if first and second language learners are asked to name it, it is the presence of difficult words in texts that is the most important single factor in the perceived difficulty level. Students and their teachers freely admit that in order to become "successful managers of sign systems" the priority task is to master the rules of use of the signs themselves (Saville-Troike, 1984; Garcia, 1991). There are many attributes of word difficulty covered in this book. These imply ways for formal education to promote the wider learning of the many G-L signs that teachers say are needed for showing access to the rules of use of academic knowledge categories.

It is the integration of these G-L words into certain highly precise and limited areas of discourse that gives them their rules of use. So their learnability really depends on the learner having a rich acquaintance with the specialist areas of discourse in which they appear, as well as frequent and motivated contact with the words themselves. Their meanings become clearer by trying them out in motivated acts of discourse and by hearing them used in reply in original acts of discourse. In this way, their semantic difficulty can be overcome, especially if learners are able to negotiate their own meanings with more experienced users when trying out new words with one another. This approach to learning difficult words is as experience-based as any learning can be that touches on the abstract. And it suggests a clear conclusion for education: We overcome our inadequate grasp of publicly available concepts, by engaging in conversations on the subject matter using the signs that give a name to those concepts.

### Extending Classroom Conversations

Although this idea is still making its way forward rather slowly in contemporary educational practice, it is far from new. In the form above, it comes from *The Concept of Education* (1967), in which R. S. Peters recommended a wider use of the *ad hominem* method used by Socrates. Peters advised that the classical way of ensuring an integrated outlook is not through explicit learning situations, not through courses, but through conversation. Also in *The Relevance of Education* (1972), Bruner argued that the crucial way in which a culture aids intellectual growth is by internalizing dialogue in thought. This prompted him to conclude that "the courtesy of conversation may be the major ingredient in the courtesy of teaching".

Some of my own work in this area has tried to change initial teacher education, so that different oral language practices can gradually enter classrooms (Corson, 1984; 1987). Indeed the growth of research and informed opinion about extending oral discourse practices in first-language, in ESL, and in other second-language contexts in schools, underlines the importance that is now given to it (Wells, 1989; 1992). Research also points to the inherent dangers of excessive teacher control of talk in classrooms: In conventional question-and-answer whole-class sessions, speakers' rights are distributed so unequally that students have few opportunities for any sustained interaction that might encourage them to put specialist words to use or even learn their uses (Sinclair & Coulthard, 1975). At the same time, the one-sided validity claims that teachers make and which students must accept uncritically when drawn into these interrogation sessions, often mean that the process is little more than one of intellectual indoctrination (Young, 1992).

Edwards & Westgate (1994) offer an extensive review of the research on classroom talk. They give special attention to the advances in England that accompanied the 'National Oracy Project' and show how these developments have been hindered by reactionary governmental policies. One of their general conclusions stands out for my discussion: the widely attested finding that normal patterns of classroom language provide interactions that are highly abstracted, in style and meaning, from interactions in the everyday world. Clearly the formality, strangeness, and abstractness of specialist G-L words contribute a great deal to this excessive abstraction, since they are the very stuff of the curriculum in many subject areas. Perhaps it is inevitable that the language of senior school classrooms is decontextualized and 'free-floating', since teachers are trying to give students a fast track into specialist meaning systems without exploring many real-world contexts that connect with those systems. In trying to do this, teachers themselves and school texts of all kinds may use specialist words appropriately on most occasions, but the actual rules of use are often missed by students, especially if the words that integrate the rules are low in frequency and morphologically unmotivated.

Some students are advantaged in their word learning by their sociocultural positioning outside schools. Borrowing from those experiences, they manage to fill in the rules of use that teachers may only roughly communicate. Moreover, those who meet relatively few linguistic discontinuities between home and school will have wider opportunities outside the school for using or at least meeting specialist words. But by extending the courtesy to all students of more relaxed and regular forms of classroom conversation centred on their subject areas, teachers can also extend the vocabulary advantages that some students have, to all students.

Cazden (1988) offers a review of research on classrooms as contexts for the language of teaching and learning. Like many current commentators on the importance of oral language in classrooms, Cazden sees language structure enmeshed with language use, and she sees linguistic means as a reflection of social and cognitive purposes. Although she makes no mention of specialist word learning, two themes that she develops seem directly relevant to vocabulary learning and use: the idea, from Vygotsky, that discourse provides a scaffold for learning; and the idea that, while early discourse provides an initial conceptualization of the world, later discourse provides a series of reconceptualizations.

The first theme is linked closely to Vygotsky's idea about the 'zone of proximal development'. This is the difference between what people can do on their own in using language, and what they can do with the help of an older or more experienced language user, working closely with them. The informal 'scaffolding' that the other person's discourse provides, is clearly the most basic kind of assistance that specialist vocabulary learning can get. In this kind of interaction, the special rules of use for words are being outlined, displayed, and negotiated across contexts, which means that these all-important rules are being 'taught' and learned in the natural language contexts of the utterances exchanged. As well, if this scaffolding is regular and continuous, the words themselves are heard and used over and over, raising their real frequency levels for the word learner. Finally, the motivation to try out the words, to put their rules of use to work, and to begin to get the rules right, is resident in the interaction itself.

The second theme, to do with extending conceptualizations through reconceptualizations, relates as much to student/student interaction as it does to teacher/student interaction. Discourse with the teacher, working with an entire class or large group, is useful for introducing specialist words and their meanings. This provides initial conceptualizations of the specialist vocabulary, set within the specialist meaning systems. It offers the kind of preliminary contact with new words that help locate them passively in verbal memory. But it gives little more than this. It is later discourse that provides the necessary elaboration. This later discourse with classmates, or even with friends or family outside the class, provides the much more important series of reconceptualizations that is needed to master rules of use across different contexts, and across the many subtle changes in sense that words have when they appear in different texts. So group work or some other dialogue activity needs to follow the initial conceptualization, not just to reinforce the passive word learning, but to add the more important benefits that come when quality input is followed by quality output. These conclusions are supported by second language research.

Kowal & Swain (1994) offer a wide summary of research on the use of student conversations in second language classrooms. The many studies not only show that learners have many more opportunities to use the target language in groupwork than in teacher-led activities. They also show that the modifications that occur in student/student interactions make the input from the teacher much more comprehensible, while student output is modified by specific conversational features of interaction, such as requests from others for clarification. Kowal & Swain extend these findings in their own study. They find that in a task in which students work together to reconstruct a second language text that was read to them by the teacher, vocabulary and morphology each become the focus of student attention, and their attention becomes focused by talking about the problem.

In first-language or ESL classrooms, word learning takes place when students engage in purposeful talk with others, addressing some aspect of a specialist meaning system, or knowledge category, or second language text that embeds the target vocabulary and the appropriate rules of use.

*The Place of Literacy and Oral Discourse in Vocabulary Growth*

Olson & Astington (1990) take the point about conversations much further, relating it both to literacy and to the lexical bar studies reported in this book. While they highlight the role that literacy has in achieving educational success in present-day schools, they see literacy having more of a mediating role in vocabulary growth. In this section, I compare their position with another strong position advanced by Stanovich & Cunningham that gives literacy a more direct influence on vocabulary growth.

Stanovich & Cunningham are careful not to attribute too much influence to literacy as a universal solvent:

> There was, in earlier writings, a tendency to attribute every positive outcome that was historically correlated with the rise of literacy - economic development, for example - to the effects of literacy itself . . . Simply put, high levels of societal literacy are correlated with too many other good things" (1992: 53).

At the same time, they do argue that the processing mechanisms exercised during reading get lots of practice, through its effects on things like phonological coding, semantic activation, parsing, and induction of new vocabulary. Because avid readers see millions of words a year (Anderson, Wilson & Fielding, 1988), these processes are being put to work many times each day. Stanovich & Cunningham (1992) and Cunningham & Stanovich (1991) report extensive studies that find print exposure to be a strong predictor of verbal fluency. They offer several reasons why reading itself has this direct link with verbal acquisition. Of relevance here, they argue that the distribution of the language structures that print exposes readers to, are different from those that people meet in speech; and they cite the findings of the lexical bar studies, among others (Biber, 1986; Chafe & Danielewicz, 1987; and Hayes, 1988) as evidence for the claim that moderate to low-frequency words appear much more often in common reading materials than they do in common speech.

These arguments are strong, and the correlation studies undertaken clearly suggest a major role for reading experience in vocabulary development (West, Stanovich & Mitchell, 1993). But the findings have less salience here than they might elsewhere. This is because Stanovich and Cunningham report work with pre-adolescent and adult level respondents, not the early and middle adolescents approaching the climax of their compulsory schooling that are of direct concern here.  In their senior education, adolescents encounter specialist word learning demands that are very unlike the more moderate demands placed on younger children. They are also unlike the demands placed on young adult university students, who are well inside specialist meaning systems to a much greater extent.

As well as mastering the background knowledge of a number of complex and apparently discrete fields, adolescents are asked to master the rules of use for huge numbers of new words, whose meanings are novel, unusual, and often changeable across contexts and systems. In this regard, Peel's research, cited in Chapter 2, is more relevant: mature concept formation from written contextual materials (i.e. from reading) is only achieved at the earliest by the age of 15 years. Children will certainly take a great many words into their passive vocabularies from their reading before 15 years, and these will show up in tests of recognition vocabulary of the kind used by Stanovich & Cunningham. But the important development in knowing how to apply the rules of use for words in discourse, needs far more than an encounter with words in print.

Prior to 15 years, 'talk about text' plays a much greater role in promoting specialist active vocabulary growth than exposure to print. According to Olson & Astington, literacy has only an indirect impact on verbal cognition through elaborating ways for talking about talk, and talking about thought. For example, they find that important metalinguistic distinctions found in the corpus of mentalistic and speech act verbs of English, are not acquired through learning to read and write. Nor are they needed for becoming literate. Rather they believe that metalinguistic distinctions of this sort are part of the discourse in any literate culture. Children acquire them if they encounter them in speech. They do not even need to learn to read and write to do so, although I should add that obviously that helps immeasurably.  In other words, participation in the discursive practices of a literate culture changes "linguistically expressed propositions into objects of thought" (1990: 705) thereby creating a discursively active vocabulary that is connected to the meaning systems of literate thought.

Let me underline my belief that the role of print exposure is still very important, since reading experience clearly does a great deal to build knowledge bases within meaning systems (Ceci, 1990; Cipielewski & Stanovich, 1992). But it is participation in the discursive practices of a literate culture that gives children the lexico-semantic range necessary for minimal success in an education within the academic culture of literacy. This participation provides regular contact with the rules of word use; these rules of use become embodied in the individual as cultural capital; and the display of this linguistic capital then distinguishes those who have participated widely in the discursive practices of a literate culture from those who have not. As their central goal, schools themselves should be providing this participation, especially where students' sociocultural positioning outside schools cuts them off from everyday or wide participation in the discursive practices of the academic culture of literacy.

**Equity Factors Outside Language: Gender and Race**

Yet even wide participation in the discursive practices of a literate culture is not enough for many. Participation on its own cannot provide the institutionalized forms of cultural capital that give official recognition and sanction, within specific fields, to the individual's embodied capital. Matters to do with class, culture, gender, and race also add or subtract value from people's linguistic capital, so that differences in educational attainment rates are only partly based on language on display. Often, as I have argued, there is an interaction of social class with culture and language.

Chapter 5 reports one study that was conducted in Australia's most cosmopolitan city. It looked at immigrant children (Italian, Spanish, Portuguese and Macedonian) from low-income backgrounds, who had learned their English in school as a second language. These ESL-program graduates out-performed their Anglo-Australian classmates from equally low-income backgrounds, on a battery of language instruments and also in school achievement examinations. This happened even though the Anglo-Australian Wollongong adolescents spoke English as their mother tongue, were matched in non-verbal reasoning ability with the immigrant children, and shared identical educational backgrounds, except for ESL exposure. Another similar effect can be seen in Canadian research: Cummins (1984) reports that across all socio-economic categories, groups of Canadian-born children from immigrant language backgrounds (Italian, Chinese, Ukrainian and German) out-perform groups of children whose mother tongue was English. Clearly class, culture and language interact in complex ways; and this complexity increases when gender and race appear as factors.

For example, school achievement in the southwest and west of the United States is clearly stratified, with African Americans, as a group, at the bottom, Hispanics in the middle, and Anglo-Americans at the top. Yet while the African Americans are native speakers of English and the Hispanics have usually gone through a program of subtractive bilingual education that might not augur well for their educational achievement relative to native speakers of English, it is the Hispanics who achieve better as a group than the African Americans in schools. Clearly in this case, there are other influential factors at work, beyond class, culture, and language: On the one hand, the Hispanic children have experiences in two languages, a contact that the monolingual African American children do not have. This might give real advantages to the Hispanics that are similar to those that I noted in the Wollongong setting in Chapter 5.

On the other hand, in many parts of the United States, African Americans as a group are the victims of structural and personal racial discrimination in almost every social context, not least in schools. For example, slavery was officially abolished by the Mississippi legislature only in

1995 (sic). The highly prejudiced discursive practices in the wider society that derive from this kind of structural injustice, could easily outweigh any English language strengths that African Americans might have relative to Hispanics. Teacher attitudes towards a particular group, coupled with other forms of discrimination, will raise or depress academic achievement in ways that modify many of the linguistic advantages or disadvantages that students possess. Gender too is another highly influential factor.

This book has widely discussed the role of discursive positioning in determining life chances. Girls and young women, especially from working class and minority culture backgrounds, often experience gendered childhood narratives that all but determine sociocultural relations for them. They see the roles that are created for them, within the limited range of narratives that they hear, as the only future roles available to them. Even when these narratives provide wide access to the meaning systems that display the rules of use of specialist G-L words, in science and mathematics for example, many girls and young women do not see a space for themselves as individuals who are really free to operate within those meaning systems. Instead, they become observers of many of the meaning systems of the school's culture of literacy, rather than participants and contributors. Often, as a result, they develop perceptions of their own powerlessness in school which reinforce their sense of powerlessness outside the school. Many girls are routinely disempowered in this way, so that the same school experiences that give boys advantages, both subtle and blatant (Corson, 1993), finish off a long process of discursively distorted socialization for many young women. They go on to accept roles which they perceive to be their lot in life, because most of the structural narratives that they have encountered leave them with few alternatives.

Perhaps the groups in pluralist societies most disempowered in this way, are girls and women who come from certain immigrant and refugee backgrounds. Often they are doubly marginalized through the discursive positioning that they receive: first as members of minority cultures; and then as females within those cultures. Their invisibility in education is increased by their marginal place in educational research and practice: On the one hand, the study and practice of multicultural education tends to treat members of any single culture as a homogeneous group, with little regard for sex. On the other hand, early feminist theory and practice tended to minimize the cultural differences between women, in the need to treat broad issues of gender discrimination that affect all women.

So while formal education is much concerned with people's ability to put meanings together in thought and to communicate them in words, many other factors affect educational success unjustly. Matters of race, culture, gender, region of living, and class, often interfere with people's educational progress unfairly. But, as I mentioned in Chapter 1, if these other things could be taken out of the equation, one thing would stand out as the most important factor in educational success or failure: The more diverse the meanings that people communicate, through the use of words as signs, and the more appropriate those meanings are to the specialist meaning systems given high status in education, the more impressed and the more rewarding the institution of education will be.

## Language Awareness, Learning Other Languages, and Vocabulary Growth

As discussion in Chapters 5 and 6 confirms, differences in sociocultural background correlate significantly with differences in adolescent children's vocabularies. But this is no deterministic conclusion. The evidence also suggests that linguistic experiences independent of sociocultural positioning can also give some groups of children the advantages they need. Here there is a definite role for formal education. Proficiency in another language, as a first language, followed by wide exposure to the formal processes of learning English-as-a-second-language, seems to be helpful in promoting vocabulary growth, on the evidence of studies reported in Chapter 5, especially if the first language is maintained and used regularly (Cummins & Swain, 1986; Hancin-Bhatt & Nagy, 1994). Alternatively as I have already suggested, a rich language environment provided as part of the courtesy of good teaching for all students in schools will help. This environment could be akin in its intensity, its motivation, and perhaps in some of its methods to that provided for immigrant children through good integrated ESL teaching practices. It could promote all students' vocabulary growth by lowering the activation levels in the mental lexicon that specialist G-L words seem to need, and by giving wide encounters with the conventions for their use.

The best language learning environment would also develop students' critical language awareness, especially in regard to the use and functions of specialist G-L words. As mentioned in Chapter 6, it is important that novice users of these words know that sometimes they can be used in rather negative ways, as instruments of unnecessary formality, or of power. Making this critical kind of language awareness available to students would help strip these words of some of the unwanted rules of use that they have acquired over time: rules of use that exclude people from interaction; rules of use that create a high status for the word user that is not justified by the context; and rules of use that offer a means of language evaluation that is not required by the subject matter. But novices also need to know that when a specialist G-L word suits the meaning of the moment, then its use really does help them to communicate meaning.

### *The Value of Romance Languages*

Studying and learning second languages also seems helpful for removing the bar. There are two vocabulary advantages that studying Latin and Ancient Greek used to offer to students of English. These advantages still seem relevant to learning and using morphologically complex and low-frequency words. But in the present day, these advantages are more widely available elsewhere, through the study of Romance languages. I present these two advantages below:

### Developing metacognitive and metalinguistic skills

Students used to get wide exposure to the etymology of English when translating into and out of Latin and Greek. This was always seen as an interesting if minor bonus that accompanied the teaching of these subjects. But on the evidence of these studies, this process of analyzing words into their stems and affixes seems very important. It helps establish certain conscious and habitual metacognitive and metalinguistic skills that seem necessary for word acquisition and use. Getting access to the concrete roots of abstract words in this way makes words more morphologically motivated for a language user. A word's meaning also becomes more transparent when we analyze it into components that have some meaning themselves. Without this linguistic motivation, specialist G-L words will often remain 'hard' words whose form and meaning appear alien and bizarre. This kind of metacognitive development, which improves practical knowledge about word etymology and relationships, seems very relevant to removing both sides of the lexical bar.

Metacognition includes those learning strategies and other matters of metalinguistic awareness that allow people to control their knowledge of language, so that they can use language better to serve their purposes. As Bruner (1987) concludes, metacognition can be taught successfully as a skill, and this may be necessary for most people to acquire it, since Bruner also observes that metacognitive activity is very unevenly distributed among people. In other words, it varies according to sociocultural background or lexico-semantic positioning: We get it from the narratives and stories told to us during interactions within the meaning systems of a culture. Getting this type of language awareness about words means discovering patterns that directly help lexical thinking processes. These patterns act as cues or easily activated nodes for placing and retrieving words in the mental lexicon. They increase word semantic transparency and they reduce the levels of activation needed to put words to use. Acquiring these patterns in natural ways is rather unusual, and it is rarely provided outside the institution of formal education.

### Conceptual development within specialist meaning systems

Most specialist G-L words have meanings that are low in imageability, difficult to grasp, and often subtly changeable across meaning systems or contexts. The process of learning specialist words develops through wide and regular encounters with the rules for their use as found in specialist discourses. In this kind of language exchange, the rules of use for one expression are set against other expressions that contrast with them or complement them. But in natural language settings, this kind of discourse is quite rare. In its place, prolonged courses of second language study can offer rich benefits for first language development, especially if the cultural contrasts in meaning preserved in the two languages are significant ones. In the classical curriculum, setting the ancient languages alongside the English was doubly useful in this way, because the cultural contrasts between the ancient and the modern extended across both time and space.

Sharwood Smith (1977) describes the effect of Latin translation on English conceptual development: The outlook on the world and the unexamined assumptions of members of a modern society necessarily become explicit when ideas have to be expressed in language which would have meaning for a reader in a pre-Christian, pre-industrial society. There is an inevitable explication of the concepts involved. Gramsci (1948) also suggests similar reasons for the study of Latin, reasons still relevant to the study of Romance languages. For him, this sort of study not only invites students to engage prior intellectual traditions and supersede them in their thinking. It can also accustom them to reason, to think abstractly and schematically, and to distinguish the concept from a specific instance of its application.

But Latin and Greek are now the property of a dwindling few, while the Romance languages are more widely available and are seen as more relevant and useful. But even proficient students of the major Romance languages - French, Spanish, Italian, Portuguese, and Romanian - mainly come from rather privileged sociocultural backgrounds and are often already successful students, perhaps without the second language study. Probably Romance language students will continue to comprise only a small minority of students in school systems. Other approaches are needed if all students are to have a more equal chance to develop their metacognitive and metalinguistic skills, and to receive wide conceptual development within specialist meaning systems.

To give all students access to these two aspects of 'knowledge about language', formal studies in 'language awareness' could be very helpful. Indeed language awareness is not just for learning about words and their morphological relationships. There are many things that language learners need to know about language itself, that studies in formal language awareness and critical language awareness can give them (Corson, 1990; 1993). If all the many areas of language awareness always appeared in the natural language experiences of people, then courses of language awareness would not be needed in formal education. But these experiences are rarely provided for first language learners in natural settings, and they are even more rarely provided for second language learners in natural settings.

## Are There Lexical Bars in Other Languages?

Chapter 2 mentioned other languages that have large numbers of G-L words in them. Most European languages that have deliberately augmented their vocabularies, have turned to Graeco-Latin sources for the new vocabulary, often by way of English. These languages include Czech, Russian, and Macedonian. They also include many of the small minority languages in Europe that are undergoing systematic revival in the present era of increased tolerance for minorities and their languages.

In my studies of Sámi language and culture education in Arctic Norway (Corson, 1995c), I found that Sámi language planners are borrowing words not just from Finnish and Norwegian, but also from English. In particular, they are borrowing its G-L vocabulary to provide a lexical basis for conducting higher levels of education using the Sámi languages. This policy is very necessary, but it could create the kind of vocabulary problem for the Sámi languages that already exists for other Scandinavian languages. For example, Frick & Malström (1976) report difficulties with the Latinate words flooding into Swedish from English. They sometimes replace equivalent Swedish words entirely and always lack motivation for most speakers of Swedish. Haugen (1981) also notes the effect of "the Anglo-American empire and its Latinised English" (p. 114) on Norwegian, where almost 90% of new words in the language come from English (Norstrøm, 1992). These new words cause major problems, and the problems are not just confined to linguistic errors. Mix-ups in their meanings can even cause life-threatening mistakes in reading safety warnings (Flydal, 1983).

Nevertheless in all these cases, as in German, the incidence of G-L words nowhere near approaches their incidence in English. For this reason, none of these languages so far has a specifically G-L lexical bar that literally separates the vocabulary of the academic culture of literacy from the more everyday vocabulary of the languages. If there are 'lexical bars' in other languages, they will take very different forms from the one in English. What could these forms be?

The point to remember is that every language has its high status academic meaning systems. Because of the difficulty of gaining admission to those systems, they are always set apart to some extent from the meaning systems that include a language's everyday vocabulary. Almost all modern users of a language have to cross this barrier at some stage in their lives, and become inducted into those meaning systems and the high status linguistic capital that goes with them. For many, this induction occurs only through education. It is a large enough barrier on its own, since crossing it requires prolonged immersion in the meaning systems. But this barrier is severely reinforced when there is some feature in the language itself, such as the G-L and Anglo-Saxon divide, that sets the high status vocabulary of English apart from its ordinary language vocabulary.

Let me raise several possibilities from the very long list of factors that might divide the vocabularies of different languages. One is suggested in the quote from Meneghello in Chapter 2, when he speaks of words in his vocabulary that provide 'ancient wounds' in his verbal memory. These are his native dialect words, which are the residue of his regional variety of Italian that is quite distant from standard Italian and its Latinate vocabulary. Gramsci (1948) also points to this division between Italian and his Sardo dialect, saying that it creates a barrier that has direct educational consequences for dialect-speaking children in Italy. No doubt this kind of bar in Italian has its parallel in other languages, where regional or social differences separate the standard variety from the non-standard.

This separation in vocabulary often happens because of conquest, unification, and imperial expansion, when another language or another variety of a language is imposed on the conquered as a language of power. Many former European colonies in Africa and Asia have the intellectual vocabularies of their colonizers' languages grafted onto the indigenous language. Because these imperial vocabularies are very unlike the indigenous, there is certainly a bar that hinders ready access to a relaxed engagement with the language of the high status meaning systems that were largely introduced by the colonizers. In the former British colonies, there is the double lexical bar created by the English vocabulary itself, and by the G-L bar within it.

Finally, many native German speakers have suggested to me that word length in German is the lexical bar of that language, and perhaps also of some kindred languages. Word length in German separates most everyday words from most specialist words, and this may create educational problems for German speakers coming from some sociocultural positions. This possibility invites serious research.

## Conclusion

The lexical bar studies give us a basis on which to plan that could recommend in a number of directions. All the suggestions for practice and further research mentioned in this chapter are well within reach in countries where English is the first language. They are also relevant to language developments in the many countries where English has become the lingua franca or the language of international communication. In these places, the lexical bar in English often creates an additional bar beyond the one first established by the need to learn English itself.

The teaching and learning of English as a second or foreign language has become so important to the world community that nothing less than deliberate language policymaking and planning can guarantee a flow of proficient speakers for many countries. As in English-as-a-first-language education, these policies need to give proficient learners wide access to the everyday and the specialist signs established in the language. This means giving them wide access to the rules of use of those signs, and thereby access to the alternative meaning systems that embed them. Giving access to alternative meaning systems is what education is all about.

# References

ADAMSON, J. W. (1922) *A Short History of Education.* Cambridge University Press: London.

AITCHISON, J. (1987) *Words in the Mind: An Introduction to the Mental Lexicon.* Blackwell: Oxford.

ANDRESKI, S. (1974) *Social Science as Sorcery.* Penguin: Harmondsworth.

ANGLIN, J. M. (1993) *Vocabulary Development: A Morphological Analysis.* The University of Chicago Press: Chicago.

AKINNASO, F. N. (1982) "On the differences between spoken and written language". *Language and Speech* **25**, pp. 97-125.

ALEXANDER, M. (1990) *The Growth of English Education 1348-1648.* Pennsylvania State University Press: University Park.

ALLEN, L., CIPIELEWSKI, J. & STANOVICH, K.E. (1992) "Multiple indicators of children's reading habits and attitudes: construct validity and cognitive correlates". *Journal of Educational Psychology* **84**, pp. 489-503.

ALLPORT, D. A. (1983) "Language and cognition". In *Approaches to Language,* edited by R. Harris. Pergamon Press: Oxford.

ALLWRIGHT, D. & BAILEY, K.M. (1991) *Focus on the Language Classroom.* Cambridge University Press: Cambridge.

ALTMANN, G. & SHILCOCK, R. (1994) *Cognitive Models of Speech Processing.* Erlbaum: Hillsdale NJ.

ALTHUSSER, L. (1971) *Lenin and Philosophy and Other Essays* (translated by B. Brewster). Monthly Review Press: New York.

ANDERSON, B. & SOLER, J. (1989) "Gender, vocabulary and school success". unpublished paper. Massey University: Palmerston North.

ANDERSON, R. C., WILSON, P. T. & FIELDING, L. G. (1988) "Growth in reading and how children spend their time outside of school". *Reading Research Quarterly* **23**, pp. 285-303.

ANDERSON, S. R. (1982) "Where's morphology?". *Linguistic Inquiry* **13**, pp. 571-612.

ANDREWS, S. (1986) "Morphological influences on lexical access: lexical or non-lexical effects". *Journal of Memory and Language* **25**, pp. 726-740.

APPLE, M. (1982) *Education and Power.* Routledge: New York.

APPLEBEE, A., LANGER, J. & MULLIS, I. (1987) *The Nation's Report Card: Learning to be Literate: Reading.* Educational Testing Service: Princeton NJ.

ARD, J. & HOMBURG, T. (1983) "Verification of language transfer". In *Language Transfer and Language Learning* (157-176) edited by S. Gass & L. Selinker. Newbury House: Rowley, Mass.

ARONOFF, S. (1976) *Word Formation in Generative Grammar.* MIT Press: Cambridge.

ARONOWITZ, S. (1981) "Preface". In *Ideology, Culture and the Process of Schooling* edited by H. Giroux. Temple University Press: Philadelphia.

AUSTIN, J. L. (1962a) *How To Do Things With Words.* Clarendon: Oxford.

AUSTIN, J. L. (1962b) *Sense and Sensibilia.* Clarendon: Oxford.

BALESTER, V. M. (1991) "Hyperfluency and the growth of linguistic resources". *Language and Education* 5, pp. 81-94.

BARBER, C. L. (1965) *The Story of Speech and Language.* Apollo: New York.

BARBER, C. L. (1976) *Early Modern English.* Deutsch: London.

BARNES, D. (1976) *From Communication to Curriculum.* Penguin: London.

BARNES, D., BRITTON, J. ROSEN, H. (1971 revised) *Language the Learner and the School.* Penguin: London

BAUER, L. (1983) *English Word-Formation.* Cambridge University Press: Cambridge.

BEAUVILLAIN, C. (1994) "Morphological structure in visual word recognition: evidence from prefixed and suffixed words". *Language and Cognitive Processes* 9, pp. 317-339.

BECK, I. L., PERFETTI, C. & MCKEOWN, M. G. (1982) "The effects of long-term vocabulary instruction on lexical access and reading comprehension". *Journal of Educational Psychology* 74, pp. 506-521.

BECK, I. L., MCKEOWN, M. G. & OMANSON, R. C. (1987) "The effects and uses of diverse vocabulary instruction techniques". In *The Nature of Vocabulary Acquisition* edited by M. G. McKeown and M. E. Curtis. Erlbaum: Hillsdale, N.J.

BEILBY, Lord Bishop of Chester. (1786) *A Letter to the Clergy of the Diocese of Chester concerning Sunday Schools.* Payne & Sons: London.

BENEDICT, H. (1979) "Early lexical development: comprehension and production". *Journal of Child Language* 6, pp. 183-200.

BENSON, J. D. & GREAVES, W. S. (1981) "Field of discourse: theory and application". *Applied Linguistics* 2, pp. 45-55.

BERGMAN, M. W., HUDSON, P. T. W. & ELING, P. A. T. M. (1988) "How simple complex words can be: morphological processing and word representations". *The Quarterly Journal of Experimental Psychology* 40A, pp. 41-72.

BERNBAUM, G. (1967) *Social Change and the School.* Routledge & Kegan Paul: London.

BERNSTEIN, B. (1977 revised) *Class, Codes and Control,* Vol. 1 *Theoretical Studies towards a Sociology of Language.* Routledge & Kegan Paul: London.

BERNSTEIN, B. (1973) *Class, Codes and Control,* Vol. 2 *Applied Studies towards a Sociology of Language.* Routledge & Kegan Paul: London.

BERNSTEIN, B. (1990) *Class, Codes and Control,* Vol. 4 *The Structuring of Pedagogic Discourse.* Routledge & Kegan Paul: London.

BERRIAN, R. W. *et al.* (1979) "Estimates of imagery, ease of definition and animateness for 328 adjectives", *Journal of Experimental Psychology: Human Learning and Memory* **5**, pp. 435-447.

BERTINETTO, P. M. (1994) "Phonological representation of morphological complexity: alternative models". *Cognitive Linguistics* **5**, pp. 77-109.

BHASKAR, R. (1986) *Scientific Realism and Human Emancipation*. Verso: London.

BHASKAR, R. (ed.) (1990) *Harré and his Critics: Essays in honour of Rom Harré with his commentary on them*. Basil Blackwell: Oxford.

BIBER, D. (1986) "Spoken and written textual dimensions in English". *Language* **62**, pp. 384-414.

BOSWORTH, J. & TOLLER, T. N. (1972 revised) *Anglo-Saxon Dictionary*. Oxford University Press: London.

BOURDIEU, P. (1971) "Systems of education and systems of thought". In *Knowledge and Control*, edited by M. F. D. Young. Collier Macmillan: London.

BOURDIEU, P. (1977) *Outline of Theory and Practice*. Cambridge University Press: London.

BOURDIEU, P. (1981) *Ce Que Parler Veut Dire: L' 'Economie des 'Echanges Linguistique*. Fayard: Paris.

BOURDIEU, P. (1984) *Distinction: A Social Critique of the Judgement of Taste*. Harvard University Press: Cambridge, MA.

BOURDIEU, P. & WACQUANT, L. (1992) *An Invitation to Reflexive Sociology*. University of Chicago Press: Chicago.

BOWLES, S. & GINTIS, H. (1976) *Schooling in Capitalist America*. Basic Books: New York.

BRADLEY, D. C. (1979) "Lexical representations of derivational relation". In *Juncture*, edited by M. Aronoff and M. L. Kean. MIT Press: Cambridge, MA.

BRADLEY, D. (1987) "Review of *The Lexical Bar*". *Australian and New Zealand Journal of Sociology*. **23**, pp. 142-145.

BRAH, A., FULLER, M., LOUDON, D. & MILES, R. (1977) "Experimenter effects and the ethnic cueing phenomenon" *Working Papers on Ethnic Relations* (University of Bristol), **3**, pp. 1-31.

BRANDIS, W. 7 HENDERSON, D. (1970) *Social Class, Language and Communication*. Routledge & Kegan Paul: London.

BRINSLEY, J. (1612) *Ludus Literarius or The Grammar Schoole*. Thomas Man: London.

BRITTON, J. (1970) *Language and Learning*. Penguin: London.

BROWN, G. & YULE, G. (1983) *Discourse Analysis*. Cambridge University Press: London.

BROWN, R. (1959) *Words and Things*. Free Press of Glencoe: New York.

BROWNE, SIR THOMAS (1646) *Pseudoxica Epidemica*. London.

BRUNER, J. S. (1973) *Beyond the Information Given: Studies in the Psychology of Knowing*. Norton: New York.

BRUNER, J. S. (1983) *In Search of Mind: Essays in Autobiography*. Harper & Row: New York.

BRUNER, J. S. (1987) "The transactional self". In *Making Sense: The Child's Construction of the World*, edited by J. S. Bruner and H. Haste. Methuen: London.

BRUNER, J. S. (1990) *Acts of Meaning*. Harvard University Press: Cambridge MA.

BRUNER, J. S., OLIVER, R. R. & GREENFIELD, P. M. (1967) *Studies in Cognitive Growth*. John Wiley: New York.

BULL, W. E. (1964) "The use of vernacular language in education". In *Language in Culture and Society: A Reader in Linguistics and Anthropology*, edited by Dell Hymes. Harper & Row: New York.

BURANI, C., SALMASO, D. & CARAMAZZA, A. (1984) "Morphological structure and lexical access". *Visible Language* **4**, pp. 348-358.

BURANI, C. & LAUDANNA, A. (1992) "Units of representation for derived words in the lexicon". In *Orthography, Phonology, Morphology and Meaning*, edited by R. Frost & L. Katz. Elsevier Science: Oxford.

BYRAM, M. (1989) *Cultural Studies in Foreign Language Education*. Multilingual Matters: Clevedon, Avon.

BUTTJES, D. & BYRAM, M. (Eds) (1991) *Mediating Languages and Cultures*. Multilingual Matters: Clevedon, Avon.

CARAMAZZA, A., LAUDANNA, A. & ROMANI, C. (1988) "Lexical access and inflectional morphology". *Cognition* **28**, pp. 297-332.

CARDWELL, J. H. (1899) *The Story of a Charity School 1699-1899*. St Anne's School Soho: London.

CARLISLE, J. F. & LIBERMAN, I. Y. (1989) "Does the study of Latin affect spelling proficiency". *Reading and Writing* **1**, pp. 179-191.

CARROLL, J. B. (1964a) "Words, meanings and concepts", *Harvard Educational Review* **34**, pp. 178-202.

CARROLL, J. B. (1964b) *Language and Thought*. Prentice Hall: New York.

CARROLL, J. B., DAVIES, P. and RICHMAN, J. B. (1971) *The American Heritage Word Frequency Book*. Houghton-Mifflin: Boston.

CARTER, R. & McCARTHY, M. J. (1988) *Vocabulary in Language Teaching*. Longmans: London.

CAZDEN, C. B. (1988) *Classroom Discourse: The Language of Teaching and Learning*. Heinemann: Portsmouth, NH.

CECI, S. J. (1990) *On Intelligence . . . More or Less: A Bio-Ecological Treatise on Intellectual Development*. Prentice Hall: Englewood Cliffs NJ.

CHAFE, W. & DANIELEWICZ (1987) "Properties of spoken and written language". In *Comprehending Oral and Written Language*, edited by R. Horowitz and S. J. Samuels. Academic Press: San Diego.

CHALL, J. S. (1987) "Two vocabularies for reading: recognition and meaning". In *The Nature of Vocabulary Acquisition*, edited by M. G. McKeown and M. E. Curtis. Lawrence Erlbaum: Hillsdale, NJ.

CHAPMAN, R. L. (ed.) (1979) *Roget's International Thesaurus*. Harper & Row: London.

CHOMSKY, N. (1980) *Rules and Representations*. Blackwell: London.

CHRISTIAN, J. *et al.* (1978) "Measures of free recall of 900 English nouns: correlations with imagery, concreteness, meaningfulness and frequency", *Memory and Cognition* 6, pp. 379-390.

CIPIELEWSKI, J. & STANOVICH, K. E. (1992) "Predicting growth in reading ability from children's exposure to print". *Journal of Experimental Child Psychology* 54, pp. 74-89.

CLARK, E. V. & BERMAN, R. A. (1987) "Types of linguistic knowledge: interpreting and producing compound nouns". *Journal of Child Language* 14, pp. 547-567.

CLARK, E. V., HECHT, B. F. & MULFORD, R. C. (1986) "Coining complex compounds in English: affixes and word order in acquisition". *Linguistics* 24, pp. 7-29.

CLASSIFICATION OF OCCUPATIONS, Registrar General (1980) Office of Population Censuses and Surveys. H.M.S.O.: London.

COLE, P., BEAUVILLAIN, C. & SEGUI, J. (1989) "On the representation and processing of prefixed and suffixed derived words: a different frequency effect". *Journal of Memory and Language* 28, pp. 1-13.

COOK-GUMPERZ, J. (1973) *Social Control and Socialization — A Study of Class Differences in the Language of Maternal Control.* Routledge & Kegan Paul: London.

CORSON, D. J. (1972) "Teaching spelling through etymology and word relationships", *Tasmanian Journal of Education* 6, pp. 69-71.

CORSON, D. J. (1980) "Chomsky on education", *Australian Journal of Education* 24, pp. 164-185.

CORSON, D. J. (1981) "Social Dialect, the Semantic Barrier and Access to Curricular Knowledge". unpublished PhD thesis: University of London.

CORSON, D. J. (1982) "The Graeco-Latin (G-L) Instrument: a new measure of semantic complexity in oral and written English", *Language and Speech* 25, pp. 1-10.

CORSON, D. J. (1983a) "The Corson Measure of Passive Vocabulary", *Language and Speech* 26, pp. 3-20.

CORSON, D. J. (1983b) "Social dialect, the semantic barrier and access to curricular knowledge", *Language in Society* 12, pp. 213-222.

CORSON, D. J. (1984) "A case for oral language in schooling". *Elementary School Journal* 84, pp. 458-467.

CORSON, D. J. (1985) *The Lexical Bar.* Pergamon Press: Oxford.

CORSON, D. J. (1987) *Oral Language Across the Curriculum.* Multilingual Matters: Clevedon, Avon.

CORSON, D. J. (1989) "Adolescent lexical differences in Australia and England by social group". *Journal of Educational Research* 82, pp. 146-157.

CORSON, D. J. (1991) "Bhaskar's critical realism and educational knowledge". *British Journal of Sociology of Education* 12, pp. 223-241.

CORSON, D. J. (1993) *Language, Minority Education and Gender: Linking Social Justice and Power.* Multilingual Matters: Clevedon, Avon.

CORSON, D. J. (Ed.) (1995a) *Discourse and Power in Educational Organizations.* Hampton Press: Cresskill, NJ.

CORSON, D. J. (1995b) "A review of *The Discursive Mind* by Rom Harré and Grant Gillett". *Language in Society* **24** (in press).

CORSON, D. J. (1995c) "Norway's Sámi Language Act: emancipatory implications for the world's aboriginal peoples". *Language in Society* **24** (in press).

COURTENAY, W. J. (1987) *Schools and Scholars in Fourteenth-Century England.* Princeton University Press: Princeton, NJ.

CUMMINS, J. (1981) "Age on arrival and immigrant second language learning in Canada: a reassessment". *Applied Linguistics* **11**, pp. 132-149.

CUMMINS, J. (1984) "The minority language child." In *Bilingual and Multicultural Education: Canadian Perspectives,* edited by S. Shapson, and V. D'Oyley. Multilingual Matters: Clevedon, Avon.

CUMMINS, J. & SWAIN, M. (1986) *Bilingualism in Education: Aspects of Theory, Research and Practice.* Longman: London.

CUNNINGHAM, A. E. & STANOVICH, K.E. (1991) "Tracking the unique effects of print exposure in children: associations with vocabulary, general knowledge and spelling". *Journal of Educational Psychology* **83**, pp. 264-274.

CURTIS, M. E. (1987) "Vocabulary testing and vocabulary instruction". In *The Nature of Vocabulary Acquisition,* edited by M. G. McKeown and M. E. Curtis. Lawrence Erlbaum: Hillsdale, NJ.

CUTLER, A. (1981) "Degree of transparency in word formation". *Canadian Journal of Linguistics* **26**, pp. 73-77.

CUTLER, A. (1983) "Lexical complexity and sentence processing". In *The Process of Language Understanding* edited by G. B. F. d'Arcais and R. J. Jarvella. John Wiley: Chichester.

CUTLER, A. (1994) "Language-specific processing: does the evidence converge?" In *Cognitive Models of Speech Processing,* edited by G. Altmann and G. Shilcock. Erlbaum: Hillsdale NJ.

DALE, P. S. (1976) *Language Development — Structure and Function.* Holt Rinehart & Winston: New York.

D'ANDRADE, R. G. (1984) "Cultural meaning systems". In *Culture Theory: Essays on Mind, Self, and Emotion,* edited by R. A. Shweder and R. A. LeVine. Cambridge University Press.

DANIELS, H. A. (1983) *Famous Last Words: The American Language Crisis Reconsidered.* Southern Illinois University Press: Carbondale.

DAVIE, R., BUTLER, N. & GOLDSTEIN, H. (1972) *From Birth to Seven — The Second Report of the National Child Development Study* (1958 Cohort). Longmans: London.

DERWING, B. L. & BAKER, W. J. (1979) "Recent research on the acquisition of English morphology". In *Language Acquisition: Studies in First Language Development,* edited by P. Fletcher and M. Garman. Cambridge University Press.

DERWING, B. L. & BAKER, W. J. (1986) "Assessing morphological development". In *Language Acquisition: Studies in First Language Development,* (second edition) edited by P. Fletcher and M. Garman. Cambridge University Press.

DES (Department of Education and Science) (1975) *A Language for Life* (The Bullock Report). HMSO: London.

DICTIONNAIRE DES FRÉQUENCES de la Trésor de la Langue Française (1971) CNRS: Nancy.

DITTMAR, N. (1976) *Sociolinguistics.* Arnold: London.

DRUM, P. A. & KONOPAK, B. C. (1987) "Learning word meanings from written context". In *The Nature of Vocabulary Acquisition,* edited by M. G. McKeown and M. E. Curtis. Lawrence Erlbaum: Hillsdale, NJ.

DUNN, L. M. & DUNN, L. M. (1981) *Peabody Picture Vocabulary Test - Revised.* American Guidance Service: Circle Pines, MN

DUPOUX, E. (1994) "The time course of prelexical processing: the syllabic hypothesis revisited". In *Cognitive Models of Speech Processing.,* edited by G. Altmann and G. Shilcock. Erlbaum: Hillsdale NJ.

DURKHEIM, E. (1893) *The Division of Labour in Society* (translated by George Simpson). Free Press of Glencoe: London (1964 edition).

EAGLESHAM, E. J. R. (1967) *The Foundations of Twentieth Century Education in England.* Routledge & Kegan Paul: London.

EDWARDS, A. D. (1976) *Language in Culture and Class — The Sociology of Language and Education.* Heinemann: London.

EDWARDS, A. D. & WESTGATE, D. (1994) *Investigating Classroom Talk.* Falmer Press: Brighton.

EDWARDS, J. R. (1979) *Language and Disadvantage.* Arnold: London.

EDWARDS, J. R. (1989) *Language and Disadvantage.* (second edition) Cole & Whurr: London.

EDWARDS, V. (1986) *Language in a Black Community.* Multilingual Matters: Clevedon, Avon.

ELBRO, C. (1990) *Differences in Dyslexia.* Munksgaard: Copenhagen.

ELSHOUT-MOHR, M. & VAN DAALEN-KAPTEIJNS, M. M. (1987) "Cognitive processes in learning word meanings". In *The Nature of Vocabulary Acquisition,* edited by M. G. McKeown and M. E. Curtis. Lawrence Erlbaum: Hillsdale, NJ.

ELYOT, SIR THOMAS (1531) *The Boke Named the Governour.* Kegan Paul: London (1883 edition).

ERVIN-TRIPP, S. (1972) "On sociolinguistic rules: alternation and co-occurrence". In *Directions in Sociolinguistics,* edited by J. J. Gumperz and D. Hymes. Holt, Rinehart & Winston: New York.

ESLAND, G. (1971) "Teaching and learning as the organisation of knowledge". In *Knowledge and Control,* edited by M. F. D. Young, Collier Macmillan: London.

FAIRCLOUGH, N. (1992) *Critical Language Awareness.* Longman: London.

FASOLD, R. (1984) *The Sociolinguistics of Society.* Basil Blackwell: Oxford.

FEAGANS, L. and FARRAN, D. C. (Eds) (1982) *The Language of Children Reared in Poverty: Implications for Evaluation and Intervention.* Academic Press: New York.

FEBVRE, L. & MARTIN, H-J. (1976) *The Coming of the Book: The Impact of Printing 1450-1800.* New Left Books: London.

FELDMAN, L.B. (1991) "The contribution of morphology to word recognition". *Psychological Research* **53**, pp. 33-41.

FERGUSON, C. A. (1959) "Diglossia". *Word*, **15**, pp. 325-340.

FLYDAL, E. (1983) *Oljespråk.* Universitetsforlaget: Oslo.

FORD, J. (1969) *Social Class and the Comprehensive School.* Routledge & Kegan Paul: London.

FORSTER, K. I. (1976) "Accessing the mental lexicon". In *New Approaches to Language Mechanisms,* edited by E. C. J. Walker and R. J. Wales. North Holland Press, Amsterdam.

FREEBODY, P. & ANDERSON, R. C. (1983) "Effects on text comprehension of differing propositions and locations of difficult vocabulary". *Journal of Reading Behaviour* **15**, pp. 19-39.

FREGE, G. (1970) *Translations from the Philosophical Writings of Gottlob Frege,* edited and translated by P. Geach and M. Black. Blackwell: London.

FREYD, P. & BARON, J. (1982) "Individual differences in acquisition of derivational morphology", *Journal of Verbal Learning and Verbal Behaviour,* **21**, pp. 282-295.

FRICK, N. & MALSTRÖM, S. (1976) *Språkklyftan* [The Language Gap]. Tidens Forlag: Kristianstad.

FUSSELL, P. (1983) *Class.* Ballantine: New York.

GARCIA, G. (1991) "Factors influencing the English reading test performance of Spanish-speaking Hispanic students". *Reading Research Quarterly* **26**, pp. 371-392.

GASS, S. & SELINKER, L. (Eds) (1983) *Language Transfer and Language Learning.* Newbury House: Rowley Mass.

GEE, J. P. (1988) "The legacies of literacy: from Plato, to Freire, through Harvey Graff". *Harvard Educational Review* **58**, pp. 195-212.

GINSBURG, H. (1972) *The Myth of the Deprived Child.* Prentice Hall: New York.

GILES, H. & POWESLAND, P. F. (1975) *Speech Style and Social Evaluation.* Academic Press: London.

GILLETT, G. (1992) *Representation, Meaning and Thought.* Oxford University Press: Oxford.

GOLDTHORPE, J. H. (1980) *Social Mobility and Class Structure in Modern Britain.* The Clarendon Press: Oxford.

GOODY, J. (1987) *The Interface Between the Written and the Oral.* Cambridge University Press.

GORDON, P. & LAWTON, D. (1978) *Curriculum Change in the Nineteenth and Twentieth Centuries.* Hodder & Stoughton: London.

GOULDEN, R., NATION, P. & READ, J. (1990) "How large can a receptive vocabulary be?". *Applied Linguistics* **11**, pp. 341-363.

GRAMSCI, A. (1948) *Opere di Antonio Gramsci, (Quaderni del Carcere XVIII)* Vols. I-XI. Einaudi: Turin (1966 edition).

GRAVES, M. F. (1986) "Vocabulary learning and instruction". *Review of Research in Education* **13**, pp. 58-89.

GRAVES, M. F., RYDER, R. J., SLATER, W. H. & CALFEE, R. C. (1987) "The relationship between word frequency and reading vocabulary using six metrics of frequency". *Journal of Educational Research* **81**, pp. 81-91.

GROBE, C. (1981) "Syntactic maturity, mechanics, and vocabulary as predictors of quality ratings". *Research in the Teaching of English* **15**, pp. 75-85.

GROVE, V. (1949) *The Language Bar.* Routledge & Kegan Paul: London. (1950 edition)

GUMPERZ, J. (1982) *Discourse Strategies.* Cambridge University Press: London.

GUMPERZ, J., KALTMAN, H. & O'CONNOR, M. C. (1984) "Cohesion in spoken and written discourse". In *Coherence in Spoken and Written Discourse,* edited by D. Tannen. Ablex: Norwood, NJ.

GUSDORF, G. (1967) *Speaking (La Parole)* (translated by P. T. Brockelman). Northwestern University Press: Evanston.

HALL, W. S., NAGY, W. E. & LINN, R. (1984) *Spoken Words: Effects of Situation and Social Group on Oral Word Usage and Frequency.* Erlbaum: Hillsdale NJ.

HALLE, M. (1973) "Prolegomena to a theory of word formation". *Linguistic Inquiry* **4**, pp. 3-16.

HALLIDAY, M. A. K. (1978) *Language as Social Semiotic: The Social Interpretation of Language and Meaning.* Arnold: London.

HAMLYN, D. W. (1967) "The logical and psychological aspects of learning". In *The Concept of Education,* edited by R. S. Peters. Routledge & Kegan Paul: London.

HAMILTON, M. , BARTON, D. & IVANIC (1993) *Worlds of Literacy.* Multilingual Matters: Clevedon, Avon.

HAMMOND, J. L. & HAMMOND, B. (1947) *The Bleak Age.* Penguin: London.

HANCIN-BHATT, B. & NAGY, W. (1994) "Lexical transfer and second language morphological development". *Applied Psycholinguistics* **15**, pp. 289-310.

HARRÉ, R. (1990) "Exploring the human Umwelt". In *Harré and his Critics: Essays in honour of Rom Harré with his commentary on them,* edited by Roy Bhaskar. (pp. 297-364) Basil Blackwell: Oxford.

HARRÉ, R. & GILLETT, G. (1994) *The Discursive Mind.* Sage: Thousand Oaks, California.

HAUGEN, E. (1981) "Language fragmentation in Scandinavia: revolt of the minorities". In *Minority Languages Today,* edited by E. Haugen, J. D. McClure and D. S. Thompson. Edinburgh University Press.

HAWKINS, E. (1988) *Awareness of Language: An Introduction.* Cambridge University Press: London.

HAWKINS, P. R. (1977) *Social Class, the Nominal Group and Verbal Strategies.* Routledge & Kegan Paul: London.

HAYES, D. P. (1988) "Speaking and writing: distinct patterns of word choice". *Journal of Memory & Language* **27**, pp. 572-585.

HAYES, D. P. & AHRENS, M. (1988) "Vocabulary simplification for children: a special case of 'motherese'?". *Journal of Child Language* **15**, pp. 395-410.

HAYES, D. P. & GRETHER, J. (1983) "The school year and vacations: when do students learn?". *Cornell Journal of Social Relations* **17**, pp. 56-71.

HEATH, S. B. (1983) *Ways with Words.* Cambridge University Press.

HEATH, S. B. (1986) "Critical factors in literacy development". In *Literacy, Society and Schooling,* edited by S. de Castell, A. Luke and K. Egan. Cambridge University Press.

HEIM, A. W. *et al.* (1974) *Manual of Instruction — AH4 Group Test of General Intelligence.* NFER: London.

HENDERSON, E. H. (1985) *Teaching Spelling.* Houghton Mifflin: Boston.

HENDERSON, L. (1982) *Orthography and Word Recognition in Reading.* Academic Press: London.

HENRY, M. K. (1993) "Morphological structure: Latin and Greek roots and affixes as upper grade code strategies". *Reading and Writing* **5**, pp. 227-241.

HIRST, P. H. (1974) *Knowledge and the Curriculum — A Collection of Philosophical Papers.* Routledge & Kegan Paul: London.

HODGES, J. (1971) "Some influences on the performance of West Indian children in London schools". MSc dissertation: University of London.

HOGGART, R. (1958) *The Uses of Literacy.* Pelican: Harmondsworth.

HOLLAND, D. & QUINN, N. (Eds) (1987) *Cultural Models in Language and Thought.* Cambridge University Press: Cambridge.

HOLMES, V. M. & O'REGAN, J. K. (1992) "Reading derivationally affixed French words". *Language and Cognitive Processes* **7**, pp. 163-192.

HOLT, M. (1978) *The Common Curriculum: Its Structures and Style in the Comprehensive School.* Routledge & Kegan Paul: London.

HOPE, T. E. (1971) *Lexical Borrowing in the Romance Languages,* Vols. I and II. Blackwell: Oxford.

HSIA, S., CHUNG, P. K. & WONG, D. (1995) "ESL learners' word organisation strategies: a case of Chinese learners of English words in Hong Kong". *Language and Education* **9** (in press).

HUDSON, R. A. (1980) *Sociolinguistics.* Cambridge University Press: London.

HURT, J. (1979) *Elementary Schooling and the Working Class 1860-1918.* Routledge & Kegan Paul: London.

HYMES, D. (Ed.) (1964) *Language in Culture and Society: A Reader in Linguistics and Anthropology.* Harper & Row: New York.

HYMES, D. (1968) "The ethnography of speaking". In *Readings in the Sociology of Language,* edited by J. A. Fishman. Mouton: The Hague.

HYMES, D. (1972) "On communicative competence". In *Sociolinguistics,* edited by J. Pride and J. Holmes. Penguin: Harmondsworth.

HYMES, D. (1974) "Review of Noam Chomsky". In *On Noam Chomsky — Critical Essays,* edited by G. Harman. Anchor Books: New York.

ISAACSON, S. (1988) "Assessing the writing product: qualitative and quantitative measures". *Exceptional Children* **54**, pp. 528-534.

JACKENDOFF, R. (1975) "Morphological and semantic regularities in the lexicon". *Language* **51**, pp. 639-671.

JACKSON, B. & MARSDEN, D. (1966) *Education and the Working Class.* Penguin: Harmondsworth.

JAKUBOWICZ, A. & WOLF, E. (1980) *Immigrant Parents and Port Kembla Schools.* Wollongong Centre for Multicultural Studies: Wollongong.

JARVELLA, R. J. & MEIJERS, G. (1983) "Recognizing morphemes in spoken words: some evidence for a stem-organized mental lexicon". In *The Process of Language Understanding* edited by G. B. F. d'Arcais and R. J. Jarvella. John Wiley: Chichester.

JOHNSON, J. (1991) "Developmental versus language-based factors in metaphor interpretation". *Journal of Educational Psychology* **83**, pp. 470-483.

KAESTLE, C. F. (1991) *Literacy in the United States.* Yale University Press: New Haven, CT.

KAKAR, S. (1982) *Shamans, Mystics and Doctors.* Beacon Press: Boston.

KINTSCH, W. (1972) "Abstract nouns: imagery versus lexical complexity", *Journal of Verbal Learning and Verbal Behaviour* **11**, pp. 59-65.

KLEIN, J. (1965) *Samples from English Cultures*, Vols. I and II. Routledge & Kegan Paul: London.

KOWAL, M. & SWAIN, M. (1994) "Using collaborative language production tasks to promote students' language awareness". *Language Awareness* **3**, pp. 73-93.

KRASHEN, S. (1989) "We acquire vocabulary and spelling by reading: additional evidence for the input hypothesis". *The Modern Language Journal* **73**, pp. 440-464.

KUCERA, F. & FRANCIS, W. N. (1967) *Computational Analysis of Present-day American English.* Brown University: Providence, R. I.

KUHN, T. S. (1962) *The Structure of Scientific Revolutions.* University of Chicago Press: Chicago.

LABOV, W. (1966) *The Social Stratification of English in New York City.* Washington Center for Applied Linguistics: Washington.

LABOV, W. (1972a) *Language in the Inner City: Studies in the Black English Vernacular.* University of Pennsylvania Press: Philadelphia.

LABOV, W. (1972b) "The logic of non-standard English". In *Language and Social Context*, edited by P.P. Giglioli. Penguin: Harmondsworth..

LABOV, W. (1978) "Gaining access to the dictionary". In *Speech and Language in the Laboratory, School and Clinic*, edited by J. F. Kavanagh and W. Strange. M. I. T. Press: Cambridge, MA.

LABOV, W. (1982) "Objectivity and commitment in linguistic science: the case of the Black English trial in Ann Arbor". *Language in Society* **11**, pp. 165-201.

LABOV, W. & FANSHEL, D. (1977) *Therapeutic Discourse.* Academic Press: New York.

LAUDANNA, A., BURANI, C. & CERMELE, A. (1994) "Prefixes as processing units". *Language and Cognitive Processes* **9**, pp. 295-316.

LAWSON, J. & SILVER, H. (1973) *A Social History of Education in England.* Methuen: London.

LAWTON, D. (1965) "Social class differences in individual interviews". Unpublished paper, University of London Institute of Education.

LAWTON, D. (1968) *Social Class, Language and Education*. Routledge & Kegan Paul: London.

LAWTON, D. (1973) *Social Change, Educational Theory and Curriculum Planning*. Unibooks: London.

LEECH, G. H. (1974) *Semantics*. Pelican: Harmondsworth.

LEHRER, A. (1974) *Semantic Fields and Lexical Structure*. North Holland: London.

LÉVI-STRAUSS, C. (1966) *The Savage Mind*. Weidenfeld & Nicholson: London.

LEUNG, C. (1993) "ESL in primary education in England: a classroom study". *Language and Education* 7, pp. 163-180

LEVIN, H., LONG, S. & SCHAFFER, C. A. (1981) "The formality of the Latinate lexicon in English". *Language and Speech* 24, pp. 161-171.

LEVIN, H. & NOVAK, M. (1991) "Frequencies of Latinate and Germanic words in English as determinants of formality". *Discourse Processes* 14, pp. 389-398.

LEVINE, R. A. (1984) "Properties of culture: ethnographic view". In *Culture Theory: Essays on Mind, Self, and Emotion*, edited by R. A. Shweder and R. A. LeVine. Cambridge University Press: Cambridge.

LEWIS, C. T. & SHORT, C. (1955 revised) *A Latin Dictionary*. Oxford University Press: London.

LIDDELL, H. G. & SCOTT, R. (1961 revised) *A Greek English Lexicon*. Oxford University Press: London.

LIMA, S. D. & POLLATSEK, A. (1983) "Lexical access via an orthographic code? The Basic Orthographic Syllabic Structure (BOSS) reconsidered". *Journal of Verbal Learning and Verbal Behaviour* 22, pp. 310-332.

LOCKE, J. (1690) *Some Thoughts Concerning Education*. London (1732 edition).

LO DUCA, M. G. (1990) *Creatività e regole: Studia sull'acquisizione della morphologia derivativa dell'italiano* Mulino: Bologna.

LUKATELA, G., GLIGORIJEVIC, B., KOSTIC, A. & TURVEY, M. T. (1980) "Representation of inflected nouns in the internal lexicon". *Memory and Cognition* 8, pp. 415-423.

LUKE, A. (1994) "On reading and the sexual division of literacy". *Journal of Curriculum Studies* 26, pp. 361-381.

LURIA, A. R. (1973) *The Working Brain*. Penguin: Harmondsworth.

LURIA, A. R. & YUDOVICH, F. IA. (1956) *Speech and the Development of Mental Processes in the Child*. Penguin: Harmondsworth. (1971 edition).

LYONS, J. (ed.) (1970) *New Horizons in Linguistics*. Pelican: Harmondsworth.

LYONS, J. (1977) *Semantics* Vols. I and II. Cambridge University Press: London.

MACKAY, D. G. (1978) "Derivational rules and the internal lexicon". *Journal of Verbal Learning and Verbal Behaviour*, 17, pp. 61-71.

MARSLEN-WILSON, W., TYLER, L. K., WAKSLER, R. & OLDER, L. (1994) "Morphology and meaning in the English mental lexicon". *Psychological Review* **101**, pp. 3-33.

MARLAND, M. (1990) "All one world: Michael Marland on multicultural publishing". *The Times Educational Supplement.* (May 25) p. B11.

MASCIANTONIO, R. (1977) "Tangible benefits of the study of Latin: a review of research", *Foreign Language Annals,* **10**, pp. 375-382.

MASON, M., MASON, B. & QUAYLE, T. (1992) "Illuminating English: how explicit language teaching improved public examination results in a comprehensive school". *Educational Studies* **18**, pp. 341-353.

MAVROGENES, N. A. (1987) "Latin and language arts: an update". *Foreign Language Annals* **20**, pp. 131-137.

MAYLATH, B. A. R. (1994) "Words make a difference: effects of Greco-Latinate and Anglo-Saxon lexical variation on post-secondary-level writing assessment in English". PhD thesis: University of Minnesota.

MCCARTHY, M. J. (1988) "Review of *The Lexical Bar*". *Language in Society* **17**, pp. 143-146.

MCCARTHY, M. J. (1990) *Vocabulary.* Oxford University Press: Oxford.

MCCLELLAND, J. L. (1987) "The case for interactionism in language processing". In *Attention and Performance XII,* edited by M. Coltheart. Erlbaum: London.

MCCLELLAND, J. L. & RUMELHART, D. E. (1981) "An interactive activation model of context effects in letter perception". *Psychological Review* **88**, pp. 375-407.

MCDONALD, M. (1989) "The exploitation of linguistic mis-match: towards an ethnography of customs and manners." In *Social Anthropology and the Politics of Language,* edited by R. Grillo. Routledge: London.

MEARA, P. (1983) *Vocabulary in a Second Language. Volume III 1986-1990.* Centre for Applied Language Studies: Swansea.

MEARA, P. (1986) "Review of *The Lexical Bar*". *JACT Review* **5**, Autumn.

MEARA, P. and BUXTON, B. (1987) "An alternative to multiple choice vocabulary tests". *Language Testing* **4,** pp. 142-151.

MENEGHELLO, L. (1963) *Libera Nos a Malo.* Fetrinelli: Milan.

MENYUK, P. (1977) *Language and Maturation.* MIT Press: Cambridge, MA.

MERCY, J. & STEELMAN, L. (1982) "Familial influence on the intellectual attainment of children". *American Sociological Review* **47**, pp. 532-542.

MILLER, G. A. (1991) *The Science of Words.* Scientific American Library: New York.

MILLS, C. W. (1940) "Situated actions and vocabularies of motive". *American Sociological Review* **5**, pp. 904-913.

MILROY, J. (1987) *Language and Social Networks.* Blackwell: Oxford.

MILROY, J. (1992) *Linguistic Variation and Change* Blackwell: Oxford.

MORAVCSIK, E. A. (1977) "'Semantic Fields and Lexical Structure' by Adrienne Lehrer, Tucson 1974 — A review", *General Linguistics* **17**, pp. 94-107.

MUCH, N. C. (1992) "The analysis of discourse as methodology for a semiotic psychology". *American Behavioural Scientist* **36**, pp. 52-72.

MÜHLHAUSLER, P. & HARRÉ, R. (1990) *Pronouns and People*. Blackwell: Oxford.

MULCASTER, R. (1582) *The First Part of the Elementary*. Scolar Press: Menston (1970 edition).

NAGY, W. E. & ANDERSON, R. C. (1984) "The number of words in printed school English". *Reading Research Quarterly* 19, pp. 304-330.

NAGY, W. E., ANDERSON, R. C. & HERMAN, P. A. (1987) "Learning word meanings from context during normal reading". *American Educational Research Journal* 24, pp. 237-270.

NAGY, W. E., HERMAN, P. A. & ANDERSON, R. C. (1985) "Learning words from context". *Reading Research Quarterly* 20, pp. 233-253.

NAGY, W. E. & HERMAN, P. A. (1987) "Breadth and depth of vocabulary knowledge: implications for acquisition and instruction". In *The Nature of Vocabulary Acquisition*, edited by M. G. McKeown and M. E. Curtis. Lawrence Erlbaum: Hillsdale, NJ.

NASH, R. (1987) "Review of *The Lexical Bar*". *New Zealand Sociology* 2 pp. 154-162.

NATION, I. S. P. (1990) *Teaching and Learning Vocabulary*. Newbury House: Rowley, MA.

NATION, P. & CARTER, R. (1989) *Vocabulary Acquisition (AILA Review 6)*. Free University Press: Amsterdam.

NIDA, E. A. (1948) "The identification of morphemes". *Language* 24, pp. 414-441.

NIELSEN, L. & PICHÉ, G. L. (1981) "The influence of headed nominal complexity and lexical choice on teachers' evaluation of writing". *Research in the Teaching of English* 15, pp. 65-73.

NIEMI, J., LAINE, M. & TUOMINEN, J. (1994) "Cognitive morphology in Finnish: foundations of a new model". *Language and Cognitive Processes* 9, pp. 423-446.

NISBET, R. A. (1967) *The Sociological Tradition*. Heinemann: London.

NORDSTRØM, M. (1992) "Engelsk alt sammen". *Aftenposten* 25, p. 34.

NORRIS, R. A. (1974) "The vocabulary of disadvantaged children: a comparative study of the vocabulary ability of children of English and of West Indian origin". unpublished MA thesis. University of Birmingham.

OGBU, J. (1987) "Variability in minority school performance: a problem in search of an explanation." *Anthropology and Education Quarterly* 18, pp. 312-334.

OGILVIE, R. M. (1964) *Latin and Greek — A History of the Influence of the Classics on English Life from 1600 to 1918.* Routledge & Kegan Paul:London.

OHALA, M. & OHALA, J. J. (1987). "Psycholinguistic probes of native speaker's phonological knowledge". In *Phonologica* edited by W. Dressler et al. Cambridge University Press: Cambridge.

OLSON, D. R. (1977) "From utterance to text: the bias of language in speech and writing", *Harvard Educational Review* 47, pp. 257-281.

OLSON, D. R. (1994) *The World On Paper.* Cambridge University Press: Cambridge.

OLSON, D. R. & ASTINGTON, J. W. (1990) "Talking about text: how literacy contributes to thought". *Journal of Pragmatics* **14**, pp. 705-721.

ORME, N. (1989) *Education and Society in Medieval and Renaissance England.* The Hambledon Press: London.

OXFORD ENGLISH DICTIONARY (Compact edition, 1991 revised), Vols I-XII. Oxford University Press: London.

PAIVIO, A., YUILLE, J. C. & MADIGAN, S. A. (1968) "Concreteness, imagery and meaningfulness values for 925 nouns", *Journal of Experimental Psychology Monograph Supplement* **76**, 1, part 2.

PALERMO, D. S. & MOLFESE, D. L. (1972) "Language acquisition from age five onward", *Psychological Bulletin,* **78**, pp. 409-428.

PALMER, F. R. (1976) *Semantics: A New Outline.* Cambridge University Press: London.

PEACHAM, H. (1622) *The Compleat Gentleman.* London.

PEEL, E. A. (1971) *The Nature of Adolescent Judgment.* Staples: London.

PEEL, E. A. and DE SILVA, W. A. (1972) "Some aspects of higher learning processes during adolescence". In *Advances in Educational Psychology,* edited by W. D. Wall and V. P. Varma. University of London Press: London.

PEEL, E. A. (1975) "Predilection for generalising and abstracing", *British Journal of Educational Psychology* **45**, pp. 177-188.

PEEL, E. A. (1978) "Generalising through the verbal medium", *British Journal Educational Psychology* **48**, pp. 36-46.

PEIRCE, B. (1995) *Language Learning and Social Identity.* Multilingual Matters: Clevedon, Avon.

PHILIPS, S. (1983) *The Invisible Culture: Communication in Classroom and Community on the Warm Springs Indian Reservation.* Longman: New York.

PLATTS, M. (1979) *Ways of Meaning — An Introduction to a Philosophy of Language.* Routledge & Kegan Paul: London.

POSTMAN, L. (1975) "Verbal learning and memory", *Annual Review of Psychology* **26**, pp. 291-335.

POSTMAN, L.& KNECHT, K. (1983) "Encoding variability and retention", *Journal of Verbal Learning and Verbal Behaviour* **22**, pp. 133-152.

POTTER, S. (1966) *Our Language.* Pelican: Harmondsworth.

PURVES, A. C. (1988) "Commentary - Research on written composition: a response to Hillocks' report". *Research in the Teaching of English* **22**, pp. 104-108.

QUINE, W.V.O. (1966) *The Ways of Paradox and Other Essays.* Random House: New York.

QUIRK, R. (1974) *The Linguist and the English Language.* Arnold: London.

QUINN, N. & HOLLAND, D. (1987) "Culture and cognition". In *Cultural Models in Language and Thought,* edited by D. Holland and N. Quinn. Cambridge University Press.

REGISTRAR GENERAL (1980) Classification of Occupations. Office of Population Censuses and Statistics: London.

REID, I. (1977) Social Class Differences in Britain. Open Books: London.

RICHARD, C. J. (1994) The Founders and the Classics: Greece, Rome and the American Enlightenment. Harvard University Press: Cambridge, MA.

RIDGE, E. (1986) "Review of The Lexical Bar". Journal of Language Learning 2, pp. 32-33.

ROBERTS, E. (1970) An Evaluation of Standardised Tests as Tools for the Measurement of Language Development. Language Research Foundation, Northwestern University Press: Evanston.

ROBERTS, T. J. (1986) "Review of The Lexical Bar". Language and Speech 29, pp. 93-94.

ROBINSON, W. P. (1978) Language Management in Education — The Australian Context. Allen & Unwin: London.

ROBINSON, W. P. (1986) "Review of The Lexical Bar". Australian Journal of Education 30, pp. 324-326.

ROLFE, G. C. (1978) "Graeco-Latin lexical elements in Russian and Czech", DPhil thesis: New University of Ulster.

ROMAINE, S. (1984) The Language of Children and Adolescents: The Acquisition of Communicative Competence. Basil Blackwell: Oxford.

ROSENTHAL, R. & JACOBSON, L. (1968) Pygmalion in the Classroom. Holt, Rinehart & Winston: New York.

RUNDLE, B. (1990) Wittgenstein and Contemporary Philosophy of Language. Basil Blackwell: Oxford.

SAMUELS, M. L. (1972) Linguistic Evolution. Cambridge University Press: London.

SANDRA, D. (1988) "Is morphology used to encode derivations when learning a foreign language". International Review of Applied Linguistics 79/80, pp. 1-23.

SANDRA, D. (1990) "On the representation and processing of compound words: automatic access to constituent morphemes does not occur". Quarterly Journal of Experimental Psychology 42A pp. 529-567.

SANDRA, D. (1993) "The use of lexical morphology as a natural aid in learning foreign language vocabulary". In Memory and Memorization in Acquiring and Learning Languages, edited by J. Chapelle and M. Claes. Centre de Langues `a Louvain-la-neuve et en Woulwe.

SANDRA, D. (1994) "The morphology of the mental lexicon: internal word structure viewed from a psycholinguistic perspective". Language and Cognitive Processes 9, pp. 227-269.

SAVILLE-TROIKE, M. (1979) "Culture, language and education". In Bilingual Multicultural Education and the Professional, edited by H. Trueba and C. Barnett-Mizrahi. Newbury House: Rowley, MA.

SAVILLE-TROIKE, M. (1984) "What really matters in second language learning for academic achievement". TESOL Quarterly 18, pp. 199-219.

SCOLLON, R. & SCOLLON, S. (1981) Narrative Literacy and Face in Inter-Ethnic Communication. Ablex: Norwood, NJ:

SCRIBNER, S. & COLE, M. (1981) *The Psychology of Literacy.* Cambridge University Press: Cambridge, MA.

SEARLE, J. R. (1969) *Speech Acts.* Cambridge University Press: London.

SEGUI, J. & ZUBIZARETTA, M. (1985) "Mental representation of morphologically complex words and lexical access". *Linguistics* 23, pp. 759-774.

SEIDENBERG, M. S. (1985) "The time, course of information activation, and utilization in visual word recognition". In *Reading Research: Advances in Theory and Practice.* Vol 5. edited by D. Besner, T. G. Waller and G. E. MacKinnon. Academic Press: London.

SEIDENBERG, M. S. *et al.* (1982) "Automatic access of the meanings of ambiguous words in context: some limitations of knowledge-based processing", *Cognitive Psychology* 14, pp. 489-537.

SELKIRK, E. O. (1982) *The Syntax of Words.* MIT Press: Cambridge MA.

SHARWOOD SMITH, J. E. (1977) *On Teaching Classics.* Routledge & Kegan Paul: London.

SILVER, P. & SILVER, H. (1974) *The Education of the Poor — The History of a National School 1824-1974.* Routledge & Kegan Paul: London.

SINCLAIR, J. M. & COULTHARD, M. (1975) *Towards an Analysis of Discourse.* Oxford University Press: Oxford.

SINCLAIR, J. M. & RENOUF, A. (1988) "A lexical syllabus for language learning". In *Vocabulary and Language Teaching,* edited by R. Carter and R. J. McCarthy. Longmans: London.

SKEAT, W. W. (1917) *A Primer of English Etymology.* The Clarendon Press: Oxford.

SMITH, P. T. & STERLING, C. M. (1982) "Factors affecting the perceived morphemic structure of written words". *Journal of Verbal Learning and Verbal Behaviour* 21, pp. 704-721.

SNOW, C. (1983) "Literacy and language: relationships during the preschool years". *Harvard Educational Review* 53, pp. 165-189.

STANNERS, R. F., NEISER, J. J. & PAINTON, S. (1979) "Memory representation for prefixed words", *Journal of Verbal Learning and Verbal Behaviour* 18, pp. 733-743.

STANOVICH, K.E. (1993) "Does reading make you smarter? Literacy and the development of verbal intelligence". *Advances in Child Development and Behaviour* 24, pp. 133-180.

STANOVICH, K.E. & CUNNINGHAM, A. E. (1992) "Studying the consequences of literacy within a literate society: the cognitive correlates of print exposure". *Memory & Cognition* 20, pp. 51-68.

STANOVICH, K.E. & CUNNINGHAM, A. E. (1993) "Where does knowledge come from? Specific associations between print exposure and information acquisition". *Journal of Educational Psychology* 85, pp. 211-229.

STEINBERG, D. B. & JAKOBOVITS, L. A. (1971) *Semantics.* Cambridge University Press: London.

STEINER, G. (1975) *After Babel — Aspects of Language and Translation.* Oxford University Press: London.

STEMBERGER, J. P. & MACWHINNEY, B. (1986) "Frequency and the storage of regularly inflected forms". *Memory and Cognition* **14**, pp. 7-26.

STEVENSON, V. (Ed.) (1983) *Words: The Evolution of Western Languages.* Methuen: London.

STIGLER, J. W., SHWEDER, R. A. & HERDT, G. (1990) *Cultural Psychology: Essays on Comparative Human Development.* Cambridge University Press: Cambridge

STORCK, P. A. & LOOFT, W. R. (1973) "Qualitative analysis of vocabulary responses from persons aged 6 to 66 plus". *Journal of Educational Psychology* **65**, 2.

STURT, M. (1967) *The Education of the People: a history of primary education in England and Wales in the nineteenth century.* Routledge & Kegan Paul: London.

SWAIN, M. (1985) "Communicative competence: some roles of comprehensible input and comprehensible output in its development". In *Input in Second Language Acquisition,* edited by S. M. Gass & C. G. Madden. Rowley MA: Newbury House.

TAFT, M. (1979) "Recognition of affixed words and the word frequency effect", *Memory and Cognition* **7**, pp. 263-272.

TAFT, M. (1985) "The decoding of words in lexical access: a review of the morphographic approach". In *Reading Research: Advances in Theory and Practice.* Vol 5. edited by D. Besner, T. G. Waller and G. E. MacKinnon. Academic Press: London.

TAFT, M. (1991) *Reading and the Mental Lexicon.* Erlbaum: Hove.

TAFT, M. (1992) "The body of the BOSS: subsyllabic units in the lexical processing of polysyllabic words". *Journal of Experimental Psychology* **18**, pp. 1004-1014.

TAFT, M. (1994) "Interactive activation as a framework for understanding morphological processing". *Language and Cognitive Processes* **9**, pp. 271-294.

TAFT, M. & FORSTER, K. I. (1975) "Lexical storage and retrieval of polymorphemic and polysyllabic words", *Journal of Verbal Learning and Verbal Behaviour* **15**, pp. 607-620.

TAFT, M., HAMBLY, G. & KINOSHITA, S. (1986) "Visual and auditory recognition of prefixed words". *Quarterly Journal of Experimental Psychology* **38A**, pp. 351-366.

TANNEN, D. (1990) *You Just Don't Understand.* Morrow: New York.

TAYLOR, I. (1990) *Psycholinguistics: Learning and Using Language.* Prentice Hall: New York.

THOMPSON, E. P. (1968) *The Making of the English Working Class.* Pelican: Harmondsworth.

THORNDIKE, E. L. & LORGE, I. (1944) *The Teacher's Word Book of 30,000 Words.* Columbia: New York.

THORNDYKE, P. W. (1975) "Conceptual complexity and imagery in comprehension and memory", *Journal of Verbal Learning and Verbal Behaviour* **14**, pp. 359-369.

TRAUGOTT, E. C. (1987) "Literacy and language change: the special case of speech act verbs". *Interchange* **18**, pp. 32-47.

TREIMAN, R., FREYD, J. J. & BARON, J. (1983) "Phonological recoding and use of spelling-sound rules in reading of sentences", *Journal of Verbal Learning and Verbal Behaviour* **22**, pp. 682-700.

TREVELYAN, G. M. (1978) *English Social History*. Longman: London (revised with new material).

TRUDGILL, P. (1975) *Accent, Dialect and the School*. Arnold: London.

TRUDGILL, P. (1983) *On Dialect: Social and Geographical Perspectives*. New York University Press: New York.

TURNER, J. (1975) *Cognitive Development*. Methuen: London.

TYLER, A. & NAGY, W. (1989) "The acquisition of English derivational morphology". *Journal of Memory and Language* **28**, pp. 649-667.

TYLER, L. K., MARSLEN-WILSON, W., RENTOUL, J. & HANNEY, P. (1988) "Continuous and discontinuous access in spoken word-recognition: the role of derivational prefixes". *Journal of Memory and Language* **27**, pp. 368-381.

TYLER, L. K., WAKSLER, R. & MARSLEN WILSON, W. D. (1994) "Representation and access of derived words in English". In *Cognitive Models of Speech Processing.*, edited by G. Altmann and G. Shilcock. Erlbaum: Hillsdale NJ.

ULLMANN, S. (1951) *The Principles of Semantics*. Blackwell: Oxford.

ULLMANN, S. (1962) *Semantics: An Introduction to the Science of Meaning.* Blackwell: Oxford (1972 edition).

VASSILYEV, L. M. (1974) "The theory of semantic fields: a survey", *Linguistics* **137**, pp. 79-93.

VERMA, G. K. & BAGLEY, C. (1975) *Race and Education Across Cultures.* Heinemann: London.

VYGOTSKY, L. S. (1962) *Thought and Language* (edited and translated by Eugenia Hanfmann and Gertrude Vakar). M. I. T. Press: Cambridge, Mass.

WALBERG, H. J. & TSAI, S. (1983) "Matthew effects in education". *American Educational Research Journal* **20**, pp. 359-373.

WATSON, F. (1908) *The English Grammar Schools to 1660: Their Curriculum and Practice*. Cambridge University Press: London.

WELLS, G. (1986) *The Meaning Makers: Children Learning Language and Using Language to Learn*. Heinemann: Portsmouth NH.

WELLS, G. (1989) "Language in the classroom: literacy and collaborative talk". *Language and Education* **3**, pp. 251-274.

WELLS, G. (1992) "The centrality of talk in education". In *Thinking Voices* edited by K. Norman. Hodder and Stoughton: London.

WEST, R. F. & STANOVICH, K. E. (1991) "The incidental acquisition of information from reading". *Psychological Science* **2**, pp. 325-330.

WHITE, T. G., SLATER, W. H. & GRAVES, M. F. (1989) "Yes/no method of vocabulary assessment: valid for whom and useful for what?". In *Cognitive and Social Perspectives for Literacy Research and Instruction*, edited by S. McCormick and J. Zutell. National Reading Conference: Chicago.

WHITE, T. G., GRAVES, M. F. & SLATER, W. H. (1990) "Growth of reading vocabulary in diverse elementary schools: decoding and word meaning". *Journal of Educational Psychology* **82**, pp. 281-290.

WHITE, T. G., POWER, M. A. & WHITE, S. (1989) "Morphological analysis: implications for teaching and understanding vocabulary growth". *Reading Research Quarterly* **24**, pp. 283-304.

WHYTE, J. (1983) "Metaphor interpretation and reading ability in adults". *Journal of Psycholinguistic Research* **12**, pp. 457-465.

WILKINS, D. A. (1972) *Linguistics and Language Teaching*. Edward Arnold: London.

WILLIS, P. (1977) *Learning to Labour*. Gower: Aldershot.

WIMMER, H., HOGREFE, J. & SODIAN, B. (1988) "A second stage in children's conception of mental life". In *Developing Theories of Mind*, edited by J. W. Astington, P. L. Harris and D. R. Olson. Cambridge University Press: Cambridge.

WINCH, P. (1958) *The Idea of a Social Science*. Routledge & Kegan Paul: London (1977 edition).

WINCH, P. (1972) *Ethics and Action*. Routledge & Kegan Paul: London.

WINTER, E. O. (1978) "A look at the role of certain words in information structure". In *Informatics 3* edited by K. P. Jones and V. Horsenell. ASLIB: London.

WITTGENSTEIN, L. (1953) *Philosophical Investigations*. (translated by G. E. M. Anscombe). Blackwell: Oxford.

WITTGENSTEIN, L. (1961) *Tractatus Logico-Philosophicus*. Routledge & Kegan Paul: London.

YOUNG, M. F. D. (1971) *Knowledge and Control*, Collier Macmillan: London.

YOUNG, R. E. (1992) *Critical Theory and Classroom Talk*. Multilingual Matters: Clevedon, Avon.

ZHOU, X. & MARSLEN-WILSON, W. (1994) "Words, morphemes and syllables in the Chinese mental lexicon". *Language and Cognitive Processes* **9**, pp. 393-422.

ZWITSERLOOD, P. (1994) "The role of semantic transparency in the processing and representation of Dutch compounds". *Language and Cognitive Processes* **9**, pp. 341-368.

# Index

Made in United States
North Haven, CT
20 October 2021